Wolfgang Schirmer (Editor)

Dunes and fossil soils

GEOARCHAEORHEIN

Eine Reihe für den Bau, Zustand und die Geschichte der Erde, die Geschichte des Menschen und sein Zusammenwirken mit der Erde im Flußgebiet des Rheins

Herausgeber: Wolfgang Schirmer

Prof. Dr. Wolfgang Schirmer
Abt. Geologie
Heinrich-Heine-Universität
Universitätsstr. 1
D-40225 Düsseldorf
E-mail: schirmer@uni-duesseldorf.de
Tel. +49-(0)211-81-12042

Wolfgang Schirmer (Editor)

Dunes and fossil soils

with contributions by

Barbara Antczak-Górka
Margot Böse
Arthur Brande
Renata Dulias
Michael Facklam
Katarzyna Issmer
Klaus-Dieter Jäger
Cornelis Kasse
Dietrich Kopp
Alojzy Kowalkowski

Marion Müller
Bolesław Nowaczyk
Iwona Okuniewska-Nowaczyk
Jolanta Pełka-Gościniak
Wolfgang Schirmer
Norbert Schlaak
Tadeusz Szczypek
Jerzy Wach
Józef Wojtanowicz
Steffen Wolters

LIT

Titelbild: Juniper Dunes Wilderness, Washington/U.S.A. (W.Schirmer, 1997)

Satz & Layout: Dr. Eva-Maria Ikinger

Die Deutsche Bibliothek – CIP-Einheitsaufnahme

Dunes and fossil soils / Wolfgang Schirmer (Editor). – Münster : LIT, 1999
  (GEOARCHAEORHEIN ; 3.)
  ISBN 3-8258-4606-7

NE: GT

© LIT VERLAG Münster – Hamburg – London
  Grevener Str. 179   48159 Münster   Tel. 0251–23 50 91   Fax 0251–23 19 72

Distributed in North America by:

Transaction Publishers
New Brunswick (U.S.A.) and London (U.K.)

Transaction Publishers
Rutgers University
35 Berrue Circle
Piscataway, NJ 08854

Tel.: (732) 445 – 2280
Fax: (732) 445 – 3138
for orders (U.S. only):
toll free 888-999-6778

Inhaltsverzeichnis

2

Prologue

Shifting dune

A sharp dune's walk from left to right
on thousand feet through country wide,
foot, knee and neck,
head, heart and leg
are through and through fine sand so light.

Each single grain jumps towards the crest,
slides down the face to come to rest,
is overrolled and buried deep
to have an earth-historic sleep.

Uncovered to the shiny world,
the surface nicely ripple-curled,
the grain prepares to jump and slide
to darkness and again to light.

Wanderdüne

Auf tausend Füßen wandert sie
von links nach rechts durchs Land.
Fuß, Nabel, Kopf,
Herz, Hals und Schopf
sind nichts als feiner Sand.

Ein jedes Korn springt auf zum Grat,
rutscht rechts die Wand hinab,
wird tausendfach dort überrollt,
ruht tief im Dünengrab.

Nach langem Schlafe freigeweht
gelangt das Korn zum Tag
und springt ins Grab und kehrt zum Licht,
so oft der Wind das mag.

Juniper Dunes Wilderness, Washington/U.S.A.
Texts & photo: W. Schirmer 1997

GeoArchaeoRhein, **3**: 5–9; Münster 1999

The Symposium „Dunes and fossil soils"

WOLFGANG SCHIRMER

In former years the Eurosiberian Subcommission (ESSC) for the study of the Holocene visited individual countries to study the progress in Holocene research of this country. During the eighties and nineties a certain satisfaction in symposiums arose. This was because of an immense augmentation of individual scientific groups, augmentation of interdisciplinary meetings and international connections in a way that an essential progress in research in an intersymposium period was no longer possible. During the same time a big financial recession underwent the whole world and, naturally, hit the scientific world to a special degree.

Research and its presentation need a certain balanced rhythmicity. Thus, time was mature to reduce the amount of meetings and to concentrate them to certain scientific topics. A scheduled meeting of the ESSC on Holocene river deltas in the Rhine delta of Germany and the Netherlands in summer 1993 was cancelled due to little participation. Since the last presentations in the ESSC by BOB HAGEMAN and others in 1969 and 1974, huge new work was done in the Rhine delta. But there was neither real international interest on that topic nor enough money respectively financial support for possibly interested participants.

In 1994 a symposium „Glacier and debris flow activity in alpine regions" led from August 27 – September 10 through the Swiss, Austrian and Italian Alps with a lecture day in St. Vigil/South Tyrol. A small group of 17 participants were guided by eleven Swiss, Austrin and German scientists. It was a scientifically very effectful field trip in an excellent natural setting.

After that symposium by looking at the huge Eurosiberian group and the small amount of scientists involved into those symposia I felt the need to organize short field trips with low costs but again on distinct topics. In discussions with KLAUS-DIETER JÄGER it turned out that there was a real need to gather data on eolian activity in the so-called European sand belt especially in eastern Germany and Poland, where a lot of work has been done by different groups with only little inter-institutional contacts.

Thus, from August 24 to 28, 1998, I organized a symposium „Dunes and fossil soils of Vistulian and Holocene age between Elbe and Wisła". This symposium was meant to be short in time and concentrate to well prepared outcrops with fossil soils of Late Glacial and Holocene age. Aim of the symposium was to compare the Holocene dune activity to that of the Pleni-Weichselian and Late Weichselian. It included the correlation of Weichselian and Holocene eolian sand deposits by means of their sedimentology and fossil soils, moreover the climatic history and history of soil development since the Pleni-Weichselian and the history of human clearance activity in dune sand areas.

The following topics were outlined in the first circular:
- Late Weichselian soils in dunes
- Holocene soils in dunes caused by naturally induced sand movements
- Holocene soils in dunes caused by human clearence activity
- Sedimentological differentiation of late Weichselian and Holocene eolian deposits
- Conclusions respecting climate and man's clearence activity.

The symposium was generously funded by the German-Polish Cooperation Foundation in Warszawa. For promotion getting this fund I am indebted especially to ALOJZY KOWALKOWSKI and BOLESŁAW NOWACZYK.

The local organizers of the field trip were KLAUS-DIETER JÄGER, Halle, ALOJZY KOWALKOWSKI, Kielce, and BOLESŁAW NOWACZYK, Poznań. 38 participants from 4 countries, Germany, Iceland, Poland and The Netherlands, attended the symposium. Field presentations were given by 16 local guides from Germany, Poland and The Netherlands. For the symposium a guide-book has been prepared in advance:

JÄGER, K.-D., KOWALKOWSKI, A., NOWACZYK, B. & SCHIRMER, W. [ed.] (1998): Dunes and fossil soils of Vistulian and Holocene age between Elbe and Wisła. — 106 p., 1 map; Poznań (AMUniv, Quaternary Res. Inst.). — This guidebook is still available at the following address (costs: 10 $): Prof. Dr. Bolesław Nowaczyk, Department of Geomorphology, Institute of Quaternary Research, Adam Mieckiewicz University, ul. H. Wieniawskiego 17/19, PL-61-713 Poznań. E-mail: geomorf@man.poznan.pl

Content of the guide-book

BUSSEMER, S. & THIEKE, H. U. (1998): Golßen — example for morphological and pedological development of the oldest Weichselian outwash plains and glacial spillways.

GRAMSCH, B. (1998): Golssen — A Late Paleolithic site in the Baruth–Głogów ice marginal valley.

BOER, DE W. M. (1998): Aeolian land forms in the Baruth ice-marginal valley and the dune profile in the Picher Berge near Schöbendorf (Brandenburg).

BÖSE, M., BRANDE, A., FACKLAM, M. & MÜLLER, M. (1998): Bliesendorf — dune-section on the Glindow moraine plain southwest of Bliesendorf.

SCHLAAK, N. (1998): Sites in the Toruń–Eberswalde ice marginal valley.

ISSMER, K. (1998): Plenivistulian and Late Vistulian loess covers and their relation to the dunes.

NOWACZYK, B. (1998): Eolian cover sands in the vicinity of Cedynia.

OKUNIEWSKA-NOWACZYK, I. (1998): The history of Late Vistulian vegetation in the vicinity of Cedynia.

NOWACZYK, B. (1998): Dunes and eolian cover sands in the vicinity of Jasień.

OKUNIEWSKA-NOWACZYK, I. (1998): Late Vistulian history of vegetation in the vicinity of Jasień (Preliminary analysis).

KOWALKOWSKI, A. (1998): Soil sequences in the Jasień dune.

ANTCZAK-GÓRKA, B. (1998): Corrasion on deflation surfaces in southern Wielkopolska.

KASPRZAK, L. (1998): Epigenetic structures of sand-wedge casts with primary mineral filling.

NOWACZYK, B. (1998): Holocene transformations of dunes in the vicinity of Osiecza near Konin.

MANIKOWSKA, B. (1998): Aeolian deposits and fossil soils in dunes of Central Poland — the dune in Kamion.

GOŹDZIK, J. (1998): Pleni-Vistulian and Late-Vistulian aeolian processes in the vicinity of Bełchatów.

The field symposium

Schedule of the field symposium (for location of the scientific localities see Fig. 1):

23-8   Arrival at Luckenwalde south of Berlin. Accomodation: Luckenwalde.

24-8   Outcrops around Berlin: Golssen, Schöbendorf, Bliesendorf, Postdüne and Melchow. Accomodation: Helenenau

25-8   Outcrops along the German-Polish Oder/Odra: Schiffmühle, Klępicz/Klemzow, Jasień/Gassen. Accomodation: Zielona Góra/Grünberg.

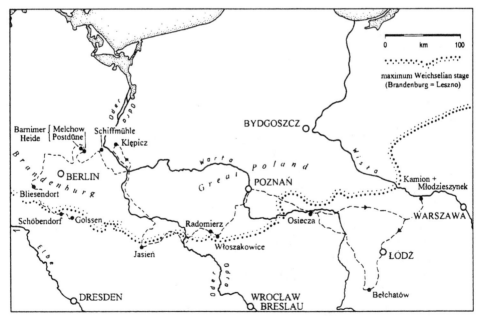

Fig. 1: Location map and route of the field symposium „Dunes and fossil soils of Vistulian and Holocene age between Elbe and Wisła" August 24 to 28, 1998.

26-8 Outcrops in southern Wielkopolska: Radomierz and Włoszakowice. The scheduled conference workshop at the Science Center of the Polish Academy of Science (PAS) had to be cancelled due to an intermittent repair of the excursion bus. Visit to Poznań downtown. Accomodation: PAS Poznań.

27-8 Outcrops in Middle Poland: Osiecza near Konin, Kamion and Młodzieszynek near Wyszogród W Warszawa. Accomodation: Łódź.

28-8 Open cast mine of Bełchatów S Łódź. Reception in the Uniejów castle near Koło. Return to Poznań.

Participants:

Dr. Barbara Antczak-Górka, Poznań
Prof. Dr. Margot Böse, Berlin
Dr. Wierd Mathijs de Boer, Utrecht
Dr. Arthur Brande, Berlin
Dr. Renata Dulias, Sosnowiec
Prof. Dr. Thorleifur Einarsson, Reykjavik
Prof. Dr. Peter Felix-Henningsen, Gießen
Dipl.-Geogr. Ute Fischer Zujkov, Eberswalde
Dr. Renate Gerlach, Bonn
Dr. Jan Goździk, Łódź
Alexandra Hilgers, Köln
Dr. Alexander Ikinger, Düsseldorf
Dr. Eva-Maria Ikinger, Düsseldorf
Dr. Katarzyna Issmer, Poznań
Prof. Dr. Klaus-Dieter Jäger, Halle (Saale)
Dr. Andreas Janotta, Köln
Dipl.-Geogr. Holger Kampmann, Berlin
Dr. Kees Kasse, Amsterdam
Hanne Kayser, Grötsch
Prof. Dr. habil. Kazimierz Klimek, Sosnowiec
Dr. hab. Anna Kollender-Szych, Gießen
Dr. habil. Dietrich Kopp, Tewswoos
Prof. Dr. Alojzy Kowalkowski, Kielce
Assoc. Prof. Maria Lanczont, Lublin
Prof. Dr. Herbert Liedtke, Bochum
Prof. Dr. Joachim Marcinek, Berlin
Prof. Dr. Bolesław Nowaczyk, Poznań
Dr. Iwona Okuniewska-Nowaczyk, Poznań
Dr. Jolanta Pełka-Gościniak, Sosnowiec
Prof. Dr. Ulrich Radtke, Köln
Dr. Ursula Schirmer, Düsseldorf

Prof. Dr. Wolfgang Schirmer, Düsseldorf
Dr. Norbert Schlaak, Altenhof
Dr. Thomas Scholten, Gießen
Prof. Dr. Tadeusz Szczypek, Sosnowiec
Dr. Günter Wetzel, Potsdam-Babelsberg
Prof. Dr. Józef Wojtanowicz, Lublin
M. Sc. Barbara Woronko, Warszawa

In addition the following colleagues acted as field guides:

Dr. Sixten Bussemer, München
Dipl.-Ing. Michael Facklam, Berlin
Dr. Bernhard Gramsch, Potsdam-Babelsberg
Dr. Lech Kasprzak, Poznań
Prof. Dr. Barbara Manikowska, Łódź
Dipl.-Geogr. Marion Müller, Berlin
Dr. Hans-Ulrich Thieke, Berlin.

During this field trip some international connections were formed concerning the inverstigation of fossil soils and TL dating of dune sand.
The following contributions underwent reviewing. Additionally all papers were carefully read whereby I was kindly supported by Eva-Maria Ikinger and my wife Ursula Schirmer.

Address of the author:

Prof. Dr. WOLFGANG SCHIRMER, Abt. Geologie, Heinrich-Heine-Universität, Universitätsstr. 1, D-40225 Düsseldorf, e-mail: schirmer@uni-duesseldorf.de

GeoArchaeoRhein, **3**: 11–42; Münster 1999

Dune phases and soils in the European sand belt

WOLFGANG SCHIRMER

Abstract: The time span between dissipation of the permafrost and development of dense vegetation was the favoured period for eolian sand accumulation. It is the period from the late Pleni-Weichselian until early Preboreal. Similar conditions existed during the earlier Weichselian prior to the Last Glacial Maximum (LGM). Dune formation has been preserved since the early Upper Weichselian in southeastern Poland.

From the LGM on, six periods of eolian activity can be recognized (Tab. 1). Period 1: Fluvio-eolian period (28,000–ca.14,000 a BP): Period with much deflation, sand deposition as niveo-eolian and fluvio-eolian accumulation, thin-bedded as well as homogenous fine, silty sand and cold-climate indicators. Period 2: Eolian coversand period (~14,000–12,200 a BP): Period producing flat and widespread sand veneers with small dunes, silty sand and small frost indicators. Period 3: Dune period (Dryas 2: 12,200–11,800 a BP): First major dune period besides coversand deposition. Period 4: Dune and dune transformation period (Dryas 3 and early Preboreal: 10,800–9,500 a BP): Period of mainly dune transformation besides formation of new dunes, also river dunes. Period 5: Little dune transformation period (Preboreal–early Atlantic): Period of quiescence with thick brown and podzolic soils, with local and little dune transformation. Period 6: Man-triggered dune period (mid-Atlantic to recent times): Period of predominant soil formation as arenosols (regosols) and podzols on vegetated dunes, scattered human forest clearing and consequent dune transformation.

Soil formation within the eolian deposits starts during late Pleni-Weichselian interstadials with arenosols or very faint cambisols. The Finow Soil of Allerødian age presents the first thicker cambisol. The next younger one is the rusty soil of Preboreal age. A possible share of Holocene pervasive soil formation on these brown soils has to be checked. Since the Boreal period the soil development changes to podzolic soils due to changing sand properties, vegetation and climate. In case of short pauses in-between eolian sand movements arenosols (regosols) are formed only during all periods mentioned.

The following report preferably reflects on the objectives gathered during the field symposium „Dunes and fossil soils of Vistulian and Holocene age between Elbe and Wisła" August 24 to 28, 1998 (SCHIRMER 1999a) (location map in Fig. 1) as well as on the details of the Proceedings Volume presented here (location map Fig. 2).

The dune activity in the north Central European Lowland, the European sand belt, shows conspicuous spatial facies differentiation from the western to the eastern part. This is due to the climatic gradient from more atlantic to more continental climate. A

Tab. 1: Various schemes outlining periods of eolian activity in the north Central European Lowland, arranged from west to east.

Dylikowa (1969)	Manikowska			Schirmer (1999)	Chrono-stratigraphy ^{14}C years
	(1991b)	(1995)	(1998)		
Dune destruction phase	VI	Eolian stages		6 Man triggered dune period	Holocene
	V		V	5 Little dune-transformation period	
Dune transformation phase	IV	III	IV	4 Dune and dune transformation period	— 10,000 —
Dune-forming phase	III	II	III	3 Dune period	Late Glacial
initial phase	II		II	2 Eolian coversand period	— 12,700 —
	I	I	I	1 Fluvio-eolian period	Upper Pleniglacial

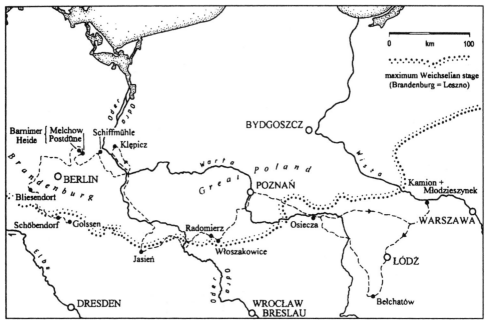

Fig. 1: Location map and route of the field symposium „Dunes and fossil soils of Vistulian and Holocene age between Elbe and Wisła" August 24 to 28, 1998.

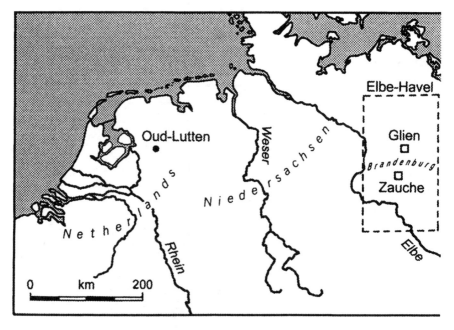

Fig. 2: Location map of the places and areas presented in this Proceedings Volume.

certain differentiation in age from south to north is due to the rejuvenation of the landscape following the northward melting ice. Moreover, some of the investigated varieties may be due to differences in specialization of regional research.

The oldest eolian activity[1] documented in this area are sand wedge fills of late Saalian age. In Bełchatów in middle Poland (Fig. 1) they cut Warthian till (GOŹDZIK 1998). From the Eemian through Middle Weichselian (Fig. 3) there is a gap of records of eolian activity concerning sand transport. Yet, as eolian activity is documented through the Upper Pleni-Weichselian glaciation period (UWG), comparable activity can be assumed for the Lower Pleni-Weichselian cold period (MWG 1 or MIS 4[2]), too. The lack of eolian documentation may be due to the loose consistence of eolian sand deposits, easily erodable by solifluction, delution[3] and wind.

The later Middle Weichselian period (MIS 3) is characterized by a vivid alternation of interstadials and short stadial periods in-between (Fig. 3). It should likewise have produced eolian sand. Then climatic conditions close to that of the early Late Glacial should have existed. However, deposits of the Middle Weichselian period are scarsely preserved at all due to immense erosion during the following Upper Pleni-Weichselian period with the last glacial maximum.

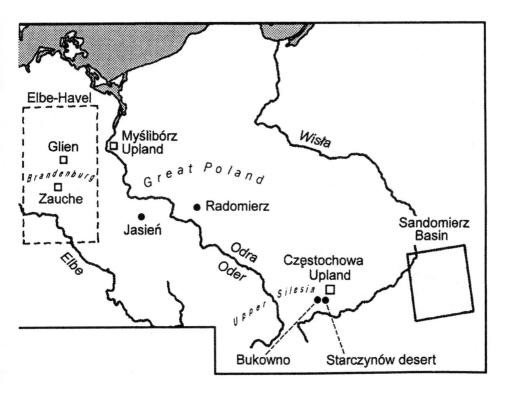

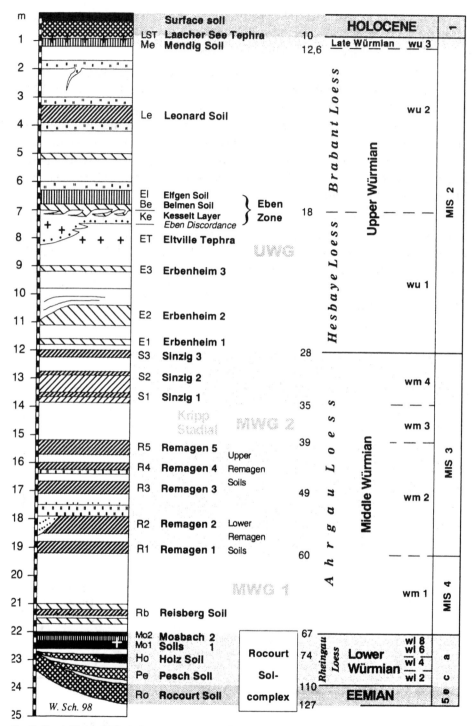

Fig. 3: Last Glacial Rhein loess sequence (from SCHIRMER 1999b).

1. Eolian activity periods since the Upper Weichselian

The eolian deposits recorded up till now range in age from the boundary Middle Weichselian/ Upper Weichselian up till recent times, starting with about 30,000 years BP.

The main objectives presented during the dune symposium and in this Proceedings Volume are gathered in Fig. 4. According to these results the eolian deposits can be grouped into six eolian activity periods with individual characteristics (Tab. 1).[4] To each of the six eolian periods outlined below, a short item is attributed that marks a typical, although not exclusive, feature of that period.

Period 1: Fluvio-eolian period (28,000–~14,000 a BP)

Period with much deflation, sand deposition as niveo-eolian and fluvio-eolian accumulation, thin-bedded as well as homogenous fine, silty sand and cold-climate indicators.

The period around the Last Glacial Maximum (LGM) is thought to be a period of strong wind activity that produced mainly deflation (abrasion). Consequently gravel and ventifact horizons forming residual deposits are assigned to the LGM, e. g. the Beuningen Gravel Bed of The Netherlands (cf. KASSE 1999) and the ventifact horizons described by DÜCKER & MAARLEVELD (1957), DE BOER (1995), SCHLAAK (1999), KOZARSKI & NOWACZYK (1991), ANTCZAK-GÓRKA (1998, 1999) and MANIKOWSKA (1995: 134). It is generally assumed that the topsoil was under continuous permafrost conditions while being deflated. Several records of ice wedge casts of this period (Fig. 4 and BÖSE 1991) support this opinion.

The deflation produced eolian coversand that locally was transformed into thin-bedded niveo-eolian sand layers. Runoff transformed them into thin-bedded fluvio-eolian layers or thicker-bedded deluvial[5] sand layers. All mentioned sediment types give evidence of their primary eolian origin by the grain-size and well sorting of the sand and matted surface of the quartz grains. According to MANIKOWSKA (1995: 132) this abrasion period supplied the braided river beds of that time with sand to a high degree. It corresponds to the fact that the Maxiwürm Terrace of the Central European rivers is topped by a rather sandy and less silty flood sediment (SCHIRMER 1995a: 37).

A proper sediment trap during deflation periods are frost wedges. Thus the eolian activity is also documented as infill of sand wedges (BLUME & HOFFMANN 1977, MANIKOWSKA 1995: 133, GOŹDZIK 1998, KASPRZAK 1998). In rare cases little dunes are recorded from eastern Poland where they occur as independent dunes (WOJTANOWICZ 1999). DE BOER (1995: 118) gives record of longitudinal dune complexes that parallel meltwater drains of Urstromtäler between the Brandenburg and Frankfurt glacier stages. On the other hand mere abrasion prevailed in middle Poland (MANIKOWSKA 1995: 135).

The sand deposit is generally finer than the following younger eolian sand layers and is marked by a high silt content. The silt content often occurs in laminae (KASSE 1999). DE

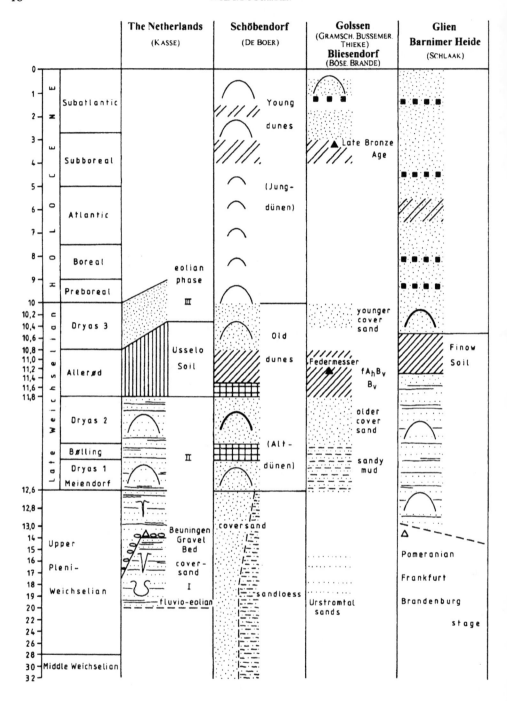

Fig. 4: Correlation of eolian sand deposits and fossil soils in the north Central European Lowland presented during the Dune Symposium and in this Proceedings Volume arranged from west to east.

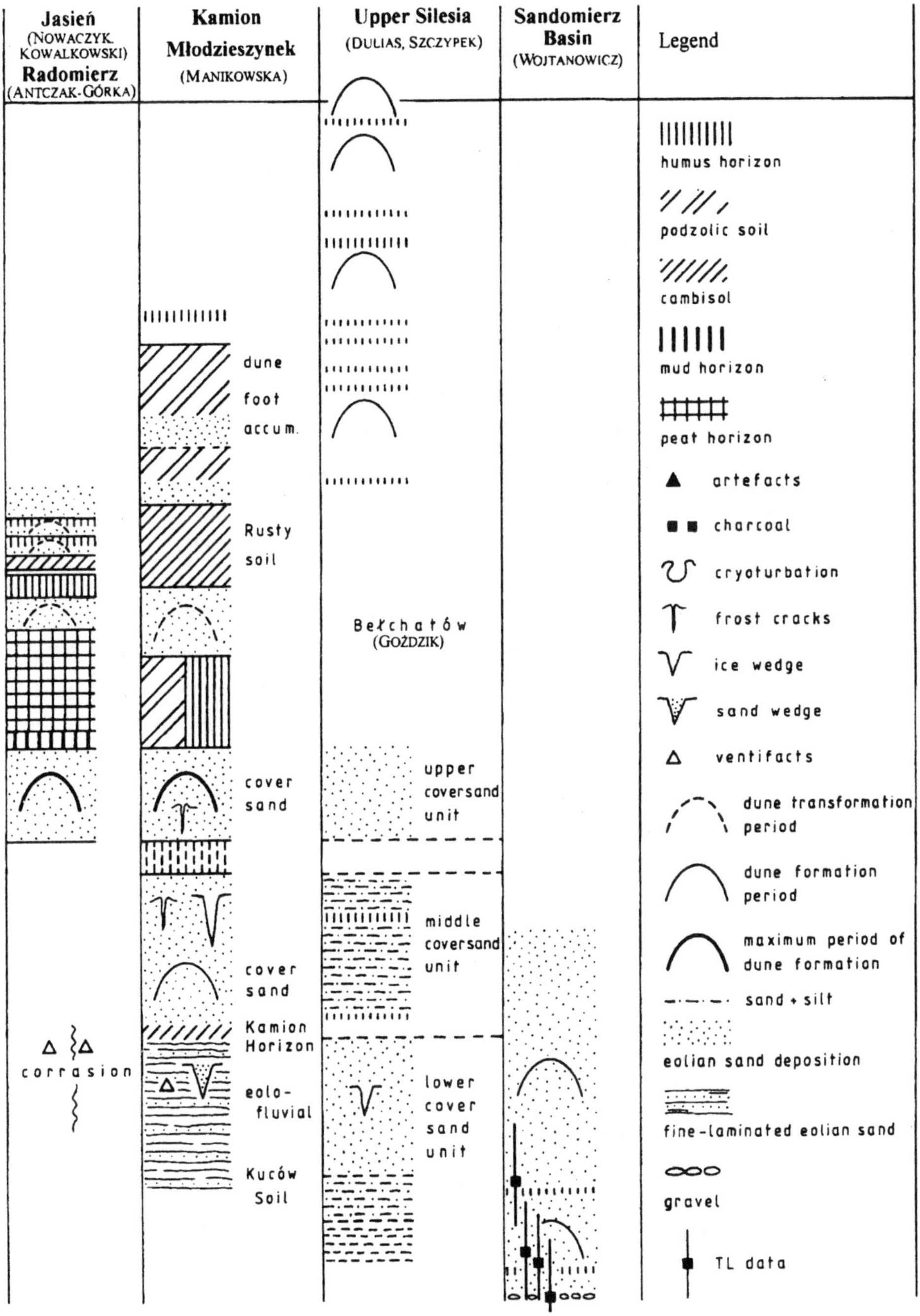

Jasień (NOWACZYK, KOWALKOWSKI) Radomierz (ANTCZAK-GÓRKA)	Kamion Młodzieszynek (MANIKOWSKA)	Upper Silesia (DULIAS, SZCZYPEK)	Sandomierz Basin (WOJTANOWICZ)	Legend

Legend:

humus horizon
podzolic soil
cambisol
mud horizon
peat horizon
▲ artefacts
■ ■ charcoal
ʊ cryoturbation
↑ frost cracks
V ice wedge
W sand wedge
△ ventifacts
dune transformation period
dune formation period
maximum period of dune formation
–·–·– sand + silt
eolian sand deposition
fine-laminated eolian sand
∞∞ gravel
TL data

Kamion Młodzieszynek:
dune foot accum.
Rusty soil
cover sand
cover sand
Kamion Horizon
eolo-fluvial
Kucόw Soil

Upper Silesia:
Bełchatόw (GOŹDZIK)
upper coversand unit
middle coversand unit
lower cover sand unit

Jasień/Radomierz:
corrasion
△ △

BOER (1995, 1998) gives record of sandloess[6], an eolian facies that mediates between loess and eolian sand. KASSE (1999) notes as characteristics for this period concave lenses of coarse sand, small-scale current ripple lamination and clayey-silty drapes, frequent cryogenic structures as cryoturbations and vertical platy structures.

WOJTANOWICZ (1999) presents TL ages of an eastern Polish dune embracing the time span between 32 ± 5.4 and 22 ± 3.7 ka BP — thus giving the oldest ages of eolian activity in the north Central European Lowland up till now. His sand sequence is interrupted by two interstadial soils, the older one at about 29 ka, the younger one at about 22 ka according to TL data of overlying sand. The latter may correspond to the Kuców Soil, a tundra soil of 21,200 ± 220 a BP and 21,970 ± 810 a BP noted by MANIKOWSKA (1998: 97 = 1995: Tab. 1). WOJTANOWICZ (1999) connects the two soils with the Dutch Hengelo and Denekamp interstadials. In case their ages are correct, only the lower one is of late Middle Weichselian age and may be connected with the Denekamp Interstadial respectively with one of the Sinzig interstadial soils of the Rhein loess sequence (Fig. 3). The younger soil is of Upper Weichselian age and cannot be connected with a Middle Weichselian interstadial. However the Rhein loess sequence shows that the Upper Weichselian period likewise encompasses several interstadial soils to be connected with. Unfortunately reliable absolute dates of these soils are absent up till now.

The fluvio-eolian sequence of the eolian period 1 ends up in a non-deposition period at about 14.5 ka BP. In The Netherlands this time is marked by the end of the residual Beuningen Gravel Bed. In Middle Poland it is marked by the Kamion Horizon ^{14}C dated to 14,500–14,000 a BP (cf. Chapter 3).

Period 2: Eolian coversand period (~14,000–12,200 a BP)

Period producing flat and widespread sand veneers with small dunes, silty sand and small frost indicators.

During this period coversand prevails besides little dunes. The sand relief remains generally low. MANIKOWSKA (1995: 144) describes a dune hillock up to 4 m high covered by a Bølling soil. DE BOER (1995: 119) reports of pre-Bølling dune cores. On the other hand BÖSE (1991: 21) considers the Oldest Dryas to be the time of main dune formation in the Berlin area. She explains the start of the dune formation as consequence of the dissipation of permafrost and the lack of fluvial and melt water in the Urstromtäler. DE BOER (1995: 106) combines the beginning of bow-shaped dunes during this period with the start of scattered vegetation. On the other hand it could be demonstrated (e. g. WALTER 1951, STENGEL 1992) that bow-shaped dunes form in barren landscapes, too, depending from gustiness of wind, from mechanical cluster formation and electrostatic attraction and repulsion of electrically charged sand grains. In addition there are examples that plant growth is able to promote dune formation (e. g. WALTER 1951, SCHELLING 1957, MEYER 1984). Within the course of period 2 the augmentation of vegetational growth should have started with the Meiendorf Interstadial (cf. U. SCHIRMER 1999). It follows that hence formation of dune forms should increase.

The fine-bedded fluvio-eolian character of the coversand decreases from west towards east. The eolian sand is still rich in silt. MANIKOWSKA (1995: 144) records up to 40 % silt that can occur as silty laminae.[7] In the west KASSE (1999) notes this period being the „most prominent phase of eolian deposition" and being the feeder for many later eolian sand reactivations. Cold-climate indicators are generally smaller than that of period 1. MANIKOWSKA (1991b: 134) notes numerous frost fissure polygons with primary sand infill.

The period ends up in the quiescence phase of the Bølling Interstadial. This interstadial is rarely represented, in Schöbendorf south of Berlin by a very weak peat (DE BOER 1995: 118) and in Kamion by an initial A horizon (MANIKOWSKA 1991a: 138), a small organic horizon dated to 12,235 a BP. KASSE (1999) explains the general lack of Bølling deposits by a scattered vegetation cover allowing the eolian work to continue.

As the Bølling Interstadial generally was a warm but short phase it is argued that vegetation encroached the European sand belt but left only a small humic cover as that of the Kamion site. This thin cover may have been widely abraded by the quickly succeeding dune period 3.

Period 3: Dune period (Dryas 2: 12,200–11,800 a BP)

First major dune period besides coversand deposition.

From the Fläming towards east, in some areas this period is suggested being the main dune phase of the inland dunes (DE BOER 1995: 117, MANIKOWSKA 1991a: 143). MANIKOWSKA (1995: 145) gives record of a parabolic dune of that age up to 15 m high and 5,000 m long. In addition, coversand goes on being produced.[8] In The Netherlands (KASSE 1999) and north of Berlin (SCHLAAK 1999) a certain amount of last fluvio-eolian activity is recorded visible by a local alternation of sand and silt laminae. Permafrost seems to have dissipated.

Whether this period is to be separated from period 2 or not is questionable. KASSE (1999) brackets period 2 and 3 (Tab. 1). As the weak soil of the Bølling Interstadial has only been found in few localities KASSE argues that observations attributed to this period 3 should often also comprise period 2. On the other hand, at those localities where the Bølling soil horizon was found, period 3 was recognized being the period of main dune formation. Thus augmentation of research on this period is needed.

This period ends up in the long quiescence phase of the Allerød Interstadial during which forest vegetation fixed the dune surface. As consequence in all areas there occur fossil soils of the Allerød period (see Chapter 3).

Presence of Palaeolithic man on coversand is recorded by GRAMSCH (1998) (see Appendix 2).

Period 4: Dune and dune transformation period (Dryas 3 and early Preboreal: 10,800–9,500 a BP)

Period of mainly dune transformation besides formation of new dunes, also river dunes.

This period seems to be a great dune period in the western part of the sand belt more than in its eastern part. Forming of new dunes is recorded from The Netherlands in the west through Great Poland in the east (Kasse 1999, Schlaak 1993, de Boer 1995, Kozarski 1978). In The Netherlands and the German Niederrhein area it is a conspicuous dune phase of river dunes (see Appendix 3). In some areas this period is even recognized being the period of main dune formation, e. g. north of Berlin (Schlaak 1999). In the area west of Poznań Kozarski & Nowaczyk (1991: 118) state the Dryas 3 to be the main period of dune as well as coversand formation. Besides new dune formation older dunes were reactivated and/or transformed. On the other hand in middle and eastern Poland dune transformation activity is recorded only. After Manikowska (1995: 141) new dune forms dating to Dryas 3 have not been found in middle Poland so far.

Cold climate indicators seem to be very rare in eolian sand of this period. Böse (1991: 24) gives record of frost fissures.

After the Allerød period the eolian activity started as late as middle Dryas 3 and continued through the first part of the Preboreal period (Nowaczyk & Rotnicki 1972[9], Schlaak 1997, Nowaczyk 1998a, Kasse 1999). Likewise Kozarski & Nowaczyk (1991) give 9,700 a BP for the extinction of eolian deposits.

Eolian period 4 ends up in the Holocene soil formation. Sometimes this period is the very end of the dune activity. In case of further dune activity the Holocene soil is split into short soil formation periods (see Chapter 3).

Period 5: Little dune transformation period (Preboreal – early Atlantic)

Period of quiescence with thick brown and podzolic soils, with local and little dune transformation.

This period is dominated by the formation of the Holocene soil on top of the dunes, mostly as brown cambic soil. Locally the dune slope and dune toe areas are subject to eolian reactivation of the dune sand. Several humic horizons and charcoal horizons interbed with eolian sand. A certainly rare case is that of Upper Silesia where Dulias (1999) gives record of newly formed dunes during the early Atlantic period. Manikowska (1995: 143) records an intermittent iron podzolic soil of Boreal age. On the other hand in many areas the first eolian activity after period 4 is chronicled not earlier than period 6 thus indicating period 5 being a mere standstill phase of eolian activity.

Eolian period 5 ends up in a podzolic soil of Atlantic to Subboreal age. Manikowska (1995: 143) gives record of an iron-humus podzol of Atlantic age. Likewise a podzolic soil of this age is recorded by Schlaak (1999). In case of the Silesian dunes (Dulias 1999) this soil position is represented by a bundle of humic soils indicating that here strong eolian activity gave only short pauses of interruption for vegetational recover and soil formation.

For this eolian period the question arises what triggers the clearing of vegetation and allows the revival of eolian activity. Most of the authors suggest that natural forest fires gave rise to vegetation clearence. However, it should be taken into account that also Mesolithic gatherers and hunters took advantage from promoting forest fires. Clearence areas within a forest give rise for augmentation of special shrubs and herbs and attract animals, thus making hunting easier.

Period 6: Man-triggered dune period (mid-Atlantic to recent times) ·

Period of predominant soil formation as arenosols (regosols) and podzols on vegetated dunes, scattered human forest clearing and consequent dune transformation.

Besides places where the Holocene soil developed from the early Holocene up till now without interference, there occurs pretty often eolian sand reactivation in places where the vegetational cover has been cleared. It starts with the Neolithic settlement during the Atlantic period (e. g. Kozarski & Nowaczyk 1991: 119, Schlaak 1999). A first cumulation of sand reactivation occurs during the Bronze Age (Lusatian Culture) (Kozarski & Nowaczyk 1991: 119). Later transformations of eolian sand areas are due to the local history of human settlement or single human activites as forest clearence, plaggen manuring or sand exploitation: Clustering of eolian sand reactivation is recorded from eastern Germany and western Poland during the Slavonic period of forest clearence in the early Middle Ages (Schlaak 1998: 31), from Brandenburg during the second half of the 12th century triggered by land clearence (Brande et al. 1999) and from Nieder-sachsen during 1770–1850 AD caused by heath cultivation (Meyer 1984). In some cases new dunes arose as in abandoned sand excavation areas (Szczypek & Wach 1999) or in military training places. There is nearly no eolian sand area without dense clustering of younger Holocene fossil soils (see Nowaczyk 1998b; Dulias 1999 in Fig. 4). The increase of dune revival events towards recent times is due to augmentation of historical records. The quiescence periods in-between are represented by podzolic or humic soils and/or charcoal horizons.

This period of inland dune transformation or in rare cases also of new dune formation is exclusively bound to man's land clearence activity.

2. Sand properties

Though publications on the European sand belt show a lot of grain-size data of eolian sand, there is no comprehensive study on the grain-size variety in space and time so far. One problem is that lateral short-distance grain-size variation (e. g. Walter 1951, Stengel 1992) and vertical stratigraphical variation can equal in dimension. Consequently, grain-size data produced from vertical sections can only roughly be evaluated.

Authors agree that during period 1 through 3 the eolian sand is richer in silt than later.

Their data show that the mean values of grain-size in general are gradually increasing from Pleni-Weichselian towards Holocene. It is a clear loess component that accompanies the sand during the Pleistocene, more or less alternating with the sand by thin layers, or homogeneously incorporated into the sand. This is due to the fact that prior to the Allerød period eolian sand has been deflated from a landscape nearly unvegetated or scantily vegetated. Hence all grain-sizes were offered to be deflated. This contrasts to the Holocene period. Then sand reactivation is concentrated to preexisting eolian sand fields. By its renewed deflation the silt content is more and more separated from the saltational transport that causes the new sand body. Supply of fresh silt is cut off by the vegetational cover. Consequently, from the Late Glacial on, the more frequent the sand is reworked by the wind the poorer it gets in silt.

This is an essential prerequisite for the soil formation and one reason for the change from cambisol on Pleistocene eolian sand to podzol on Holocene eolian sand.

3. Soil formation in the European sand belt

The formation of the fossil and recent soils in eolian sand is one of the most interesting and most controversially disputed point of soil formation. On the other hand typical soils once calibrated are often the best indicators to date the underlying sand deposits.

3. 1 The controversies

The main point of controversy is due to the great pore volume of eolian sand which makes it difficult to state whether soil forming processes in a field section happened successively or simultaneously. A typical example for this fundamental discussion during the field symposium was that at the Radomierz site southwest of Poznań (Fig. 1) presented by BARBARA ANTCZAK-GÓRKA (1998, 1999).

At this site the Leszno (Brandenburg) Till Plain is buried 1.8 m below the surface and is overlain by a 0.3 m thick fossil deflation pavement the entire clast population of which comes up to 64 % of ventifacts. This residual layer is overlain up to the surface by an eolian coversand of 1.5 m thickness (inclusive a basal 20 cm thick transitional bed of medium sand with rare small pebbles).

The following soil horizons (not mentioned by ANTCZAK-GÓRKA) were noted during the symposium field visit (Fig. 5):

Ah   0.3 m coversand
Bv   1.0 m coversand
Sw   0.5 m transitional and residual layer
Bt   till

The following possible explanations were discussed in the field:

1. The soil is a so-called Fahlerde formed during one single soil forming action. The porous eolian coversand allows the formation of a brown weathered cambisol horizon

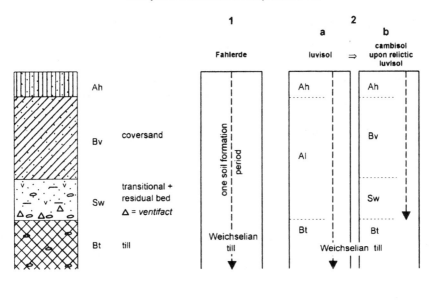

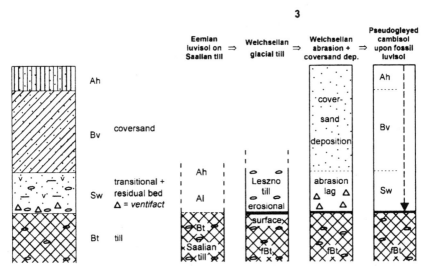

Fig. 5: Three possibilities to explain the soil formation within the Weichselian coversand overlying boulder clay by the example of the Radomierz Site.

(Bv), the underlying till causes damming of water that forms the bleached horizon (Sw). The solid till rich in silt and clay forms an illuvial horizon (Bt). This soil formed since the Late Weichselian.

2. The soil formation embraces two processes: a. Formation of a luvisol in the course of which the coversand acted as lessivé horizon (Al), the till as illuvial horizon (Bt). b. Later soil formation transformed the Al into a cambisol (Bv). Thus the studied soil

belongs to two different soil forming processes acting since the Late Weichselian.

3. A possible and quite different explanation was mine. The Bt horizon is — due to its strong development — a fossil Eem soil upon Saalian till. The Bv horizon is the Late Glacial–Holocene soil on Weichselian coversand. The residual layer is the only remnant of the Leszno till highly deflated and transformed into the ventifact horizon. The Bt horizon on top of the till caused stagnation of water (Sw horizon) since the deposition of the cover bed. Thus the studied soil belongs to two different interglacial periods, the basal luvisol to the Eemian, the topping cambisol (Pseudogley-Braunerde) to the Late Glacial/Holocene period.

ad 1. This explanation is suggested by KOPP (1970) to be the normal soil formation process in periglacial coverbeds.

ad 2. In northern Central Europe this idea is mainly promoted by ROESCHMANN (1994); however, he considers the age of the soil formation to belong to the Holocene only, not to the Late Glacial.

ad 3. This explanation would fit to many observations in Brandenburg, where the main corpus of the till plains turned out to be formed during the Saalian glaciation period, and the inland ice of the Brandenburg stage left only a small cover of deposits on top of the Saalian sedimentary body (MARCINEK et al. 1983: 16). Likewise in the northern Alpine foreland the maximum Würmian glaciation is suggested to have caused only little morphological transformation activity and left only a thin depositional cover (ELLWANGER, pers. communication).

3.2 Soil development in dunes since the Last Glacial retreat

Generally each standstill of morphological activity is marked by a certain soil formation. Successively during periods of high morphological activity those traces are mostly destroyed. However, there are some rare and very early records of fossil soils.

Kamion Horizon (MANIKOWSKA 1991a: 146, 1995: 130)

MANIKOWSKA (1991a: 138) records a decalcified brown alluvial soil formed on top of a 2 m thick flood deposit that veneers the Otwock Terrace of the river Wisła. The soil is covered by a 8 m thick dune sand. The soil consists of a 10 cm thick silty-clayey humic top soil. The underlying subsoil of 50 cm forms a sandy-silty deposit with iron oxide enrichment, homogenization and decalcification. The humus provided ^{14}C ages of 14,590 ± 270 a BP, 14,300 ± 300 a BP and 13,500 ± 290 a BP (the latter age for humic acids).

Consequently the Kamion Horizon is a floodplain soil preserved by the shelter of dune sand in a very early stage of the Weichselian ice retreat. MANIKOWSKA correlates the Kamion Horizon with the Epe Horizon (KOLSTRUP 1980: 227) from the eastern Netherlands. Perhaps correlation is possible with the Leonard Soil, the youngest fossil soil within the Rhein loess sequence (Fig. 3) (see Appendix 4).

Bølling Soil

The weak peat observed by DE BOER (1995: 118) in Schöbendorf south of Berlin forms the fluvial base of a dune field and is — like the Kamion Horizon — not an inner dune soil. The only inner-dune soil of Bølling age hence published is that from the Kamion dune field (MANIKOWSKA 1991a: 138). On top of dune sand preserved up to 1.5 m thickness, an initial A horizon was developed consisting of „one or two very thin, 0.5–1.5 cm, layers of organic material" [14]C dated to 12,235 ± 260 a BP. The soil has been buried by a 10 m high dune. [10]

Allerød Soil

There is nearly no dune area not documented by an Allerødian soil. Thus it is not the presence of an Allerød soil that is surprising but its varying soil type.

A humic horizon (A horizon) is recorded from The Netherlands and adjacent westernmost Germany (as Usselo horizon, HYSZELER 1947) as well as from Brandenburg (DE BOER 1995: 119) and Młodzieszynek (Fig. 1) close to Warszawa (MANIKOWSKA 1998). In the latter area the Allerød soil often is transformed into a humic soil sediment thus marking the interstadial position by one or several soil sediment layers. The immaturity of the soil of that area may be due to little eolian activity of intra-Allerødian age.

In other places of the same area the Allerød soil is represented as a weak podzolic soil (MANIKOWSKA 1995: 131).

A cambisol is recorded from Brandenburg north of Berlin as Finow Soil (SCHLAAK 1993: 79). Likewise it occurs south of Berlin (BUSSEMER 1998 and BUSSEMER & THIEKE 1998; see Appendix 2). The Finow Soil (SCHLAAK 1993, 1997, 1998, 1999) occurs both lying on glaciofluvial deposits and on eolian older coversand up to 5 m in thickness. Thus its morphology is mostly even to undulated (SCHLAAK 1998: 30). It is a 5–15 cm thick brownish soil, a dystric cambisol. It lacks a humus horizon. Destratification reaches down to 15 cm depth below the soil. The soil has an increased share of pelite mostly in favour of the coarse silt and clay fraction, that is higher in the upper part than in the lower part of the soil. It shows new smectite formation and enrichment of Al and Fe in comparison to its parent rock.

Laterally towards depressions the Finow Soil corresponds to a series of sand-peat layers dating from 11,400 to 10,130 a BP, in its lower part embracing the Laacher See tephra. Charcoal remnants from the soil yielded ^{14}C ages between 11,330 and 10,290 a BP. SCHLAAK (1998: 28) estimates the soil to comprise about 1,200 years ranging from the Allerød Interstadial into the Dryas 3 period (SCHLAAK 1999). JÄGER & KOPP (1999) record a lateral transition from an Allerødian peat into a gleyic gelisol.

Likewise peat (NOWACZYK 1998a, MANIKOWSKA 1995: 131) or a peaty gleyic soil (KOWALKOWSKI et al. 1999) formed in other areas in depressions on top of eolian sand. The peaty gleyic soil yielded ^{14}C ages between 10,879 ± 210 and 10,200 ± 210. [11]

Dryas 3 (Younger Dryas) soil formation ?

In the section of Werneuchen 1 situated 30 km northeast of Berlin in close extramarginal position to the Frankfurt glacier stage, BUSSEMER (1998: 34) describes an ice wedge that vertically cuts a fossil soil. The parent sand below the fossil soil yielded a TL age of 9.6 ± 1.3 ka, the sand fill of the ice-wedge a TL age of 11.3 ± 2.1 ka BP. Both the fossil soil and the ice wedge are horizontally cut by 1.5 m thick eolian sand of young Holocene age. Based on the TL ages BUSSEMER concludes an intra-Dryas 3 age of the fossil soil.

The story of the earth always provides us with surprises, even in earth science. However, a dating method in state of being newly tested should not be applied to produce new revelations of the earth history. Considering the thousands of carefully studied pollen profiles of the Dryas 3 period that show a clear decline and incline of the climate we should be cautious to change well proved results by means of two TL data. The fossil soil may also be an equivalent of the Finow Soil or might have been caused by pervasion of younger weathering processes from the recent surface through the eolian sand cover rich in pores. Later soil processes would pass through the vertically orientated fill of the ice wedge and settle in the older eolian sand aside the ice wedge that is much richer in silt than the Holocene eolian sand. This at least should be taken into account.

Holocene soil formation

The Holocene soils are the continuation of Late Glacial soil formation in those areas where no or no essential morphological dynamics acted. Therefore Holocene soils in flat areas normally embrace a component of Late Glacial soil formation. In case of a depositional socle of Dryas 3 age it is possible to check the true component of Holocene soil formation. Moreover, in case of intermittent Holocene deposition it is possible to yield distinct time sectors of the Holocene soil formation. These cases are perfectly realized in dune fields.

Older Holocene soil formation (Preboreal to Boreal)

A rusty soil, cambic arenosol, is recorded from Poland developed on top of Dryas 3 dunes and covered by Boreal eolian sand (MANIKOWSKA & BEDNAREK 1994, MANIKOWSKA 1998: 95, KOWALKOWSKI et al. 1999). The rusty soil is dated to Preboreal and early Boreal age. The ^{14}C dates of plant macroremains vary from 9,740 ± 100 to 8,630 ± 140 (MANIKOWSKA & BEDNAREK 1994: 34). It is a Bv horizon enriched in iron and Al oxides. Towards the Boreal period it changed locally into podzolization to form a podzolic-rusty soil. In places this rusty soil survives as relic subsoil for recent podzolic soils. KOWALKOWSKI et al. (1999) describe the rusty soil of Jasień as 15–20 cm thick evenly rusty coloured horizon without features of pedogenesis in situ. ^{14}C ages between 10,150 ± 80 and 9,870 ± 120 a BP are somewhat older than those of the rusty soil at Kamion. In case they are reliable they would point to earlier cease of eolian sand redeposition.

Besides brown soils there are, of course, also initial humus horizons and arenosols (regosols). These soils appear sporadicly throughout the Holocene eolian sand deposits wherever short pauses between eolian redeposition occur.

It seems that from the Preboreal on chances for eolian sand redeposition are given rather locally being controlled for example by forest fires. Consequently during the older Holocene soil forming processes are the normal. Eolian revival occurs frequently but happens sporadicly in space and time. Thus the ages of the buried soils differ while their soil types conform.

Mid Holocene soil formation (Atlantic to mid Subboreal)

The time of close forestation in Europe is certainly equivalent to the time of lowest eolian revival of sand transport. Consequently thick soils are developed on eolian sand until human interference cleared the vegetation. The change from cambisol to podzolic soils recorded by MANIKOWSKA for the Boreal period spreads obviously widely over the European sand belt. This change is known since JÄGER & KOPP (1969). Though some of the Bv horizons survived far into the later Holocene as relic horizons (e. g. MANIKOWSKA & BEDNAREK 1994: 37) the soil formation on eolian sand of this period is the podzolic soil.

This change in soil type is — as mentioned in Chapter 2 — due to tapering of the pelite content of the eolian sand towards the Holocene. For the pelite content is an essential prerequisite for the formation of a Bv horizon. MANIKOWSKA & BEDNAREK suggest that the brown soil grew under scattered trees (pine with birch and willow), rich grass vegetation and relatively dry climate. The threshold via podzolization was given by the change to a denser forest with less grass accompanied by a more humid climate. Furthermore it was promoted by the proceding decline of basic cations in the parent rock.

Dune pervasion by soil formation

The process of pervasion of eolian sand by soil formation has hardly been regarded so far. As mentioned above the Holocene eolian sand is poor in pelite content. This implies only little weathering capacity of the Holocene eolian sand and it perfectly invites rain water to pervade downdune. By downward arriving at the Pleistocene eolian sand that is richer in pelite, the pervading rain water finds a substratum proper for weathering. A good example for this process is the pervasion of the Laacher See pumice in the Mittelrhein Basin. At the base of this pumice weathering transforms the Allerødian calcaric regosol into a cambisol during Holocene times (SCHIRMER & IKINGER 1995, IKINGER 1996). Likewise in dunes with similar large porosity pervasion of weathering should be taken into account. A good deal of brown cambisol formation underneath the Holocene eolian sand may result from succeeding pervasion processes. Sometimes this pervasion leaves traces visible as small subhorizontal, undulating small brown streaks and bands — a well known feature likewise mentioned by KOWALKOWSKI et al. (1999: ch. 5).

4. The European sand belt in space and time

In central Europe a west–east extending loess belt covers the upland area with its basins. Adjoining to the north a likewise west–east extending sand belt covers the north Central European lowland forming the European sand belt. Within this sand belt there is an augmentation of dune formation from west towards east.

Both belts, the loess and the sand belt, interfinger. The loess belt encroaches the adjacent northern lowland forming a seam at its southern rim with interfingering of silt and sand. Within this rim the youngest loesses of Late Pleni-Weichselian age alternate with eolian sand (GEHRT 1998). In addition within the sand belt there occur patches of loess or sandloess e. g. along the Lower Rhein (SIEBERTZ 1992, 1998), in the Münster Basin (RABER & SPEETZEN 1992), in Niedersachsen (VIERHUFF 1967), perhaps in western Poland (ISSMER 1999; see also Appendix 1).

On the other hand within the loess belt there are basins with immense eolian sand activity nourished by different sources. The Regnitz Basin for example is nourished mainly by Keuper sand and fluvial redeposited Keuper sand (HABBE et al. 1981). The Unterfranken Basin is fed by Main river sand (HAGEDORN et al. 1991) exploited from the same Keuper sand area. The Oberrhein Basin is fed by river sand of the Rhein and Main (WALTER 1951). The Pannonian Basin is nourished by alluvial fans and river deposits of the Danube and its tributaries (BORSY 1991).

All in all the upland loess belt and the lowland sand belt are separated both in space and time. The separation in space is based on the availability of loose sand on the one hand and silty debris on the other hand inclusive their possibility to settle without being deflated anew. The separation in time seems to be based on permafrost. Under continuous permafrost in sand areas mostly deflation took place polishing ventifacts by sand and ice crystals and producing eolian coversand. In areas supplied by periglacial silty debris strong winds deflate silt enough from the permafrost surface to form loess blankets. Since the permafrost dissipated and the surface dried, augmented sand deflation could start in sand areas, whilst in areas of silty debris the surface soil becomes more and more wet and solid and starts to be vegetated by grass cover thus preventing deflation. First scattered vegetational appearence in the sand belt augmented the obstacles in the flat landscape and caused wind channels thus giving rise for changing the eolian accumulation forms. The apogee of the dune formation should lie in an optimally balanced period between dissipating of permafrost with onset of first plant growth on the one hand and encroachment of dense vegetation on the scattered vegetated land on the other hand.

Concerning the estimations of the peak of dune formation in different investigation areas the results differ highly (Tab. 2):

Tab. 2: Estimated peak of dune formation in different areas. Eolian activity periods after Tab. 1.

Eolian activity period	Chronostrati- graphical age	area	author
4	Dryas 3	north of Berlin	SCHLAAK 1999
		Polish western Pomerania	KOZARSKI & NOWACZYK 1991: 78
3	Dryas 2	south of Berlin	DE BOER 1995: 117
		Wisła river dunes of Kamion	MANIKOWSKA 1991b: 143
2	upper Plenigl.	around Berlin	BÖSE 1991: 21

On the one hand these records certainly reflect the effect of local investigation. On the other hand a certain shift from south to north is visible, too. The oldest dune formation of the European sand belt of 32 ka, recorded from southeastern Poland by WOJTANOWICZ (1999), is a period proir to the glaciation in the northern part of the European sand belt that became ice-free much later to start with dune formation. The summit of eolian activity in the Dryas 3 period is recorded from the area closely extramarginal to the Pomeranian glacier stage that started with ice retreat at about 15 ka.

During the period of dense vegetational cover since Preboreal times only sporadic sand reactivation is possible. It occurs in places of forest burning, caused either naturally or anthropogenically, and in places of human land clearence. However, these sporadic reactivations mostly happen as consequence of the great late Pleni-Weichselian – Late Glacial eolian sand period that provided the large sand masses ready to be deflated anew.

During Pleni-Weichselian and early Late Glacial the periods of eolian activity were much longer than the periods of quiescence in-between. Vice versa from the Allerød period on the periods with denser vegetation were much longer than the periods of eolian activity.

Soil formation within the eolian deposits starts during late Pleni-Weichselian interstadials with AC soils or very faint B horizons. The Finow Soil of Allerødian age presents the first thicker B horizon. The next younger one is the rusty soil of Preboreal age. A possible share of Holocene pervasive soil formation on these brown soils has to be checked. Since the Boreal period the soil development changes to podzolic soils (cf. JÄGER & KOPP 1969) due to changing sand properties, vegetation and climate. During all periods mentioned there were pauses between eolian sand movements short enough to form only arensols (regosols).

Appendix 1

Loess deposits in Polish Western Pomerania

In the midst of the sand belt within the Pomeranian end moraine belt of Polish Western Pomerania there occur silts in small basins and on south slopes within the rolling endmoraine landscape. As KOZARSKI & NOWACZYK (1991) chronicle, BERENDT (1908)[12] described them as glacial deposits, DAMMER (1941) proposed an eolian origin (so-called Flottsand), CEGŁA & KOZARSKI (1976)[13] designate them loess. ISSMER (1998, 1999) provides sedimentological details. The silts occur in a laminated and massive facies. They have to be younger than the underlying Pomeranian Phase and Chojna (resp. Angermünde) Subphase (around 15 ka BP). They exhibit periglacial structures and are covered by flow till. Therefore KOZARSKI & NOWACZYK (1991) and ISSMER (1998, 1999) assign them to the Oldest Dryas before Bølling.

A group of loess patches far beyond the northern limit of the continuous loess belt needs critical proof. High fine-sand share, an average low rate of the typical loess fraction 0,063–0,020 mm, absence of loess molluscs, prevailing bedding of the fine-sandy silts, the field-morphological facies as well as their vertical position within the melt-down phase of the glacial sequence suggest that the eolian nature of these silts is not conclusive. The previously postulated nature as glacial silt perhaps reworked by runoff should be seriously taken into account.

Appendix 2

Fossil soils at the Golssen site

GRAMSCH (1998), BUSSEMER (1998) and BUSSEMER & THIEKE (1998) present a dune area, the site Golssen, south of Berlin (Fig. 1) situated in the Głogów–Baruth Urstromtal. There, the dune area „Gehmlitz" forms a small undulated sand ridge which is a good kilometer long and up to 5 m high. The eolian sand rests upon fluvial sand of a younger level of the Urstromtal, the Younger Baruth Urstromtal.

In a section of 1996 of BUSSEMER (1998) and BUSSEMER & THIEKE (1998) a good meter of eolian coversand is overlying the fluvial sand. The coversand is subdivided by a fossil cambisol with the horizon sequence fAh-AhBv-Bv into an older and younger coversand. According to TL ages the older coversand yielded ages of 14–11 ka BP, the base of the younger coversand an age of 10.7 ± 1.0 ka BP. As consequence the intermittent cambisol should be an equivalent of the Allerødian brown Finow Soil (SCHLAAK 1993: 79).

In another section excavated in 1968 (GRAMSCH 1998) the fossil soil provided artefacts from the Late Palaeolithic Federmesser Culture. Additionally ceramic sherds of Late Bronze age were found within the same strata. GRAMSCH explains the mixture of both cultures in the same strata caused by migration downward from the surface of the fossil cambisol into its B horizon by pedomechanic processes.

However, there remains a contradiction between both groups: After BUSSEMER (1998) and BUSSEMER & THIEKE (1998) the younger coversand is much older than Bronze Age, after GRAMSCH (1998: 16) it has been deposited „soon after resp. generally after the Bronze Age". Looking at the description of the sections given by the authors, BUSSEMER (1998) and BUSSEMER & THIEKE (1998) describe a brown cambisol of the horizon sequence fAh-AhBv-Bv (Braunerde), whereas GRAMSCH presents a podzol of the horizon sequence fAh-Ae-Bs (actually, in his description of 1998: 13 he notes: „humus horizon (A-horizon) 7–9 cm...eluvial horizon 8–15 cm...brown earth horizon (Bv-horizon)" and calls the soil „sand-brown-podsol").

In a third excavation only presented for the field symposium in August 1998 we saw a single fossil soil as good podzol with the horizon sequence fAh-Ae-Bs. This excavation did not produce artefacts.

Consequently, a strong discussion started during this first stop of the field symposium. ALOJZY KOWALKOWSKI mentioned that Braunerde and podzol can occur laterally within the same soil formation, Braunerde in dryer, podzol in wetter positions. In contrast DIETRICH KOPP stated that Braunerde is of Late Glacial age, podzol of Holocene age, therein iron-rich podzol of older Holocene age, iron-poor podzol of younger Holocene age. My own statement was the proposal given in Fig. 6 that would clear the discrepancy between the two groups of excavators: Instead of two eolian sand units there might be three in the Gehmlitz dune field, an older Late Glacial one (period 2 after Tab. 1), a younger Late Glacial one (period 3) and a post-Bronze Age one (period 6). They are separated by two fossil soils, the Allerødian Braunerde of BUSSEMER's excavation and the Holocene podzol in the 1998 excavation. These two fossil soils locally converge to one soil at places where the Dryas 3 dune transformation was not active. The former Braunerde soil changed during the Holocene into a Braunerde-podzol or a podzol. And such a place of convergence of both fossil soils was possibly found in the 1968 excavation of GRAMSCH. This would explain the coexistence of Late Glacial and Young Holocene artifacts in one and only soil.

A similar soil history has been demonstrated in Bliesendorf southwest of Berlin where the soil formation starting with the Late Glacial was not fossilized earlier than the 12th century by eolian sand (BÖSE et al. 1998, BRANDE et al. 1999).

The course of the field excursion led to the Kamion dune field south of Wyszogród where BARBARA MANIKOWSKA demonstrated that during the Allerød period weak podzols developed. This soil type of Allerødian age seems to be inconsistent with KOPP's statement given above. However, his statement would be right in general, when he allows to vary it in that way, that there is a tendency of soil development since the declining Last Glacial from forming cambisols (Braunerde) during the Allerød and the Preboreal period towards strong iron podzols during the mid Holocene, changing to podzols poorer in iron towards the recent times.

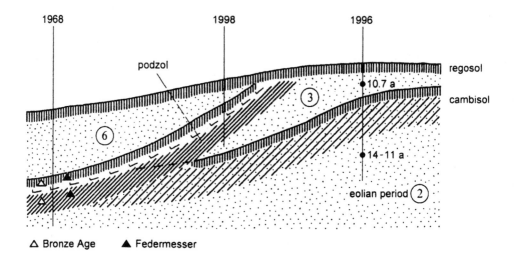

Fig. 6: Gehmlitz sand field close to Golssen south of Berlin. Proposal to clarify the discrepancy in the presentation of three excavations (1968, 1996, 1998).

Appendix 3

Climate of the Dryas 3

During the Dryas 3 (Younger Dryas) period a river terrace was deposited wide-spread in Central Europe, known from many valleys from the Alpine Foreland to the Northern Lowland. It is the Ebing Terrace, likewise called Niederterrasse 3 (SCHIRMER 1983, 1995a). According to cross sections of the terrace body the river pattern changes from meandering to braided. In both cases during the later part of the fluvial activity — whether new deposition or redeposition — the river produced sand plains enough to provide abrasion plains to be deflated. Along the river Rhein the Schönbrunn Terrace — equalling the Pomeranian phase — and the Ebing Terrace itself are crowned by dunes of the Dryas 3 period on both sides of the river. Thus one reason for the cumulation of eolian activity not earlier than in the later part of Dryas 3 is the time necessary to provide sand planes wide enough for large-scale abrasion. In addition another reason, an increased dryness in the second part of Dryas 3 mentioned by KASSE (1999), may be effective. On the other hand there are arguments for the bulk of fluvial deposition in the early Dryas 3. On top of the Ebing Terrace there are thick cold-climate flood deposits prior to the Holocene ones and epigenetic cold-climate indicators as drop soils and cryoturbations on the rivers Main and Rhein (SCHIRMER 1995a: 40).

Summarizing, there are indicators for river activity concentrating during a wet early Dryas 3 period thus providing wide sand plains that easily could be deflated during a dry second Dryas 3 period.

Appendix 4

The boundary Pleni-Weichselian/Late Weichselian

Several researchers draw the boundary with the first warming after the Last Glacial Maximum (LGM). By finding the Kamion Horizon MANIKOWSKA (1995: 131) regarded this interstadial phase as the first warming after the LGM and hence she suggested to draw the boundary between the Pleni-Weichselian and the Late Glacial with the beginning of the Kamion Horizon.

However, looking at the Rhein loess record (Fig. 3) there are at least two interstadials in the loess between the LGM and the eventual climate improvement of the Meiendorf-Bølling-Allerød group. There is the Elfgen Soil as calcaric regosol preceded by the Belmen Soil as weak humic gelic gleysol, and later follows the Leonard Soil as brown calcaric cambisol. These soils are separated by thick loess stacks of the eolian Brabantian loess rich in frost cracks and ice wedges. The largest ice wedges of the Last Glacial at all occur within this Brabantian loess.

This implies that the first part of the Last Glacial stage, the Marine Isotope Stage (MIS) 2, was obviously humid and cold thus triggering the augmentation of inland ice until the LGM. In contrast the period after the LGM was obviouly dry and cold and produced the largest ice wedges within the loess formation. Apart from the change from humid to dry there were several warm interstadials interrupting the MIS 2 cold period. One of them (probably Kesselt Layer till Elfgen Soil) caused the dissipation of continuous permafrost and might have triggered the ice to surge towards its maximum advance (SCHIRMER 1999c).

Drawing the base of the Late Glacial with the beginning of the first warming after the LGM means to draw it together with the maximum ice advance or immediately after it. In doing so the maximum cold dry climate with its large ice wedges would be included into the Late Glacial. Undoubtedly this period of cold dry loess deposition has to be part of the Pleni-Weichselian though there are some interstadial periods intercalated. Consequently the beginning of the Late Glacial should be drawn posterior to the Pleni-Weichselian, with the first interstadial that shows a traceable biological climate improvement towards the Holocene — and this is doubtless the interstadial group of Meiendorf-Bølling-Allerød (BOCK et al. 1985, U. SCHIRMER 1999).

Annotations

[1] Means: eolian activity concerning sand transport. As this article concerns eolian sand all statements on eolian activity concern sand transport and exclude loess transport if not especially noted.

[2] UWG = Upper Weichselian Glaciation, MWG 1 = Middle Weichselian Glaciation 1, MIS = marine isotope stage equaling oxygen stage.

[3] The term *colluvial* equals the German term *deluvial* (action: *delution*), also the

term *ablual* (LIEDTKE in GALBAS et al. 1980: 10), whilst the German *kolluvial* is restricted to down slope transport of soil material, mostly induced by man's impact on the landscape.

[4] Gathering observations during the field excursion for getting a scheme of the eolian deposits, the outlines of the sixfold scheme presented here came into existence during the first days. During the fourth excursion day BARBARA MANIKOWSKA presented her own scheme (MANIKOWSKA 1998: 93) of five eolian stages, by the way in her very clear and distinct manner. Both schemes matched highly. Of course, hers was better geared than mine. Later by studying more literature I found that MANIKOWSKA varied her stage scheme several times (Tab. 1: MANIKOWSKA 1991b, 1995, 1998). The 1991b paper offers a sixfold scheme that excellently matches with my own one.

[5] see annotation 3.

[6] Sandloess is an intermittent member within the range loess—eolian sand with a content of 20–50 % sand mass (AG Boden 1994: 164).

[7] To this period belong the silts of Polish Western Pomerania (Locality Klępicz in Fig. 1). See Appendix 1.

[8] After KOZARSKI & NOWACZYK (1991: 118) and NOWACZYK (1998a) in Great Poland first coversand deposition started as late as the Dryas 2 period. Also BUSSEMER & THIEKE (1998) state in Golssen south of Berlin the start of eolian sedimentation not earlier than Late Glacial. This may be due to observations from single outcrops.

[9] quotet in KOZARSKI (1978: 293)

[10] The Bølling soil is a very rare phenomenon in Europe at all. In areas of low morphological variety the soils of the Bølling and Allerød period are incorporated into the recent soil. In rare cases these Late Glacial soils were separated from the Holocene soil by thicker Late Glacial accumulations as flood deposits, slope debris, eolian sand or the Laacher See volcanic ash. The Late Allerødian Laacher See Tephra preserved the early Allerødian soil as pararendzina (calcaric regosol) on top of loess, the Mendig Soil. Moreover, after pollenanalytical data this Mendig Soil embraces the onsets of soil formation from the beginning of the Meiendorf Interstadial through the Bølling Interstadial up till the Allerød period (SCHIRMER 1996).

Deposition during the Dryas 2 period separating the Bølling and Allerød soils is even more rare.

[11] The soil formation of the Allerød period is the most intensive soil formation during the Late Glacial. Normally, it is incorporated in the surface soil. Together with the weak Meiendorf and Bølling soils, it is the first onset of the post-glacial soil formation. Consequently the Allerødian soil is only preserved in case of being covered. In most cases this happened by Dryas 3 deposits. Besides the eolian sand preservation of the Usselo Soil, the Finow Soil and related soils, preservation by floodplain deposits took place producing the fossil Trieb Soil, a pseudo-chernozem

developed along central European rivers (SCHIRMER 1977: 310, 1995a: 39). Buried by the Laacher See Tephra in 13,000 cal BP the Mendig Soil has been preserved as calcaric regosol on top of loess (SCHIRMER 1995b: 529, 1996) (cf. annotation 10).

[12] cited in KOZARSKI & NOWACZYK (1991: 110)

[13] cited in KOZARSKI & NOWACZYK (1991: 110)

References

AG Boden (1994): Bodenkundliche Kartieranleitung. — 4. Aufl., 392 S.; Hannover.

ANTCZAK-GÓRKA, B. (1998): Corrasion on deflation surfaces in southern Wielkopolska. — In: JÄGER, K.-D., KOWALKOWSKI, A., NOWACZYK, B. & SCHIRMER, W. [eds.]: Dunes and fossil soils of Vistulian and Holocene age between Elbe and Wisła: 74–77; Poznań (AMUniv, Quaternary Res. Inst.).

— (1999): Changeability of climatic conditions of the last ice-sheet decay in the light of corrasion process studies in southern Wielkopolska. — GeoArchaeoRhein, 3: 55–60; Münster.

BLUME, H.-P. & HOFFMANN, R. (1977): Entstehung und pedologische Wirkung glaziärer Frostspalten einer norddeutschen Moränenlandschaft. — Z. Pflanzenernaehr. Bodenkd., 140: 719–732; Weinheim.

BOCK, W., MENKE, B., STREHL, E. & ZIEMUS, H. (1985): Neuere Funde des Weichselspätglazials in Schleswig-Holstein. — Eiszeitalter und Gegenwart, 35: 161–180; Hannover.

BOER, W. M. DE (1995): Äolische Prozesse und Landschaftsformen im mittleren Baruther Urstromtal seit dem Hochglazial der Weichselkaltzeit. — Berliner geogr. Arbeiten, 84: 215 S.; Berlin.

— (1998): Aeolian land forms in the Baruth Ice-Marginal Valley and the dune profile in the Picher Berge near Schöbendorf (Brandenburg). — In: JÄGER, K.-D., KOWALKOWSKI, A., NOWACZYK, B. & SCHIRMER, W. [eds.]: Dunes and fossil soils of Vistulian and Holocene age between Elbe and Wisła: 17–21; Poznań (AMUniv, Quaternary Res. Inst.).

BÖSE, M. (1991): A palaeoclimatic interpretation of frost-wedge casts and aeolian sand deposits in the lowlands between Rhine and Vistula in the Upper Pleniglacial and Late Glacial. — Z. Geomorph. N. F., Suppl.-Bd. 90: 15–28; Berlin, Stuttgart.

— BRANDE, A., FACKLAM, M. & MÜLLER, M. (1998): Bliesendorf — Dune-section on the Glindow moraine plain southwest of Bliesendorf. — In: JÄGER, K.-D., KOWALKOWSKI, A., NOWACZYK, B. & SCHIRMER, W. [eds.]: Dunes and fossil soils of Vistulian and Holocene age between Elbe and Wisła: 22–26; Poznań (AMUniv, Quaternary Res. Inst.).

BORSY, Z. (1991): Blown sand territories in Hungary. — Z. Geomorph. N. F., Suppl.-Bd. 90: 1–14; Berlin, Stuttgart.

BRANDE, A., BÖSE, M., MÜLLER, M., FACKLAM, M. & WOLTERS, S. (1999): The Bliesendorf soil and aeolian sand transport in the Potsdam area. — GeoArchaeoRhein, 3:

147–161; Münster.

BUSSEMER, S. (1998): Bodengenetische Untersuchungen an Braunerde- und Lessivé-profilen auf Sandstandorten des brandenburgischen Jungmoränengebiets. — Münchener geogr. Abh., A 49: 27–93; München.

— & THIEKE, H. U. (1998): Golßen — Example for morphological and pedological development of the oldest Weichselian outwash plains and glacial spillways. — In: JÄGER, K.-D., KOWALKOWSKI, A., NOWACZYK, B. & SCHIRMER, W. [eds.]: Dunes and fossil soils of Vistulian and Holocene age between Elbe and Wisła: 4–12; Poznań (AMUniv, Quaternary Res. Inst.).

DAMMER, B. (1941): Über Flottsande in der östlichen Mark Brandenburg. — Jb. Reichsstelle f. Bodenforschung, 61, 1940: 186–197; Berlin.

DÜCKER, A. & MAARLEVELD, G. C. (1957): Hoch- und spätglaziale äolische Sande in Nordwestdeutschland und in den Niederlanden. — Geol. Jb., 73: 215–234; Hannover.

DULIAS, R. (1999): Holocene dunes in southern Poland. — GeoArchaeoRhein, 3: 137–146; Münster.

DYLIKOWA, A. (1969): Problematyka wydm śródladowych w Polsce w świetle badań strukturalnych. (Summary: Problematics of inland dunes in Poland in the light of structural examinations.) — Prace Geogr. Inst. Geografii Polskiej Akademii Nauk, 75: 39–74.

GALBAS, P. U., KLECKER, P. M. & LIEDTKE, H. (1980): Erläuterungen zur Geomorphologischen Karte 1: 25,000 der Bundesrepublik Deutschland, GMK 25, Blatt 5, 3415 Damme. — 48 p.; Berlin.

GEEL, B. VAN, COOPE, G. R. & HAMMEN, T. VAN DER (1989): Palaeoecology and stratigraphy of the Lateglacial type section at Usselo (The Netherlands). — Rev. Palaeobot. Palynol., 60: 25–129; Amsterdam.

GEHRT, E. [Hrsg.] (1998): Äolische Sedimente und Bodenentwicklung im nördlichen Harzvorland. — Arbeitskreis Paläopedologie der Deutschen Bodenkundlichen Gesellschaft, 17. Sitzung vom 21.–23.5.1998 in Braunschweig, Programm und Exkursionsführer: 127 S.; Hannover (Niedersächs. LA f. Bodenforschung).

GOŹDZIK, J. (1998): Pleni-Vistulian and Late-Vistulian aeolian processes in the vicinity of Belchatów. — In: JÄGER, K.-D., KOWALKOWSKI, A., NOWACZYK, B. & SCHIRMER, W. [eds.]: Dunes and fossil soils of Vistulian and Holocene age between Elbe and Wisła: 98–103; Poznań (AMUniv, Quaternary Res. Inst.).

GRAMSCH, B. (1998): Golssen — A Late Paleolithic site in the Baruth–Głogów Ice Marginal Valley. — In: JÄGER, K.-D., KOWALKOWSKI, A., NOWACZYK, B. & SCHIRMER, W. [eds.]: Dunes and fossil soils of Vistulian and Holocene age between Elbe and Wisła: 13–16; Poznań (AMUniv, Quaternary Res. Inst.).

HAGEDORN, H., RÖSNER, R., KURZ, J. & BUSCHE, D. (1991): Loesses and aeolian sands in Franconia, F. R. G. — Z. Geomorph. N. F., Suppl.-Bd. 90: 61–76; Berlin, Stuttgart.

HABBE, K. A., MIHL, F. & WIMMER, F. (1981): Über zwei 14C-Daten aus fränkischen Dünensanden. — Geol. Bl. NO-Bayern, 31 (1–4): 208–221; Erlangen.

HIJSZELER, C. C. W. J. (1947): De oudheidkundige opgravingen in Twente in de laatste jaren. — Oudheidkundige Bodemonderzoek in Nederland: 327–349, 3 Taf.; Meppel.

IKINGER, A. (1996): Bodentypen unter Laacher See-Tephra im Mittelrheinischen Bekken und ihre Deutung. — Mainzer geowiss. Mitt., **25**: 223–284; Mainz.

ISSMER, K. (1998): Plenivistulian and Late Vistulian loess covers and their relation to the dunes. — In: JÄGER, K.-D., KOWALKOWSKI, A., NOWACZYK, B. & SCHIRMER, W. [eds.]: Dunes and fossil soils of Vistulian and Holocene age between Elbe and Wisła: 33–41; Poznań (AMUniv, Quaternary Res. Inst.).

— (1999): Plenivistulian and Late Vistulian loess deposits in northwestern Poland (Western Pomerania). — GeoArchaeoRhein, **3**: 83–96; Münster.

JÄGER, K.-D. & KOPP, D. (1969): Zur archäologischen Aussage von Profilaufschlüssen norddeutscher Sandböden. — Ausgrabungen und Funde, **14** (3): 111–121; Berlin.

— (1999): Buried soils in dunes of Late Vistulian and Holocene age in the northern part of Central Europe. — GeoArchaeoRhein, **3**: 127–135; Münster.

KASPRZAK, L. (1998): Epigenetic structures of sand-wedge casts with primary mineral filling. — In: JÄGER, K.-D., KOWALKOWSKI, A., NOWACZYK, B. & SCHIRMER, W. [eds.]: Dunes and fossil soils of Vistulian and Holocene age between Elbe and Wisła: 78–86; Poznań (AMUniv, Quaternary Res. Inst.).

KASSE, C. (1999): Late Pleniglacial and Late Glacial aeolian phases in The Netherlands. — GeoArchaeoRhein, **3**: 61–82; Münster.

KOLSTRUP, E. (1980): Climate and stratigraphy in northwestern Europe between 30,000 B.P. and 13,000 B.P., with special reference to The Netherlands. — Meded. Rijks Geol. Dienst, **32** (15): 181–253, 1 encl.

KOPP, D. (1970): Periglaziäre Umlagerungs-(Perstruktions-)zonen im nord-mitteleuropäischen Tiefland und ihre bodengenetische Bedeutung. — Tag.-Ber. dt. Akad. Landwirtsch.-Wiss. Berlin, **102**: 55–81.

KOWALKOWSKI, A. (1998): Soil sequences in the Jasień dune. — In: JÄGER, K.-D., KOWALKOWSKI, A., NOWACZYK, B. & SCHIRMER, W. [eds.]: Dunes and fossil soils of Vistulian and Holocene age between Elbe and Wisła: 65–73; Poznań (AMUniv, Quaternary Res. Inst.).

— NOWACZYK, B. & OKUNIEWSKA-NOWACZYK, I. (1999): Chronosequence of biogenic deposits and fossil soils in the dune near Jasień, Western Poland. — GeoArchaeoRhein, **3**: 107–125; Münster.

KOZARSKI, S. (1978): Das Alter der Binnendünen in Mittelwestpolen. — In: NAGL, H. [Hrsg.]: Beiträge zur Quartär- und Landschaftsforschung (Festschrift J. FINK): 291–305; Wien.

— & NOWACZYK, B. (1991): Lithofacies variation and chronostratigraphy of Late Vistulian and Holocene aeolian phenomena in northwestern Poland. — Z. Geomorph. N. F., Suppl.-Bd. **90**: 107–122; Berlin, Stuttgart.

MANIKOWSKA, B. (1991a): Dune processes, age of dune terrace and Vistulian decline in the Vistula Valley near Wyszogród, central Poland. — Bull. Polish Acad. Sciences,

Earth Sciences, **39** (2): 137–148.

— (1991b): Vistulian and Holocene aeolian activity, pedostratigraphy and relief evolution in Central Poland. — Z. Geomorph. N. F., Suppl.-Bd. **90**: 131–141; Berlin, Stuttgart.

— (1995): Aeolian activity differentiation in the area of Poland during the period 20–8 ka BP. — Biuletyn Peryglacjalny, **34**: 127–165, Tab. 1; Łódź.

— (1998): Aeolian deposits and fossil soils in dunes of Central Poland — the dune in Kamion. — In: JÄGER, K.-D., KOWALKOWSKI, A., NOWACZYK, B. & SCHIRMER, W. [eds.]: Dunes and fossil soils of Vistulian and Holocene age between Elbe and Wisła: 92–97; Poznań (AMUniv, Quaternary Res. Inst.).

— & BEDNAREK, R. (1994): Fossil Preboreal soil on the dune sands in central Poland and its significance for the conception of rusty soils (cambic arenosols) genesis. — Roczniki Gleboznawcze (soil science annual) Suppl., **44**: 27–39; Warszawa.

MARCINEK, J., SARATKA, J. & ZAUMSEIL, L. (1983): Die natürlichen Verhältnisse der Hauptstadt der DDR, Berlin, und ihres Umlandes — ein Überblick. — 113 S., 9 Abb.; Berlin.

MEYER, H.-H. (1984): Jungdünen und Wehsande aus historischer Zeit im Gebiet nördlich des Dümmers. — Oldenburger Jb., **84**: 403–436; Oldenburg.

NOWACZYK, B. (1998a): Eolian cover sands in the vicinity of Cedynia. — In: JÄGER, K.-D., KOWALKOWSKI, A., NOWACZYK, B. & SCHIRMER, W. [eds.]: Dunes and fossil soils of Vistulian and Holocene age between Elbe and Wisła: 42–47; Poznań (AMUniv, Quaternary Res. Inst.).

NOWACZYK, B. (1998b): Holocene transformations of dunes in the vicinity of Osiecza near Konin. — In: JÄGER, K.-D., KOWALKOWSKI, A., NOWACZYK, B. & SCHIRMER, W. [eds.]: Dunes and fossil soils of Vistulian and Holocene age between Elbe and Wisła: 87–91; Poznań (AMUniv, Quaternary Res. Inst.).

PEŁKA-GOŚCINIAK, J. (1999): Influence of wind and older relief on the character of sandy deposits in the Starczynów "Desert" (southern Poland). — GeoArchaeoRhein, **3**: 163–176; Münster.

PYRITZ, E. (1972): Binnendünen und Flugsandebenen im Niedersächsischen Tiefland. — Göttinger geogr. Abh., **61**: 153 S., 3 Beil.; Göttingen.

RABER, C. & SPEETZEN, E. (1992): Flugsand, Sandlöß und Löß im zentralen Münsterland (Westfälische Bucht, NW-Deutschland). — Natur- und Landschaftskunde, **1**: Möhnesee-Körbecke.

ROESCHMANN, G. (1994): Prozesse der Bodenbildung. — In: KUNTZE, H., ROESCHMANN, G. & SCHWERDTFEGER, G. [Hrsg.]: Bodenkunde. — 5. Aufl.: 226–247; Stuttgart (Ulmer).

SCHELLING, J. (1957): Herkunft, Aufbau und Bewertung der Flugsande im Binnenlande. — Erdkunde, **11**: 129–135; Bonn.

SCHIRMER, U. (1999): Pollenstratigraphische Gliederung des Spätglazials im Rheinland. — Eiszeitalter und Gegenwart (im Druck).

SCHIRMER, W. (1977): In: BECKER, B. & SCHIRMER, W.: Palaeoecological study on the Holocene valley development of the River Main, southern Germany. — Boreas, **6**: 303–321; Oslo.

— (1995a): Valley bottoms in the late Quaternary. — Z. Geomorph. N.F., Suppl.-Bd. **100**: 27–51; Berlin.

— (1995b): Mittelrhein Basin and lower Mittelrhein. — In: SCHIRMER, W. [ed.]: Quaternary field trips in Central Europe, **1**: 524–537; München (Pfeil).

— (1996): Spätglaziale Böden unter Laacher See-Tephra. — In: Landesamt für Natur und Umwelt des Landes Schleswig-Holstein [Hrsg.]: Böden als Zeugen der Landschaftsentwicklung: 49–58; Kiel (L.-A. Natur u. Umwelt SH).

— (1999a): The Symposium „Dunes and fossil soils". — GeoArchaeoRhein, **3**: 5–9; Münster.

— (1999b): Eine Klimakurve des Oberpleistozäns aus dem rheinischen Löß. — Eiszeitalter und Gegenwart (im Druck).

— (1999c): Die Eben-Zone im Oberwürmlöß zwischen Maas und Rhein. — Mskr.

— & IKINGER, A. (1995): Gravel pit east of Torney. — In: SCHIRMER, W. [ed.]: Quaternary field trips in Central Europe, **1**: 535; München (Pfeil).

SCHLAAK, N. (1993): Studie zur Landschaftsgenese im Raum Nordbarnim und Eberswalder Urstromtal. — Berliner geogr. Arbeiten, **76**: 145 S., 14 Taf.; Berlin.

— (1997): Äolische Dynamik im brandenburgischen Tiefland seit dem Weichselspätglazial. — Arbeitsberichte Geogr. Inst. Humboldt-Univ. Berlin, **24**: 58 S.; Berlin.

— (1998): Sites in the Toruń–Ebwerswalde ice marginal valley. — In: JÄGER, K.-D., KOWALKOWSKI, A., NOWACZYK, B. & SCHIRMER, W. [eds.]: Dunes and fossil soils of Vistulian and Holocene age between Elbe and Wisła: 27–32; Poznań (AMUniv, Quaternary Res. Inst.).

— (1999): Typical aeolian sand profiles and palaeosols of the Glien till plain in the northwest of Berlin. — GeoArchaeoRhein, **3**: 97–105; Münster.

SIEBERTZ, H. (1998): Methodisch-sedimentologische Auswertungsverfahren bei der Erstellung einer äolischen Decksedimentkarte vom Niederrheinischen Höhenzug. — Decheniana, **151**: 199–212, 1 Beil. ; Bonn.

— (1992): Neue Befunde zu den sedimentologisch-stratigraphischen Lagerungsverhältnissen und zur Altersordnung der äolischen Decksedimente auf dem Niederrheinischen Höhenzug. — Eiszeitalter und Gegewart, **42**: 72–79, 1 Krt. als Beil.; Hannover.

STENGEL, I. (1992): Zur äolischen Morphodynamik von Dünen und Sandoberflächen. — Würzburger geogr. Arb., **83**: 363 S., Taf. 1; Würzburg.

SZCZYPEK, T. & WACH, J. (1999): Human impact and development of a modern scarp dune. — GeoArchaeoRhein, **3**: 177–186; Münster.

VIERHUFF, H. (1967): Untersuchungen zur Stratigraphie und Genese der Sandlößvorkommen in Niedersachsen. — Mitt. Geol. Inst. TH Hannover, **5**: 99 S.; Hannover.

WALTER, W. (1951): Neue morphologisch-physikalische Erkenntnisse über Flugsand und Dünen. — Rhein-Mainische Forschungen, **31**: 4–34, 1 Taf.; Frankfurt a. M.

WOJTANOWICZ, J. (1999): Problem of occurrence and age (TL) of inland Plenivistulian dunes in Poland (on the example of Sandomierz Basin). — GeoArchaeoRhein, **3**: 43–53; Münster.

Address of the author:

Prof. Dr. WOLFGANG SCHIRMER, Abt. Geologie, Heinrich-Heine-Universität, Universitätsstr. 1, D-40225 Düsseldorf, e-mail: schirmer@uni-duesseldorf.de

GeoArchaeoRhein, **3**: 43–53; Münster 1999

Problem of occurrence and age (TL) of inland Plenivistulian dunes in Poland (on the example of Sandomierz Basin)

Józef Wojtanowicz

Abstract: The opinion of S. Z. Różycki (1967) about the occurrence of Plenivistulian inland dunes in Poland can be confirmed. In the Sandomierz Basin (SE Poland) a complex of low and long sand ridges consists of longitudinal dunes elongated in WNW–ESE direction. One of them, i. e. the dune at Żuków, was dated to 22–32 ka BP. The Plenivistulian dunes contain three times more silt fraction than the dunes of the Late Glacial. Sand in the Plenivistulian dunes is distinctly weaker sorted.

1. Introduction

Despite of over a hundred years' history of very successful studies on inland dunes in Europe it seems that not all problems have been resolved. One of the essential questions is the age of dunes. It is accepted that the inland dunes in Europe were formed in the Late Glacial but the controversial question is the beginning of the dune-forming processes, i. e. age of the initial stage of dune development. Recently, new data have been published in Poland, from which we can determine the age of the initial stage at 14–15 ka BP (Manikowska 1991, 1995) or even at about 16 ka BP (Wojtanowicz 1996).

However, the problems connected with inland dunes should be considered in relation to aeolian activity during the Vistulian, and especially the Plenivistulian. In the non-glaciated area under in periglacial conditions the aeolian processes were the main relief-forming processes besides the fluvial ones (Goździk 1991).

At that time the youngest and thickest loess covers were formed in upland areas and aeolian coversands in river valleys, pradolinas and denudation plains of the European Lowland. Fluvial sediments were subjected to aeolian processes (Goździk 1995; Buraczyński 1994). Strong deflation and corrasion processes resulted in formation of denudation pavements built of ventifacts.

Were dunes formed during the Plenivistulian? Have they persisted in recent relief? The investigations in the Sandomierz Basin (S Poland) allowed the author to give affirmative answers to these questions.

2. Problem of Plenivistulian dunes in Poland in the light of former research

The earliest studies on the Plenivistulian dunes were published by Różycki (1967) who thought that "excellently developed systems of parabolic dunes... were however only one of the last stages of their development" (p. 185). He considered the narrow, elongated dune ridges several metres high and extending in W–E direction in the Błonie Plain (west of Warsaw) to be the oldest persisted dune generation. RÓŻYCKI recognized these sandy ridges as longitudinal dunes formed by winds of higher velocities on bare ground "in conditions quite different from those which occurred during the formation of parabolic inland dunes" (p. 186). He stated that these longitudinal dunes were formed before the Leszno phase of the last glaciation. Thus, they should be older than 20 ka BP.

Persistence chances of the Plenivistulian dunes were also discussed by MARUSZCZAK (1968, 1983). He noticed that these dunes were characterized by weaker grain sorting than the Late Glacial dunes and contained an admixture of silt, though nobody found any example of loess covering dunes in Poland. However, MYCIELSKA-DOWGIAŁŁO (1965) observed in southern Poland not only dune sands of the main stage encroaching on loesses (well-known and rather common phenomenon) but also silty inserts in aeolian sands.

In the opinion of GOŹDZIK (1991) in Central Poland the first dunes could be formed in land depressions during the Upper Plenivistulian from 19 to 13.5 ka BP. In the other recent Polish papers dealing with aeolian activity during the Vistulian (KOZARSKI 1990; KOZARSKI & NOWACZYK 1991; MANIKOWSKA 1991, 1995) the problem of Plenivistulain dunes was not mentioned.

3. Dunes of the Sandomierz Basin

The Sanomierz Basin is a lowland situated between the Carpathians in the south and the Middle Polish Upland belt (Małopolska Upland, Lublin Upland and Roztocze Upland) in the north. The main relief forms of the basin are the wide valleys of the Vistula river and its Carpathian tributaries the longest of which is the San river. In these valleys extensive Pleistocene sand terraces occur. Especially wide proluvial plains exist at the foot of the Roztocze Upland. Outside the river valleys rolling plateaux are covered by various Pleistocene deposits. This area was not glaciated during the Vistulian.

The Sandomierz Basin is characterized by a strong dune relief. It is one of the largest complexes of inland dunes in Poland. They were investigated by the author (WOJTANOWICZ 1969, 1970).

3.1. Beginning of the main stage of inland dune development

When studying the dunes of the Sandomierz Basin in the 60's the author correlated the first stage of dune-forming processes with the Oldest Dryas (WOJTANOWICZ 1969). Recently several dunes were thermoluminescence-dated (Tab. 1). The TL datings were made by mgr JAROSŁAW KUSIAK in the TL Laboratory of the Department of Physical Geography and Paleogeography, UMCS, Lublin, ul. Akademicka 19, 20-033 Lublin. Their distribution is shown in Fig. 1. Beside the dunes in the Sandomierz Basin (at Niwiska, Pikuły, Piskorowy Staw) also those occurring in the neighbouring Roztocze region (at Górecko Kościelne, Józefów, Zawadki) were investigated. The dunes are of

Tab. 1: TL datings from the bottom parts of dunes in SE Poland.

Region	Profile	Depth [m]	Annual dose Dr [Gy/ka]	Paleodose ED [Gy]	TL age [ka BP]	Laboratory sample No.
Sandomierz Basin	Niwiska	12.5	0.922	11.5±1.7	12.5±1.9	LUB-3049
	Pikuły	5.4	0.818	7.5±1	9.2±1.3	LUB-3557
	Pikuły	6.0	0.786	9.2±1.3	11.7±1.7	LUB-3558
	Pikuły	6.2	0.792	9.8±1.4	12.4±1.9	LUB-3559
	Pikuły	6.4	0.967	12.8±1.8	13.2±2.0	LUB-3560
	Pikuły	7.0	0.878	14.8±2.1	16.9±2.5	LUB-3561
	Piskorowy Staw	0.8-1.0	0.805	11±2.3	14±3	LUB-3013
	Piskorowy Staw	1.2-1.4	0.828	10±2.5	12±3	LUB-3014
Roztocze Upland	Górecko Kośc.	6.0	0.657	11±3	16.7±5	LUB-3072
	Józefów	10.5	0.568	6±1.5	10.5±3	LUB-3073
	Zawadki	17.8-18.0	0.494	5.5±1	11±2.3	LUB-3211
	Zawadki	18.3-18.4	0.878	9±1.5	10.2±2	LUB-3213

parabolic and transversal ridge types, well developed, strongly marked in relief. Some of them are high. Only the bottom or basal parts of the dunes were dated. The obtained datings range from 10.5 to 16.9 ka BP. These are the first results of absolute dating (by the TL method) of dunes in south-eastern Poland. These preliminary results indicate that all studied dunes were formed during the Late Glacial. However, the beginning of dune-forming processes should be shifted before the Oldest Dryas, and also before the Kamion phase (= Epe) after MANIKOWSKA (1991, 1995). It should be determined at about 16–16.5 ka BP.

3.2. Plenivistulian dunes near Żuków

A very interesting complex of relief forms recognized as aeolian relief has been found near Żuków on the Tarnogród Plateau in the eastern part of the Sandomierz Basin (Figs. 1, 2). Sand ridges, sometimes discontinuous and consisting of separate hummocks, are elongated in WNW–ESE direction and form parallel series. Their length ranges from several hundred metres to several kilometres (2.5-6.5 km), and width from 20 to 60 m; 40 m on average. Their ridges are low, they reach a height of 1–4 m.
The sand ridges are situated in different morphological positions. They occur in

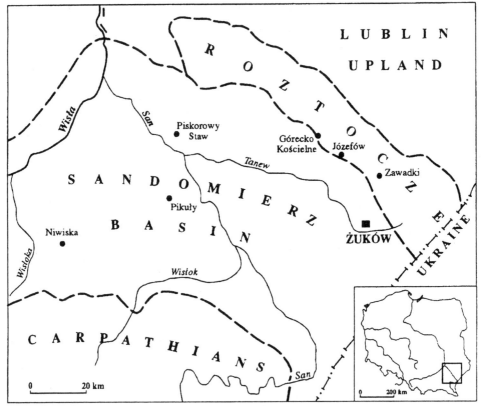

Fig. 1: Location sketch of the Plenivistulian dune at Żuków and of TL-dated Late Glacial dunes.

depressions, mainly in valleys which here have flat, swampy bottoms, but they also occur encroaching on slopes and low watershed areas. It is well visible in Fig. 2 that a sand ridge can join different relief forms; for example a longer ridge in the centre of Fig. 2 between Żuków and Nowy Lubliniec extends from the valley of the Buszcza and Łówcza rivers to the east and encroaches on a several metres high watershed area. Thus, it seems that the studied ridges do not belong to natural levees built up by aeolian sands. Similar forms studied by MYCIELSKA-DOWGIAŁŁO (1978) in the northern part of the Sandomierz Basin were recognized as natural levees. There are some ridges, for example in the Gnojnik valley near Żuków, which follow the valley line. However their orientation is adapted to relief forms.

The studied sand ridges differ from the Late Glacial dunes. They are considerably less visible in the relief. Their lines correspond with lines of the Plenivistulian dune ridges in the Błonie Plain investigated by RÓŻYCKI (1967). They also correspond entirely with the WNW direction of aeolian sand transport during the Plenivistulian, recognized in Central Poland by GOŹDZIK (1991, 1995), in the Roztocze and Sandomierz Basin by BURACZYŃSKI (1993).

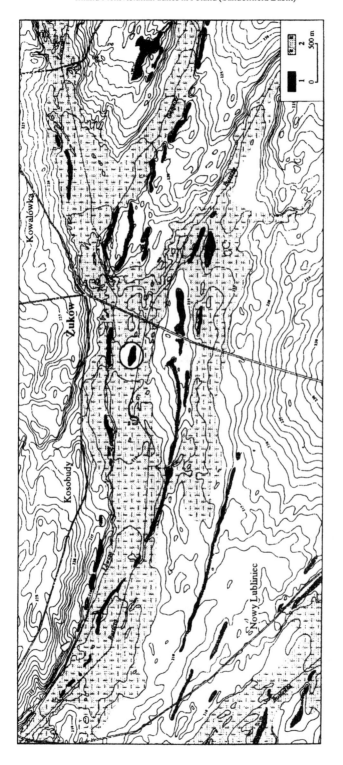

Fig. 2: Situation of dunes in the environs of Żuków.
1 – dunes, 2 – Holocene river accumulation plains. Isohypses every 1.75 m.

The structure of the described ridges was examined in an exposure in the Żuków dune ridge (Fig. 3) — a low but distinctly visible hummock about 4 m high (216.5 m a.s.l.), 60 m wide, 22 m long and extending in WNW–ESE direction. It emerges from the wet, swampy plain of the Łówcza and Buszcza rivers — tributaries of the Wirowa river. The dune is situated between the rivers and looks as if it had sunk into the river alluvia. And that is the fact. More detailed analysis of a map indicates that the examined hummock is not the only thereabout; it is the highest one of several hummocks forming an about 3 km long train extending in WNW–ESE direction. Some of these hummocks are almost completely "drowned". Those situated west of Kosobudy lie at the base of the valley edge.

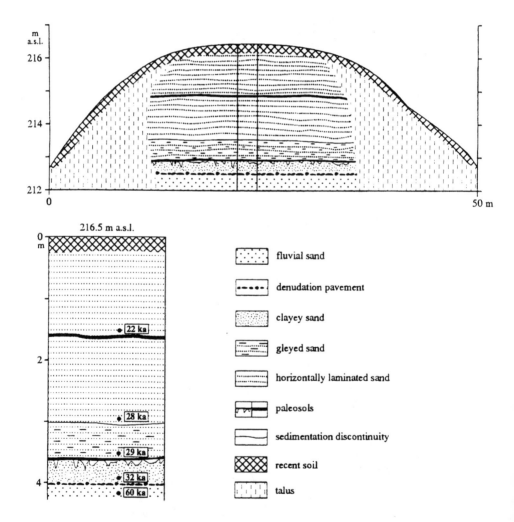

Fig. 3: Cross-section and profile of the Żuków dune.

The structure of the Żuków dune has been studied in detail (Fig. 3). On top occurs a very well developed soil of brown or eroded podzol type with a thick illuvial horizon. Partially it has features of a subfossil soil because it is covered by younger sands in places. Yellow-brown, medium-grained sand with horizontal wavy lamination occurs to the depth of 3 m (Photo 1). Darker laminae consisting of finer sand and of silty-clayey fraction are characteristic here. In the whole profile the content of silt is higher than in typical dunes. This is visible even in the field. In the main 3 m thick sandy series, at a depth of 1.5 m there occurs a horizon of a weakly developed soil or a vegetation horizon 10 cm thick, in which lamination is not visible. At a depth of 3.0–3.7 m, a layer of white, gleyed, streaky sand occurs. A thin humus horizon lying below is disrupted by "fingers" — root traces (?). Ferrugineous, streaky, somewhat clayey sand occurring at a depth of 3.7–4.0 m is underlain by a denudation pavement consisting of rounded gravel overlying medium-grained, laminated fluvial sands.

Five samples repesenting all essential layers were dated by TL method (Tab. 2, Fig. 3). The fluvial sand below the denudation pavement was dated to about 60 ka BP, i. e. to the beginning of the Plenivistulian. The clayey sand over the denudation pavement was dated to 32 ka BP. It marks the beginning of dune accumulation. The age of the sand lying directly over the older paleosol (thin humus horizon with "fingers") was determined at 29 ka BP. The dating obtained from the bottom of the main 3 m thick sand series was 28 ka BP. The younger paleosol (from a depth of 1.5 m) was dated to 22 ka BP. Thus, the examined paleosols were probably formed during the Hengelo and Denekamp interstadials, respectively.

All the datings of the dune sediments range from 22 to 32 ka BP. Therefore, they indicate that the studied dune was created during the Plenivistulian.

Tab. 2: TL datings of the Żuków dune.

Lithology Situation	Depth [m]	Annual dose Dr [Gy/ka]	Paleodose ED [Gy]	TL age [ka BP]	Laboratory sample No.
Sand from the younger paleosol	1.5-1.6	1.158	25±4	22±3.7	LUB-3068
Yellow-brown, horizontally laminated sand	2.9-3.0	0.919	26±4	28±4.3	LUB-3069
Sand over the older paleosol	3.6-3.7	0.904	26±4	29±4.7	LUB-3070
Clayey sand over the pavement	3.8-4.0	0.932	30±4.8	32±5.4	LUB-3071
Sand below the pavement	4.5	1.140	68±13.6	60±12	LUB-3016

JÓZEF WOJTANOWICZ

Tab. 3: Grain size distribution of investigated dunes.

Situation	Depth (cm)	Content of fraction in %; diameter in mm							Granulometric indices according to FOLK & WARD			
		>1	1-0.5	0.5-0.25	0.25-0.1	0.1-0.05	0.05-0.02	<0.02	Mz	σ_I	Sk_I	K_G
Piskorowy Staw	0.8-1.0	0.70	4.28	39.71	52.15	1.92	0.83	0.41	2.14	0.77	0.00	0.74
Piskorowy Staw	1.2-1.4	0,00	3.57	39.72	50.97	3.17	2.49	0.08	2.18	0.81	0.05	0.81
Górecko Kościelne	6.0	0.20	2.63	48.82	46.82	0.59	0.45	0.00	2.06	0.75	0.14	0.74
Józefów	10.5	0.00	2.65	54.48	42.33	0.20	0.22	0.12	0.96	0.72	0.20	0.76
Żuków	1.5-1.6	0.40	3.66	48.01	30.28	1.04	0.53	4.82	2.36	1.16	0.19	1.33
Żuków	2.9-3.0	0.83	10.47	40-76	46.35	4.75	0.17	1.69	2.02	0.99	0.13	1.00
Żuków	3.6-3.7	0.13	6.44	41.90	39.40	3.88	1.83	2.40	2.10	0.84	0.04	0.80
Żuków	3.8-4.0	0.47	16.50	31.52	49.54	7.89	2.17	3.17	1.82	0.91	0.13	0.93

Photo 1: Structure of the Żuków dune.

Granulometric analysis confirmed a greater content of silt and clay fraction (almost three times on average) in the Żuków dune in comparison with dunes of Late Glacial age (Tab. 3). The percentage of these fine fractions was greatest at the beginning of the sedimentation and decreased towards the top of the Żuków dune. The sand of this dune is distinctly weaker sorted ($\sigma_1 = 0.84$–1.16) than the sand of the other examined dunes ($\sigma_1 =$ 0.72–0.81).

Taking into account all the information about structure and texture of the Żuków dune it can be stated that this dune was formed under different paleogeographic conditions than the Late Glacial dunes. It was accumulated under periglacial conditions when permafrost occurred. Silt was important in the aeolian sedimentation because a lot of silt material was produced during the cryolithogenesis.

4. Conclusions

In south-eastern Poland, in the Sandomierz Basin a dune complex forms low and up to several kilometres long sand ridges elongated in WNW–SES direction as longitudinal dunes. They differ in conditions of occurrence, relief and structure from the Late Glacial parabolic and transversal dunes. Field investigations, granulometric analysis and TL datings show that the longitudinal dune ridges were formed during the Plenivistulian. One of these forms was TL-dated to 32–22 ka BP.

It seems that the dune site at Żuków is the first one in Poland which is TL-dated to Plenivistulian age.

5. References

BURACZYŃSKI, J. (1993): Rozwój procesów eolicznych piętra Wisły na Roztoczu i w Kotlinie Sandomierskiej (Summ.: Development of eolian processes during the Vistulian stage in Roztocze Upland and Sandomierz Basin). — Wyd. UMCS, Lublin: 64 p.

— (1994): Rola procesów eolicznych w rozwoju pokryw piaszczystych na Roztoczu Tomaszowskim (Summ.: Role of aeolian processes in the development of cover sands on Tomaszów Roztocze Upland). — In: NOWACZYK, B. & SZCZYPEK, T. [eds.]: Vistuliańsko-holoceńskie zjawiska i procesy eoliczne — wybrane zagadnienia: 13–23; Poznań.

GOŹDZIK, J. (1991): Sedimentological record of aeolian processes from the Upper Plenivistulian and the turn of Pleni- and Late Vistulian in Central Poland. — Z. Geomorph. N. F., Suppl.-Bd. 90: 51–60; Berlin, Stuttgart.

— (1995): Wpływ procesów eolicznych na genezę górnoplenivistuliańskich aluwiów w środkowej Polsce (Summ.: Impact of aeolian processes on the formation of Upper Plenivistulian alluvium in Central Poland). — Acta Univ. Lodz., Folia Geographica, 20: 99–107; Łódź.

KOZARSKI, S. (1990): Pleni and Late Vistulian aeolian phenomena in Poland: new occurrences, palaeoenvironmental and stratigraphic interpretations. — Acta

Geographica Debrecina, **26-27**: 31–45; Debrecen.

— & Nowaczyk, B. (1991): Lithofacies variation and chronostratigraphy of Late Vistulian and Holocene aeolian phenomena in northwestern Poland. — Z. Geomorph. N. F., Suppl.-Bd. **90**: 107–122; Berlin, Stuttgart.

Manikowska, B. (1992): Vistulian and Holocene aeolian activity, pedostratigraphy and relief evolution in Central Poland. — Z. Geomorph. N. F., Suppl.-Bd. **90**: 131–141; Berlin, Stuttgart.

— (1995): Aeolian activity differentiation in the area of Poland during the period 20-8 ka BP. — Biul. Perygl., **34**: 125–165.

Maruszczak, H. (1968): Przebieg zjawisk w strefie peryglacjalnej w okresie ostatniego zlodowacenia w Polsce (Summ.: The course of phenomena in the periglacial zone during the last glaciation). — Prace Geogr. IG PAN, **74**: 157–200; Warszawa.

— (1983): Procesy rzeźbotwórcze na obszarze Polski w okresie ostatniego zlodowacenia i w holocenie. — In: Kozłowski, J. K. & Kozłowski, S. K. [eds.]: Człowiek i środowisko w pradziejach: 32–42; Warszawa.

Mycielska-Dowgiałło, E. (1965): Mutual relation between loess and dune accumulation in Southern Poland. — Geogr. Polon., **6**: 105–115.

— (1978): Rozwój rzeźby fluwialnej północnej części Kotliny Sandomierskiej w świetle badań sedymentologicznych (Summ.: Development of the fluvial relief in the north part of the Sandomierz Basin in the light of sedimentological research). — Dissertationes Universitatis Varsoviensis, **120**: 167 p.; Warszawa.

Różycki, S. Z. (1967): Plejstocen Polski Środkowej (Summ.: The Pleistocene of Middle Poland). — PWN: 251 p.; Warszawa.

Wojtanowicz, J. (1969): Typy genetyczne wydm Niziny Sandomierskiej (Rés.: Types génétiques de dunes dans le Bassin de Sandomierz). — Annales Univ. Marie Curie-Skłodowska, sec. B, **24**: 1–45; Lublin.

— (1970): Wydmy Niziny Sandomierskiej w świetle badań granulometrycznych (Rés.: Les dunes du Bassin de Sandomierz á la lumiére de l'examin granulométrique). — Annales Univ. Marie Curie- Skłodowska, sec. B, **25**: 1–49.

— (1996): Wiek inicjalnej fazy wydm śródlądowych późnoglacjalnych i problem wydm plenivistuliańskich w Polsce południowo-wschodniej w świetle datowań TL (Summ.: Age of the initial phase of the Late Glacial intracontinental dunes and problem of the Plenivistulian dunes in south-eastern Poland in the light of TL datings). — In: Szczypek, T. & Waga, J. M. [eds.]: Współczesne oraz kopalne zjawiska i formy eoliczne — wybrane zagadnienia . — Uniwersytet Śląski: 157–169; Sosnowiec.

Address of the author:

Prof. Dr. Józef Wojtanowicz, Instytut Nauk o Ziemi, ul. Akademicka 19, PL-20-033 Lublin, Poland.

GeoArchaeoRhein, **3**: 55–60; Münster 1999

Changeability of climatic conditions of the last ice-sheet decay in the light of corrasion process studies in southern Wielkopolska

BARBARA ANTCZAK-GÓRKA

Abstract: The process of corrasion is recorded in the area of the Pleistocene glaciation mainly in the form of the ventifacts. This event has been studied in the marginal zone of the last glaciation in the Leszno Till Plateau. There occur wind-polished stones on the surface as well as in a fossil deflation horizon. The till underlying the horizon shows fossil structures of epigenetic frost fissures. Detailed studies of the ventifacts' morphology were carried out as well as simple petrographical analysis and comparison of both in different morphological situations.

1. Introduction

Corrasion is a process mainly recorded in solid rocks. However, traces of corrasion are generally found in former glaciated areas. These are mainly wind-polished stones occurring in different geomorphological situations. They are found outside of sedimentation areas, i. e. they are related to genetically different forms and deposits. Their sites are known both from areas of older moraine till plains, from outwashes, river terraces and proglacial marginal valleys. As was stated by KOZARSKI & NOWACZYK (1992), they occur in the top parts of the upper pleni-Vistulian and late-Vistulian series and are formed as a series of ventifacts. Likewise their sites are commonly found in series older than the Vistulian, particularly in fossil levels of deflation horizons (NITZ 1965; KUBIŚ 1978; ANTCZAK-GÓRKA 1995).

2. Study site

In the Leszno Till Plateau corrasion within the area of maximum extent of the last glaciation is mainly related to the recession period from the maximum Vistulian phase although, undoubtedly, its effects are the consequences of processes older than the last glaciation. The time of periglacial climatic conditions which formed these series is also difficult to define. However, the maximum of corrasion processes was in the period of most severe periglacial desert. Conditions for extensive distribution of this periglacial domain existed in Wielkopolska throughout the period of Vistulian deglaciation (KOZARSKI 1993). About 20 km north of Wschowa there is the Radomierz site (Fig. 1) being part of the Śmigiel Plain (KRYGOWSKI 1961). KRYGOWSKI defines that region as an area with slight periglacial transformation. The plain consists of uplands representing till plateaus flanked by outwash plains. Absolute heights of the area vary from 100 to 116 m above sea level.

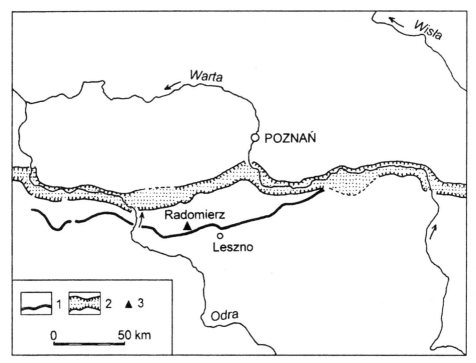

Fig. 1: Location map.
1 – limit of the last glaciation, 2 – Warsaw-Berlin ice marginal valley, 3 – study site.

3. Aeolian coversands

Very common in this area are aeolian coversands with an average thickness of 1.0 to
1.5 m. Fine sands alternate with medium ones. At the Radomierz site the thickness of
this series is 1.3 m. Under this layer one finds a transient zone formed as medium grain
sand with singular stones of 3 cm in diameter. At a depth of 1.5 m a fossil deflation
pavement with a thickness of up to 30 cm was found. In the transient zone only single
small stones with traces of eolian microrelief are found, whereas in the deflation horizon
the number of ventifacts increases to 64 % of the entire clast population (Tab. 1).

Tab. 1: Population of eologlyptoliths in different morphological situations.

	transitional zone	deflational horizon
clasts	119	461
eologlyptoliths (%)	26	64
ventifacts (%)	17	49

4. The ventifacts' morphology

Tab. 2 and 3 demonstrate a detailed analysis of the shape and size of rocks at the Radomierz site. This analysis was made both in the deflation pavement horizon where rocks modeled by the wind occur in situ and on the surface of forested and farmland areas. This procedure intends to find out to what extent the variability of ventifacts differs in natural and anthropogenically affected layers.

Tab. 2: Variety of ventifact shapes in different morphological situations (in %).

	1-faceted	2-faceted	3-faceted	multi-faceted
deflational horizon	46,2	24,9	20,8	8,1

Tab. 3: Range of ventifact diameters in different geomorphological situations (in %).

	0 cm to 4 cm	4cm to 8 cm	≥ 8 cm
deflational horizon	34,2	29,8	36,0
surface	47,1	30,6	23,3

One- and two-faceted ventifacts are dominant both within the surface test fields and in the fossil horizon; only three- and multifaced ventifacts occur approximately 6 % more often in the fossil horizon than on the surface. This may be an indication of a more advanced corrasion in the fossil level or of a greater dynamics of clasts, as is stated by DYLIK (1952). One- and two-edged ventifacts with one polished wall are dominant on the surface whereas in the fossil horizon the number of polished walls increases insignificantly (4.7 %). In both horizons simple edges are dominant, arch-like ones are less frequent, s-shaped ones are least frequent.

Ventifacts of a diameter up to 4 cm are dominant on the surface, whereas the percentage of ventifacts of a diameter larger than 8 cm clearly increases (by 12.7 %) in the fossil horizon. This is undoubtedly an effect of farming.

Concerning the affected rock types wind polished stones are mainly found among porphyrites, sandstones, granodiorites, granites and gneisses. Differences between the surface and the fossil horizon were not stated.

5. The structure of the frost fissure

Below the fossil deflation pavement a till layer is connected genetically with the maximum of the last glaciation (KASPRZAK 1988). This till is cut by fossil ice wedges 1.3 m in depth with an aperture on top of 24 cm in width. These wedges are filled by fine sand similar to the aeolian coversand lying above. Those epigenetic ice-wedges are typical in this region (KASPRZAK 1988).

6. The ventifact microrelief

The corrasion process was particularly observed at the Górsko site located about 2 km south of Radomierz. On the surface of farmland a population of wind-polished stones has been found, constituting over 60 % of the population of all clasts — it is comparable to the number of wind-polished stones in the fossil deflation horizon. This particularly large intensity of aeolian transformation of small stones was also recorded in a very rich eolian microrelief. The most frequent forms are holes and grooves. However, over half of the forms have well formed flutes and cupules. Obviously the degree to which microrelief was formed is closely related to the mineral composition of rocks. Poly-mineral rocks are characterized by more complex microrelief. Laminated stones and ventifacts with concave surfaces that are indicating a very advanced process of aeolian weathering (DYLIK 1952) are common at this site. Like at the adjacent site, ventifacts are mainly formed here in porphyritic rocks, sandstones, granodiorites, granites and gneisses and single forms in quartzites.

7. The quartz grain shapes

At the Radomierz site quartz grains from aeolian coversands were examined by the graniformametry method (KRYGOWSKI 1964). The results are given in Tab. 4. They are mainly sands in which half angular grains (type β) are dominant. This type of quartz grains is also dominant at the base. The loss of young angular grains compared to the base is insignificant. No clear vertical differentiation in the roundness of the eolian coversands was observed. On this basis one can conclude that aeolian processes did not have much impact on the modelling of quartz grains in this series.

Tab. 4: Abrasion of quartz grains in the Radomierz site.

	type α	type β	type γ	Wo index of abrasion
eolian cover sands	17,0	59,6	23,4	1063
substratum	22,4	50,9	25,8	1079

8. Climatic conditions in the period of deglaciation

The corrasion process in the area under discussion was recorded as a series of wind-polished stones occurring both on the surface and in fossil deflation horizons. It was found that after a phase of intensive deflation and corrasion there was a phase of eolian accumulation, which is evidenced by layers of aeolian coversands.

The question of the variation and the timespan of the periglacial processes activity is still an open problem. On the basis of studies of the wind-created periglacial processes and the events connected with them we can state that after the recession of the last ice-sheet from the maximum phase conditions of very serverely cold desert were present. Evidence for these conditions are the epigenetic ice-wedges developed in the till deposits of the last glaciation, the ventifacts and the rather thick layers of aeolian coversand. All these events occured under conditions of a cold desert without plants or with very poor plant cover.

The question remains whether it was continous or discontinous permafrost, whether it was an only seasonal or a perenial event ?

The studies of periglacial phenomena in the zone of the Leszno Till Plain showed that there was no climatic jump after the maximum ice extent and the climatic changes were rather gradual, because there is no evidence of surficial water activity. In conclusion, the results presented show that after the recession of the maximum ice extent there existed conditions favouring permafrost development and the intensive process of corrasion and probably deflation. After this period, aeolian accumulation took place. This model is similar to that presented by KOZARSKI (1993).

9. Acknowledgments

I would like to thank M. A. MIROSLAWA LIMANÓWKA who performed the laboratory analysis, to M. A. NADSTOGA who translated the text and to JOHN CATLOW who corrected our English.

10. References

ANTCZAK-GÓRKA, B. (1995): Analiza przestrzenna i gęstość występowania eologliptolitów na obszarach testowych Polski środkowozachodniej [Spatial analysis and density of eologlyptoliths on test areas of Central and Western Poland]. — In: KOZARSKI, S. [ed.]: Deglacjacja Północno-zachodniej Polski: warunki i transformacja geosystemu (20 → 10ka BP) [Deglaciation of north-western Poland: conditions and transformation of the geosystem, 20 → 10ka BP], part II, analytical monograph KBN 603198101.

DRZEWICKA, I. (1950/51): Zagadnienie form i klasyfikacji graniaków wiatrowych [The problem of forms and classification of wind ventifacts]. — Czasopismo Geograficzne, **20/21**: 217–236.

DYLIK, J. (1952): Głazy rzeźbione przez wiatr i utwory podobne do lessu w Środkowej Polsce (Summ.: Wind worn stones and loess like formation in Middle Poland). — Biul. Inst.Geol., **67**: 173–198.

KASPRZAK, L. (1988): Dyferencjacja mechanizmów formowania stref marginalnych faz leszczyńskiej i poznańskiej ostatniego zlodowacenia na Nizinie Wielkopolskiej (Summ.: Mechanism differentiation in the formation of marginal zones Leszno and Poznań phases of the last glaciation, Great Poland Lowland). — Dokomentacja Geogr., **5–6**, Inst. Geogr. Przestrz. Zagosp. PAN, 159 p.; Wrocław, Warszawa.

KOZARSKI, S. (1993): Late Vistulian deglaciation and expansion of the periglacial zone in NW Poland. — Geol. Mijnbouw, **72**: 143–157.

— & NOWACZYK, B. (1992): Późnovistuliańskie i holoceńskie zjawiska eoliczne w rejonie dolnej Odry i dolnej Warty (Summ.: Lithofacies variation and chronostratigraphy of the Late Vistulian and Holocene phenomena in northwestern Poland). — In: SzczYPEK, T. [red.]: Wybrane zagadnienia z geomorfologii eolicznej.WNoZ UŚl.: 37–117; Sosnowiec.

KRYGOWSKI, B. (1961): Geografia fizyczna Niziny Wielkopolskiej. Cz.I (Summ.: Physical geography of the Great Poland Lowland). — Geomorfologia, PTPN Wydz.Mat.-Przyr.: 203.

KUBIŚ, W. (1978): Próba wykorzystania graniaków jako prawdopodobnego wyznacznika północnego zasięgu strefy peryglacjalnej w pełni Wurmu pomiędzy Turkiem a Koninem (Summ.: An attempt to use the ventifacts as probable indicator of the northern extent of periglacial pleni Wurm zone in the area between Turek and Konin). — Bad. Fizjogr. Pol. Zach., **31**: 103–126.

NITZ, B. (1965): Windgeschliffene Geschiebe und Steinsohlen zwischen Fläming und Pommerscher Eisrandlage. — Geologie, **14:** 686–696; Berlin.

Address of the author:

Dr. BARBARA ANTCZAK-GÓRKA, Institute of Quaternary Research, Adam Mickiewicz University, Geomorphology Section, ul. Wieniawskiego 17/19, PL-61-713 Poznań, Poland.

GeoArchaeoRhein, 3: 61–82; Münster 1999

Late Pleniglacial and Late Glacial aeolian phases in The Netherlands

Cornelis Kasse

Abstract: A new Late Glacial site Oud-Lutten with well-developed aeolian units separated by organic deposits is presented from the eastern Netherlands. The results are discussed and a comparison is made with previously established phases of aeolian activity. Three aeolian phases are distinguished during the Weichselian Late Pleniglacial and Late Glacial in the Netherlands (see Tab. 1). During phase I (c. 20–14 ka BP) aeolian activity was very important, but the preservation of primary aeolian deposits was low due to the presence of permafrost and related overland flow. Phase II (c. 14–11.9 ka BP) represents the major period of widespread aeolian deposition in sand-sheets and low-dunes. Locally, two subphases (II a and II b) have been distinguished separated by Bølling organic sediments. It is stressed that subphase II b is not strictly coinciding with the Older Dryas chronozone. During phase III (c. 11–9 ka BP) localized aeolian deposition occurred mostly as dunes. Reworking of older aeolian deposits took place on the dryer interfluves and secondly, new dunes were formed on the eastern banks of rivers by deflation from river floodplains. The time of formation, geomorphology and sedimentary environments of the aeolian deposits are discussed and compared with similar sediments in central Europe.

1. Introduction

Aeolian coversands of the end of the last glacial are a very widespread deposit in western and central Europe. The occurrence of coversands is patchy in Great Britain (BATEMAN 1995) but on the continent the coversands form a continuous deposit in the Netherlands, Germany, Poland and Russia (KOSTER 1988; KASSE 1997; ZEEBERG 1998). The source areas were situated in the large delta plains of the Rhine and Maas and in the (pro)glacial sandy deposits along the Weichselian ice sheet limit. Coversand deposition took place especially at the end of the last glacial from the Last Glacial Maximum (c. 25 ka) onwards until the beginning of the Holocene.

VAN DER HAMMEN (1951, 1971) introduced a litho- and chronostratigraphic scheme of the Late Pleniglacial and Late Glacial aeolian deposits in the eastern Netherlands (Tab. 1). Four aeolian units were distinguished: the Older Coversand I and II and Younger Coversand I and II, which were separated by phases of erosion or soil formation (Beuningen Complex, Lower Loamy Bed, Usselo Bed or Soil). The aeolian units were rather rigidly connected with distinct glacial or stadial intervals of respectively the Late Pleniglacial, Oldest Dryas, Older Dryas and Younger Dryas. Later on this scheme was used also in Germany (DÜCKER & MAARLEVELD 1957) and Poland (e. g. KOZARSKI 1990;

Tab. 1: Chrono- and lithostratigraphy of the Late Pleniglacial and Late Glacial aeolian deposits in the Netherlands. (1) is according to VAN DER HAMMEN (1971) and VAN GEEL et al. (1989); (2) is according to VAN HUISSTEDEN (1990).

¹⁴C years BP	Chronostratigraphy			Lithostratigraphy (1)			Lithostratigraphy (2)	Aeolian phases this study
9								
	HOLOCENE							
10								III
11	W E I C H S E L I A N	Late Glacial	Younger Dryas	T W E N T E F O R M A T I O N	Wierden Member	Younger Coversand II	Wierden Member	
			Allerød			Usselo Bed or Soil		
12			Older Dryas			Younger Coversand I / Lower Loamy Bed		IIb
			Bølling					II
13			Late Pleniglacial		Lutterzand Member	Older Coversand II	Lutterzand Member s.s.	IIa
14								
15						Beuningen Complex	Beverborg Member	Beuningen Gravel Bed
16 ka						Older Coversand I		I

KOZARSKI & NOWACZYK 1991). Apart from stratigraphical research the sedimentology and depositional environments of the aeolian deposits have been investigated and more dates have become available (SCHWAN 1986). In this article the supposed climatic relationship between coversand deposition and cold phases will be evaluated and it will be demonstrated that the phases of coversand deposition are not so time constrained as has been suggested previously. For example the Younger Coversand II in the Netherlands has been deposited especially in the second half of the Younger Dryas period possibly extending into the early Holocene, although the first part of the Younger Dryas was colder. Besides coldness other environmental factors like aridity, preservation potential, regional vegetation differences and changes in fluvial systems have been important as well in the formation of coversands and dunes.

2. Results

A coversand profile has been investigated near the village of Oud-Lutten in the province Overijssel in the eastern Netherlands (Fig. 1). The profile consists of several layers of aeolian sand separated by organic deposits. The peaty deposits had been found during soil mapping of the area. The investigated site is located along the northern margin of the Vecht river valley: an east-west ice-marginal valley of Saalian age. Directly north of

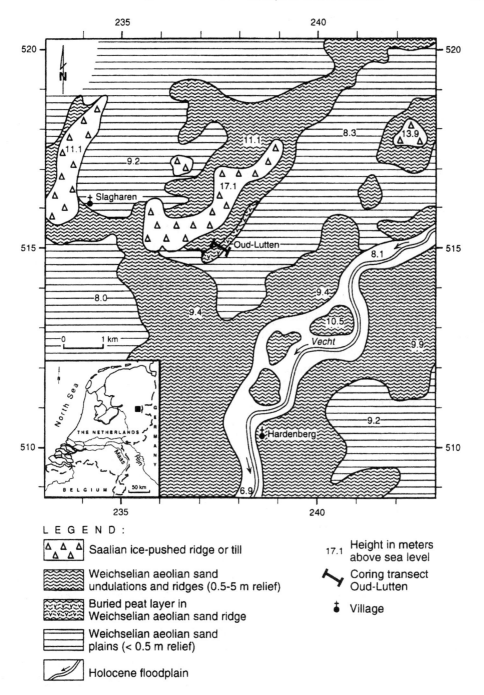

Fig. 1: Geomorphological map of the investigated area. The Oud-Lutten site is located in a coversand ridge at the boundary of the higher-lying coversand undulations to the lower-lying coversand plains.

Oud-Lutten the Saalian tills are found at the surface forming the higher landscape elements (Fig. 1). Following the Saalian, the Vecht valley south of Oud-Lutten has been filled with Eemian and Weichselian fluvial deposits c. 10–20 m thick. In the final arid stages of the Weichselian glacial the landscape was covered by wind-blown sands (so-called coversands in the Netherlands) and the Vecht river was confined to its present-day course. The coversands are up to several meters thick and especially around the ice-pushed ridges and along the Vecht floodplain the coversands are thicker and have more relief (Fig. 1). The investigated site Oud-Lutten is situated at the transition from the higher aeolian coversand relief in the northwest to the lower aeolian coversand plain in the southeast. According to the geomorphological map of the Netherlands (1:50,000) a coversand ridge is located at this transition.

Perpendicular to the coversand ridge a coring profile was made and afterwards a profile pit has been dug to sample the organic layers (Fig. 2). At the base medium to fine sand in a fining-upward sequence has been found which is interpreted as a braided river deposit of the Vecht during the Weichselian Late Pleniglacial (HUISINK 1998). This fluvial unit is overlain by a thin gravel bed, its components generally not exceeding 2 cm. This gravel bed is correlated with the Beuningen Gravel Bed which is a widespread marker horizon in the Netherlands, separating the so-called Older Coversand I and II. However, in this section the aeolian Older Coversand I is missing and the Beuningen Gravel Bed overlies fluvial deposits equivalent in age to the Older Coversand I (see also discussion). Overlying the Beuningen three aeolian units have been distinguished that are separated by organic deposits (Fig. 2). Aeolian unit A consists of fine-grained sand with loamy laminae. Especially below the organic layer the loamy laminae in unit A can be slightly organic containing some detritus and fine, possibly sedge roots. The upper boundary of unit A to the overlying organic layer is gradual; in the northwestern part of the section the upper boundary is indistinct. Aeolian units B and C are somewhat coarser grained than unit A because the loamy laminae are missing. Unit B is only present in the central part of the cross section; it forms an aeolian wedge intercalated in the organic layer. The aeolian sand grades laterally into a sandy moss peat and moss peat in a southeastern direction, indicating aeolian sand supply from the northwest. Unit B is time-equivalent with the lower part of the organic layer. The upper part of the organic layer is very pure without sand and is equivalent with the Usselo soil that overlies unit B. Aeolian unit C truncates the Usselo soil in the northwestern part of the cross section and overlies the organic layer with a sharp contact. The organic unit occurs in the central and southeastern part of the cross section and reveals a lateral and vertical differentiation in composition. It consists of peaty loam at the base with many fine sedge roots, changing upward into sandy peat with very well-preserved mosses. The upper part of the peat is more amorphous with some seeds of *Menyanthes*. Laterally, the central part is more sandy and moss-dominated, while the southeastern part is more loamy and contains less moss fragments and more sedge and *Menyanthes*.

The three aeolian units represent three fluxes of aeolian sedimentation at this site. The geomorphological position at the southeastern fringe of a coversand ridge and the cross

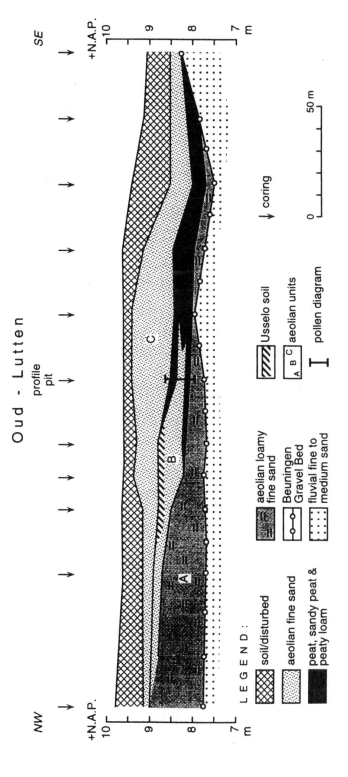

Fig. 2: Cross-section through the coversand ridge at Oud-Lutten showing three aeolian units separated by organic beds. For location see Fig. 1.

section both indicate that the described sequence has been formed by the step-wise migration of a low dune ridge to the southeast implying northwesterly winds during its formation. Because of this step-wise migration, organic deposits, that accumulated because of the wet seepage conditions at the lee side of the dune, were subsequently buried and therefore preserved only locally. To the northwest in the higher coversand area, standstill phases (e. g. soils) in the aeolian deposition have probably been eroded; to the southeast distinctive Late Glacial aeolian units have not been formed and Late Glacial organic material or soils have been incorporated in the Holocene soil profile. Only in the central part of the cross section three phases of aeolian activity are present and as a hypothesis it was proposed that the three aeolian units A, B and C might be correlated with the Older Coversand II, Younger Coversand I and Younger Coversand II respectively. In order to test this hypothesis a profile pit was excavated and two box cores (40 cm high, 10 cm wide, 10 cm deep) were taken for pollen analyses and radiocarbon dating (not available yet).

The pollen diagram shows seven pollen zones. The Cyperaceae are not included in the pollen sum. The biostratigraphic interpretations and tentative dates in conventional ^{14}C-years BP are based on HOEK (1997).

The lowermost zone 1a (102.5–137 cm) is dominated by herbs, especially Gramineae. *Pinus*, *Alnus* and *Picea* are high in the loamy lower part indicating reworking. *Artemisia* is rising towards the end of this zone, indicating the start of the Late Glacial around 12,900 BP. Therefore, this zone has been formed at the end of the Pleniglacial and beginning of the Late Glacial (Oldest Dryas). Aeolian unit A and the lower peat layer (Fig. 2) were all formed in this period.

Pollen zone 1b1 (93.5–102.5 cm) shows an increase of *Betula* and *Salix* while Gramineae is decreasing. This zone reflects the onset of the *Betula* phase of the Bølling dated at c. 12,450 BP.

Pollen zone 1b2 (70.5–93.5 cm) has lower Gramineae values and is dominated by *Betula* and *Salix*. The *Juniperus* curve is rising. This zone is interpreted as the *Betula* phase of the Bølling period between 12,450 and 12,100 BP. This means that the major part of the aeolian sand influx of unit B (Fig. 2) occurred during the Bølling in stead of the Older Dryas as was expected.

Pollen zone 1c (66.5–70.5 cm) shows a strong drop in the *Betula* values and Gramineae strongly increase. *Artemisia* attains high values. *Juniperus* attains its maximum values in this zone reflecting the stabilization of the aeolian landscape. This zone is equivalent with the Older Dryas zone (12,100–11,900 BP) (HOEK 1997). This means that only the upper part of sand unit B (Fig. 2) is of Older Dryas age.

Pollen zone 2a (63.5–66.5 cm) reveals high *Betula* values and low values of herbs. This zone is correlated with the *Betula* phase of the Allerød (11,900–11,250 BP). The aeolian sand of the previous zone has changed into a non-sandy peat indicating that the aeolian activity had ceased at the start of the Allerød.

Pollen zone 2b (57.5–63.5 cm) is dominated by *Pinus* and *Betula* has decreased. This zone reflects the *Pinus* phase of the Allerød (10,950–11,250 BP).

Pollen zone 3 (55–57.5 cm) shows a strong decrease of *Pinus* and increase of herbs. The vegetational change is in the uppermost part of the peat and marks the Allerød-Younger Dryas transition at c. 10,950 BP. Shortly afterwards the peat is covered by renewed aeolian activity (unit C in Fig. 2) during the Younger Dryas.

3. Discussion

Upper Pleniglacial (c. 25–14 ka)

The first evidence of strong aeolian activity in the Netherlands has been registered in deposits of the Last Glacial Maximum. In Oud-Lutten aeolian sediments from this phase are missing but they have been described from a nearby exposure in the Vecht valley (HUISINK 1998). In the Netherlands these deposits were formerly ascribed to the Older Coversand I (VAN DER HAMMEN 1971) and later to the Beverborg Member (VAN HUISSTEDEN 1990) (Tab. 1). Their lithostratigraphic position is below the Beuningen Gravel Bed which is a widespread erosional surface separating the Older Coversand I and II. Sedimentological studies revealed that these Older Coversand I sediments are generally not of primary aeolian origin (VAN HUISSTEDEN et al. 1986; VANDENBERGHE & VAN HUISSTEDEN 1988; SCHWAN & VANDENBERGHE 1991). They are generally found in river valleys where they form the top of a fluvial fining upward sequence (SCHWAN 1987; VAN DEN BERG & SCHWAN 1996; KASSE 1997). These aeolian sediments, therefore, have been reworked by shallow water and recently they have been described as fluvio-aeolian deposits (SCHWAN 1987; KASSE 1997). This means that the grain-size characteristics and the generally horizontal bedding resemble aeolian deposits but sedimentary structures like shallow, concave lenses of coarse sand, small-scale current ripple lamination and clayey/silty drapes indicate that the last depositional process was fluvial (KASSE et al. 1995). The rivers of this period resembled present-day High Arctic braided river systems with fluvio-aeolian sedimentation (GOOD & BRYANT 1985).

Similar deposits have been described from Germany (SCHWAN 1987; MOL 1997) and Poland. Especially in Poland the studies of quartz grain morphology clearly indicate that after 30 ka the content of wind-abraded grains strongly increases in the fluvial deposits of this period. Also here, primary aeolian deposits of this phase are very scarce or even absent (KOZARSKI 1990; MANIKOWSKA 1991; GOŹDZIK 1991).

This widespread reworking of the aeolian deposits in river valleys has been explained by the presence of continuous permafrost which could be deduced from the presence of diagnostic periglacial features like ice-wedge casts (KASSE 1997). The permafrost layer in the generally sandy subsoil will have reduced the infiltration of rain and snow-melt water and consequently overland flow will have been an important process at the surface (WOO & WINTER 1993). Under such conditions it is envisaged that aeolian sediments that had been deposited on interfluves and floodplains during winter were constantly removed by rain and meltwater in spring and summer. Consequently, despite strong aeolian activity, aeolian deposits were not frequently preserved. Especially on interfluves the Older Coversand I is often missing and only Older Coversand II deposits are frequently found overlying a gravel lag concentrate on older substratum (Tab. 1: phase I). The erosional products were transported by overland flow and shallow runoff towards the valleys and accumulated there on the floodplains. As a result, the fluvio-aeolian deposits of this period are mostly restricted to valleys, which contrasts with the following period when extensive aeolian deposits blanketed the whole landscape.

The age of the deposits is not well established. Organic remains are generally absent in the Netherlands (Van Huissteden et al. 1986; Kasse et al. 1995) and in Poland (Goździk 1991; Kozarski 1993). Lithostratigraphic units with peaty beds underlying the fluvial and fluvio-aeolian deposits have generally been dated as Middle Pleniglacial (Van Huissteden 1990; Mol 1997) and therefore the overlying fluvio-aeolian unit has been attributed to the Late Pleniglacial. The general occurrence of large ice-wedge casts in the fluvio-aeolian sediments has often been correlated with the maximal cold of the last glacial (c. 25–15 ka) which is in agreement with a Late Pleniglacial age. Luminescence dates are still rather scarce but the OSL-dates of 18 to 20 ka obtained from Germany confirm the Late Pleniglacial age (Mol & Rhodes 1997).

The general absence of datable organic material can partly be explained by the extreme coldness of the High Arctic climate, but the general tendency in most fluvial sequences, with a decrease of fluvial deposition and increase of (reworked) aeolian sediment, seems to indicate that an increase of the climatic aridity occurred as well towards the end of the period (Kasse 1997).

The bedding types are in general dominated by weak horizontal bedding of fine sand often with an alternation of loamy laminae (Van der Hammen 1971; Mol et al. 1993; Kasse et al. 1995). In this respect these Older Coversand I deposits resemble the Older Coversand II deposits. However, in contrast to the Older Coversand II the Older Coversand I deposits contain shallow, concave lenses of coarse sand, small-scale current ripple lamination and clayey/silty drapes indicative for fluvial deposition. Furthermore, the Older Coversand I deposits are frequently disturbed by cryogenic processes associated with seasonal freezing and thawing and therefore the horizontal bedding has a wavy of crinkly appearance due to water saturation and water escape and sometimes the original horizontal bedding has been almost totally erased giving the sediment a massive structure (Schwan & Vandenberghe 1991). Vertical platy structures, possibly associated with intense surface cooling of the permafrost landscape, are a common periglacial feature in this unit (Vink & Sevink 1971; Mol et al. 1993). The presence of continuous permafrost and its final degradation at the end of the period has resulted in the formation of ice-wedge casts and large-scale cryoturbations in the Older Coversand I deposits. By contrast such periglacial structures are missing in the Older Coversand II (Kasse 1997).

Late Pleniglacial and early Late Glacial (Oldest Dryas) (c. 14 ka–12.5 ka)

Aeolian sediments from this period have previously been called the Older Coversand II (Van der Hammen 1971) and later the Lutterzand Member s. s. (sensu stricto) (Van

HUISSTEDEN 1990) (Tab. 1: phase IIa). Aeolian unit A in Oud-Lutten (Fig. 2) can be correlated with this Older Coversand II unit. The occurrence of the latter unit is widespread in the Netherlands as it is found on both interfluves and in valleys covering the pre-existing landscape and therefore it has been called coversand (KOSTER 1988). It is the most prominent phase of aeolian deposition and many of the younger Late Glacial and Holocene aeolian deposits have been reworked from this Older Coversand II unit. In the Netherlands this unit forms an aeolian sand sheet with in general low relief. In Oud-Lutten (Fig. 2: unit A) the relief is less than 1 m. Also in Poland, flat aeolian covers are dominant but small dunes up to 3.5 m have been described (GOŹDZIK 1991; MANIKOWSKA 1991, 1994) from this period.

The age of the Older Coversand II is not well known, due to the general absence of datable organic material while luminescence dating has been performed only sporadically. KOLSTRUP (1980) reported a date of c. 14 ka BP for the base of the Older Coversand II in the Netherlands and MANIKOWSKA (1991) dated some organic deposits at the top of a fluvial sequence underlying the coversands at c. 14.3 to 14.6 ka BP. The end of the Older Coversand II deposition is often correlated with the start of the Bølling period at 13 ka (see e. g. VANDENBERGHE 1991: Fig. 2), however, without any dating control. VAN GEEL et al. (1989) presented two AMS-dates of c. 12.8 and 12.9 ka BP from organic laminae within the Older Coversand II unit which indicates that deposition continued into the Late Glacial (Tab. 1: phase IIa). As will be discussed below the end of this widespread coversand phase can be extended until the start of the Allerød, since in many cases there is no clear boundary in the coversands under the Allerød soil. In such cases the Older Coversand II and Younger Coversand I form one unit because Bølling age sediments or organics are not present (Tab. 1: phase II). Only in a few cases Bølling age sediments have been reported in the coversand area of the Netherlands (see below) (e. g. VAN GEEL et al. 1989) and Poland (GOŹDZIK 1991: 58; MANIKOWSKA 1994: 120). Dates of c. 12.4 to 12.0 ka BP indicate that at that time aeolian activity had decreased but not stopped. In Oud-Lutten, the aeolian activity forming unit A decreased already before the *Betula* phase of the Bølling (see Fig. 3), i. e. somewhat earlier than 12,450 BP (HOEK 1997).

As has been stated in the introduction, it has been argued previously that the aeolian phases strictly coincide with glacial or stadial conditions (e. g. KOZARSKI & NOWACZYK 1991: Tab. 3). However, this does not hold true for the most widespread and prominent Older Coversand II deposits. In contrast to the deposits of the previous period before c. 14 ka BP which are characterized by ice-wedge casts indicating permafrost, the Older Coversand II sediments only contain thin frost cracks, cm-scale wide and up to 1 m deep. These frost cracks definitely point to less severe (= warmer) climatic conditions with deep seasonal frost, so it has been concluded that the most extensive coversand/sand sheet phase occurred during the very arid waning stage of the last glacial (KASSE 1997). The bedding types in the deposits of this period are of primary aeolian origin. Structures indicative for fluvial processes are generally absent, showing the strong aridity of this

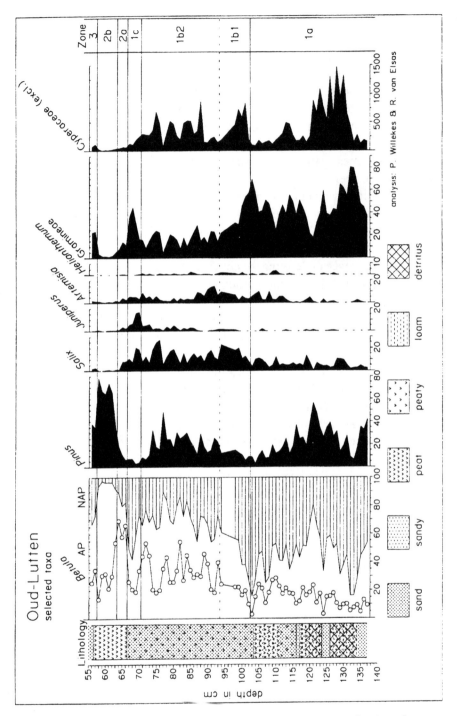

Fig. 3: Pollen diagram of the Late Glacial sequence at Oud-Lutten (selection of curves only). For location see Fig. 2.

period. Horizontal to low-angle bedding and alternating bedding of fine sand and silty fine sand are dominant in the sand-sheet deposits (KASSE 1997). The occurrence of silty fine sand or loamy laminae within the deposits has sometimes been attributed to permafrost conditions or niveo-aeolian deposition (STAPERT & VEENSTRA 1988). As has been stated above, however, evidence for the presence of permafrost has not been found. Niveo-aeolian deposits as observed in present-day arctic environments do not reveal loamy laminae and the disappearance of snow from the niveo-aeolian sediment results in sediment collapse and deformed bedding (KOSTER & DIJKMANS 1988; DIJKMANS 1990). The presence of loamy laminae in the coversands is presently explained by deposition and adherence of loessic material on a moist or wet surface (SCHWAN 1986). The coversands of lower topographic positions or poorly drained sites indeed have more frequent loamy laminae than on well-drained locations (VANDENBERGHE & KROOK 1981). The supposed strong aridity of this period seems to conflict with the widespread occurrence of loamy laminae that are indicative of surface wetness. It is postulated that despite the climatic aridity the depositional surface was wet in spring and early summer due to the combination of snow melt, thawing of deep seasonal frost and low relief of the sand sheet.

Bølling s. s. (c. 12.5–12.1 ka)

Bølling age organics or soils from the aeolian coversand landscape are extremely rare in the Netherlands, especially in comparison with the very frequent Allerød soils. The same holds true for Germany (SCHLAAK 1997) and Poland. MANIKOWSKA (1994) reported an initial soil from the Bølling period at Kamion dated at 12,235 BP. According to VAN DER HAMMEN (1971) the Lower Loamy Bed was formed during the Bølling s. l. (sensu lato) period, but this loamy layer has not been dated because organic carbon is missing. At Usselo VAN GEEL et al. (1989) reported organic deposits from the Bølling s. s. intercalated with Late Glacial aeolian sediments. More frequently Bølling age organics have been reported from pingo scars (DE GANS 1981; BOHNCKE et al. 1988).

The scarcity of Bølling age soils/organics in the aeolian district can in my opinion be explained by the continuation of aeolian deposition although with decreased intensity during that period. The land surface that was totally covered with aeolian sediments during the previous period (14–12.5 ka; Tab. 1: phase IIa) was only partly stabilized by vegetation and soil formation during the Bølling s. s. (12,5–12.0 ka). Evidence for this hypothesis is obtained from the few sites with Bølling organic deposits within the coversand region. In site Usselo the Bølling organic deposits are very sandy and contain sandy laminae which can be attributed to aeolian deposition at the same time of organic accumulation (KASSE 1997). In Oud-Lutten aeolian activity decreased and organic accumulation started before the *Betula* rise of the Bølling s. s. (see Fig. 3), this is shortly before 12,450 BP (HOEK 1997). However, already during the *Betula* zone of the Bølling (c. 12,450–12,100 BP) the aeolian deposition increased again (see Fig. 3) and most of the sand of unit B in Fig. 2 has been deposited during this *Betula* phase. This means that aeolian deposition continued during the Bølling s. s. period although perhaps at a slower rate than before so that locally organic deposits could be formed (see Tab. 1: phase II). The start of the first organic accumulation in the Bølling seems to be around 12,500 BP (site Oud Lutten; VAN GEEL et al. 1989). This moment coincides with the Late Glacial rapid climatic amelioration at c. 14,670 cal yr BP as reconstructed from ice-core records (HOEK 1997: 48). The increased organic production may reflect a temperature and humidity increase associated with this climatic improvement. The development of a (sparse) vegetation cover can explain the change in this interval and the following Older Dryas from generally flat sand sheets to low dunes.

The formation of the Lower Loamy Bed (VAN DER HAMMEN 1971) intercalated in sandy coversands may also reflect the decreased aeolian activity, due to decreased sand supply and initial surface stabilization by vegetation during the Bølling. As the sand deposition became less important the deposition of loessic material — already existing as loamy laminae in the Older Coversand II — became more important.

As has been stated above, only in a few places the aeolian activity of the Late Pleniglacial and Late Glacial was interrupted by peat formation during the Bølling s. s. Only in such cases the aeolian activity can be separated in two phases (Tab. 1: phase II a and II b). Both examples (Usselo and Oud-Lutten) are situated at the lee side of a coversand ridge and it seems possible that peat formation during the Bølling was favored by water seepage in front of the coversand ridge. Except for these local peat accumulations, aeolian activity continued in most regions and the aeolian deposits can not be differentiated (Tab. 1: phase II). Aeolian activity finally stopped at the start of the Allerød.

Older Dryas (12.1–11.9 ka)

Previously the Younger Coversand I has been attributed rather strictly to the Older Dryas period (VAN DER HAMMEN 1971) (Tab. 1). This phase of aeolian deposition was later recorded as well in Germany and Poland (KOZARSKI & NOWACZYK 1991). However, in contrast to what was expected, the Oud-Lutten site shows that aeolian unit B (Fig. 2) was not restricted to the Older Dryas, since it has been formed in both the Bølling and Older Dryas periods (Tab. 1: phase II b). Furthermore, given the standard deviations of ^{14}C dates, it is questionable if an aeolian phase can be reliably correlated with such a short event like the Older Dryas.

According to VAN DER HAMMEN & WIJMSTRA (1971) the Younger Coversand I sediments generally do not contain loamy laminae like the preceding Older Coversand II and they are somewhat coarser grained. The bedding is in general horizontal to low-angle parallel, indicating that in the Netherlands the morphology was sand sheet and low dunes (KASSE 1997). The low dunes were formed as a last-stage feature during aeolian phase II, probably related to the vegetation development during the Bølling and Older Dryas periods.

VAN DER HAMMEN & WIJMSTRA (1971) sometimes subdivided the aeolian sequences underlying the Usselo soil on the basis of differences in bedding types, in a lower loamy-laminated Older Coversand II part and an upper non-loamy horizontally laminated Younger Coversand I part (e. g. Van der Hammen & Wijmstra 1971: 96, 136). Schwan (1986), however, stressed that specific sedimentary facies need not be related to specific periods. The different sedimentary facies are the result of differences in topography, drainage and moisture conditions of the surface and these are to some extent time-independent. For instance, at the base of the Younger Dryas dunes deposits alternating bedding of loamy fine sand and sand — normally associated with the Older Coversand II — is present due to moister conditions at the dune base (Schwan 1991). So, bedding type should not be used as a time marker, but it has been noted that in any coversand sequence that formed during aeolian phase II (Tab. 1) alternating bedding of fine sand and loamy fine sand indicating a wet depositional surface, is always overlain by dry-aeolian horizontal to low-angle bedding without silty laminae (Schwan 1986: 104; Kasse 1997). This drying-up sequence in phase II seems to conflict with the assumed increase of climatic humidity at the start of the Bølling s. s. around 12.5 ka (see above). Despite the fact that the climate may have become wetter, the depositional surfaces may have become dryer due to the development of vegetation and associated low dunes during the Bølling and Older Dryas.

In contrast with the preceding Older Coversand II sands in the Netherlands, sediments dating from the Older Dryas are not so frequently reported, since so few sites exist in which both Bølling and Allerød organics underlie and overlie the Younger Coversand I. Mostly only the Usselo soil or peat of Allerød age is present overlying the coversand. Therefore, in the case of the Usselo soil overlying coversand, it is only allowed to say that the coversand predates the Allerød (Older Coversand II and/or Younger Coversand I) (Tab. 1: phase II).

In Poland on the other hand the Older Dryas period has often been ascribed as a period of major dune formation (Kozarski 1990; Manikowska 1994). Large-scale dune slipfaces covered by Allerød soils have been reported in several places and this seems to prove that the Older Dryas was a period of intense dune formation. However, as has been stated above for the Netherlands, also in Poland Bølling age sediments underlying the so-called Older Dryas dunes are rare (Bohncke et al. 1995). In many cases the dune sediments underlying the Allerød soil have been correlated with the Older Dryas period for morphological reasons without strong dating control (e. g. Nowaczyk 1986). It is the authors opinion that the difference in intensity of the Older Dryas aeolian phase in the Netherlands (low intensity) and Poland (high intensity) is only an apparent difference caused by differences in definition and insufficient dating. In Poland many dune sediments predating the Allerød soil have been assigned completely to the Older Dryas on morphological grounds, but the dune bodies could also have been formed over a longer time span covering the Bølling s. l. and the Older Dryas. In the Netherlands, aeolian sediments in the same stratigraphic position underlying the Allerød soil have often been assigned — because of the presence of loamy laminae — to the Older Coversand II of Late Pleniglacial age, but here also the aeolian deposition could have spanned the Late Pleniglacial, Bølling and Older Dryas.

The areal differentiation of sand-sheet and low-dune formation in the Netherlands and high-dune formation in Poland has been explained by climatic gradients (BÖSE 1991) and differences in vegetation development (KASSE 1997).

Allerød (c. 11.9–11.0 ka BP)

The Allerød period seems to be a period of non-deposition in the western and central European aeolian landscape (VAN DER HAMMEN 1951, 1971; VANDENBERGHE 1991; KOZARSKI & NOWACZYK 1991; MANIKOWSKA 1994; SCHLAAK 1997). The landscape was stabilized by a forest vegetation. In the Netherlands birch forests were succeeded by pine forest in the later part of the Allerød (c. 11,250 BP, HOEK 1997). In profile Oud-Lutten (Fig. 3) both the *Betula* and *Pinus* phase of the Allerød are present in the upper peat layer overlying aeolian unit B in Fig. 2. This means that aeolian activity has ceased before the *Betula* phase of the Allerød and the surroundings of the investigated site were stabilized by peat growth and soil formation (Fig. 2). Short-lived cold climatic oscillations during the Allerød like the Gerzensee oscillation did not affect the forest vegetation to such an extent that opening of the vegetation cover and deflation occurred.

The Usselo soil of Allerød age is a very common soil in Late Glacial aeolian sequences of the Netherlands. Human artefacts have been reported frequently from this soil horizon (HIJSZELER 1957). Its occurrence over the country as a whole, however, is not so widespread, because the soil has been preserved only when aeolian accumulation occurred during the Younger Dryas and the Younger Dryas aeolian deposition was rather local in comparison with especially the Older Coversand II deposition which was countrywide. In those regions where Younger Dryas deposition did not take place the Late Glacial soil has been incorporated by Holocene soil formation.

The appearance of the Allerød soil in the Netherlands can be very different. In low-lying areas in the aeolian region peat was formed (e. g. site Usselo, VAN GEEL et al. 1989; site Ossendrecht, SCHWAN 1991). In higher areas of the aeolian landscape a soil was formed (Usselo soil), 5 to 20 cm thick, that is normally characterized by a slight humus accumulation and some bleaching of the quartz grains (Ah-E-(Bw-)C profile). A weathering horizon (Bw) or weak illuviation of iron (Bs-horizon) have been found infrequently (site Weelde in Belgium, unpublished). Charcoal is a common constituent of the soil. ^{14}C-dates of 23 samples of charcoal from the Usselo soil cluster around 11,000 BP (HOEK 1997: 43). This agrees very well with the results from Poland, since MANIKOWSKA (1994: 121) reported that most of the dates of the Allerød soil are between 11,200 and 10,800 BP. The Usselo soil is intensively homogenized and the original sedimentary structures have been destroyed by bioturbation and soil forming processes. Round to oval-shaped burrows, c. 1 cm in diameter, are very frequent below the well-drained soils and they have commonly been attributed to burrowing activity by beetles (BRUSSAARD & RUNIA 1984).

In Poland the Allerød soil has been reported on the lee side of dune slip faces that were active during the Older Dryas (NOWACZYK 1986; MANIKOWSKA 1991). Recently, also in

Germany a soil of Allerød age (the Finow soil) has been found in Late Glacial dune sequences (SCHLAAK 1997). The appearance of the Allerød soils in Poland is very similar to the Netherlands. The soils are slightly enriched in organic matter, homogenized by bioturbation and locally weakly podsolized (e. g. MANIKOWSKA 1991: 136). The Allerød soils described in eastern Germany on the other hand contain a clearly developed weathering horizon (Bw) and are classified as brown soils (Braunerde). The difference between the formation of brown soils and weakly podsolized soils can be climate related — the brown soil occurring in dryer climates — but since the weakly podsolized soils occur in both the Netherlands and Poland it is concluded that the formation of the brown soils is related to another soil forming factor. The brown soils described in eastern Germany by SCHLAAK were formed within the limits of the Weichselian glaciation while the slightly podsolized soils in the Netherlands and in Poland have been formed outside the limits of the Weichselian glaciation on a older substratum. The difference in age and mineralogical composition of the parent material from which the aeolian deposits were formed can explain the difference in soil formation. The Weichselian glacial deposits in eastern Germany were not strongly leached and weathered and consequently brown soils developed on the mineralogically richer aeolian material. In the Netherlands on the other hand the substratum had been intensively weathered during the Eemian and parts of the Weichselian and consequently slightly bleached and podsolized soils developed on the poorer aeolian material.

Younger Dryas (c. 11–10 ka)

During the Younger Dryas aeolian deposition started again in both western and central Europe (VAN DER HAMMEN 1951, 1971; VANDENBERGHE 1991; KASSE 1995; ISARIN et al. 1997; SCHLAAK 1997; NOWACZYK 1986; MANIKOWSKA 1991, 1994). The pollen diagram from Oud-Lutten (Fig. 3) shows that the peat was covered by sand after the Allerød-Younger Dryas transition, i. e. after 10,950 BP (HOEK 1997). The peat-sand contact, however, is sharp and there may be a hiatus between the end of peat formation and start of aeolian accumulation. Apparently the stabilizing vegetation cover of the Allerød period was destroyed. Formerly, the formation of the Younger Coversand II was attributed to the cold stadial conditions of the Younger Dryas period (VAN DER HAMMEN 1971; KOZARSKI & NOWACZYK 1991). However, recent results from the Netherlands demonstrate that the deposition of the so-called Younger Coversand II especially occurred in the second part of the Younger Dryas period, after c. 10.5 ka BP (see Tab. 1: phase III) (BOHNCKE et al. 1993; KASSE 1995; ISARIN et al. 1997). This means that aeolian deposition did not coincide completely with stadial conditions, since the first part of the Younger Dryas seems to have been colder than the second part (ISARIN & BOHNCKE, 1997). It is suggested that despite the coldness of the first part of the Younger Dryas aeolian activity was restricted by rather wet climatic conditions, while during the second part of the Younger Dryas, despite a slight climatic improvement, aeolian activity became more prominent due to an increased aridity.

The end of the Younger Coversand II deposition in the Netherlands is not well dated. In most cases the Younger Coversand II dune sands are overlain by the Holocene soil (mostly podsols). In a few cases peat that formed in dune deflation hollows has been dated (VAN GEEL et al. 1980/1981; SCHWAN 1991). The dates of 10,150 and 9,050 BP of the base of the peat show that the end of the Younger Coversand II deposition does not coincide necessarily with the end of the Younger Dryas biozone. Dune formation may have continued, perhaps locally, during the Preboreal period (KASSE et al. 1995). This continuation of aeolian deposition in the early Preboreal was also reported in Germany and Poland (SCHLAAK 1997; KOZARSKI 1990; MANIKOWSKA 1991, 1994). This means that the reconstruction of wind directions during the Younger Dryas based on the surface dune morphology (cf. ISARIN et al. 1997) may be hazardous. Although the sediment has been deposited during the Younger Dryas, the dune morphology may be a last-stage feature of Preboreal age.

In the Netherlands aeolian deposition during this period occurred in two regions:

i. higher places within the coversand area and
ii. along river valleys.

Higher well-drained locations of the previously deposited Older Coversand II and Younger Coversand I were reworked by the wind, but no new material was added to the sites. Especially on the higher interfluves between brooks and on coversand ridges this reworking is evident (VAN DER HAMMEN 1951). Apparently, not only the coldness of the Younger Dryas stadial, but also the increased aridity of the period caused the destruction of the vegetation cover and deflation of the surface.

The second region of large-scale Younger Dryas aeolian deposition is associated with river valleys. Along the large rivers like the Maas and Scheldt but also along smaller brooks extensive dune fields were formed on the east banks, indicating a westsouthwesterly wind during the Younger Dryas (KASSE 1995; ISARIN et al. 1997). The source of these aeolian sands is not by reworking of older coversands but from the Younger Dryas floodplains. Due to the Younger Dryas stadial conditions and related higher peak discharges the floodplain morphology had changed. In the case of the Maas river the channel morphology had changed from meandering during the Allerød to multichannel during the Younger Dryas. From these wider channel belts sand was deflated and accumulated along the floodplains.

From Germany and Poland it has been reported that the impact of the Younger Dryas on aeolian activity and dune formation was not so important. The already existing dune fields of the preceding Older Dryas period were slightly transformed but new dune fields were not formed (e. g. MANIKOWSKA 1991). The reason for this limited effect of the Younger Dryas cooling and aridity on the aeolian environment may be twofold. First, in contrast to the Netherlands, the vegetation decline and opening of the vegetation cover seems to have been less severe. The Younger Dryas vegetation remained dominated by forest elements (birch and pine) and bare ground susceptible to deflation did not occur frequently (BOHNCKE et al. 1995). Secondly, a change in river pattern from meandering to braided has not been reported frequently for the Polish rivers (KOZARSKI 1983; STARKEL 1995 and references cited there). Consequently, in contrast to the Netherlands, rivers maintained their meandering pattern and sediments were not easily deflated from the meandering channels and river-connected dune belts did not form.

4. Conclusions

Previously four coversand deposits have been distinguished each associated with a distinct cold period. In the foregoing it has been discussed that these four phases are not equally important and that their timing has to be adjusted. It is proposed here to define three phases of aeolian sand deposition in west and central Europe (Tab. 1):

Phase I (c. 20–14 ka BP): In this period of the Last Glacial Maximum aeolian processes have been very important, but the preservation of primary aeolian deposits has been low. The presence of continuous permafrost resulted in strong overland flow and aeolian sediments were reworked by water and deposited in valley floodplains as shallow fluvial deposits. Locally in the valley floodplains the reworked aeolian sediments alternate with primary aeolian beds and therefore have been described as fluvio-aeolian deposits. Formerly, they have been called the Older Coversand I. The sediments are especially extensive in floodplains but they normally lack outside the river plain. The sedimentary sequences from this period show that towards the end of this phase the fluvial activity decreased and aeolian deposition increased, which has been explained by an increase of the climatic aridity culminating in the formation of the Beuningen Gravel Bed.

Phase II (c. 14–11.9 ka): In this period following the Last Glacial Maximum the climate had already ameliorated, but deep seasonal frost still occurred. The aridity during this phase was strong, especially from c. 14 to 12.5 ka, since structures indicating surficial flow are nearly absent. Aeolian deposition occurred especially in sand sheets although locally in Poland low dunes were formed. Preservation of the aeolian sediments was strong and the deposits of this phase are the most important and widespread in western and central Europe. The sediments often have a characteristic alternating bedding of fine sandy and loamy fine sandy laminae in the lower part and horizontal bedding of fine sand in the upper part. Formerly, sediments from this phase were called the Older Coversand II and Younger Coversand I. Only locally the sediments from this phase can be subdivided in a phase II a and II b because of the presence of an organic layer of Bølling age. More often, however, Bølling age sediments are not present and the aeolian activity continued during the Bølling and Older Dryas periods until the start of the Allerød (phase II). In the Netherlands mostly sand sheets and low dunes were formed while further east sand sheets and high dunes were formed because of the stronger development of the vegetation cover in central Europe.
The Bølling period, especially from c. 12.5 ka onwards, is a period of decreased aeolian activity and increased organic production perhaps due to increased climatic humidity associated with the rapid Late Glacial climatic improvement. Local accumulations of silt

and organic material occurred in lower lying areas e. g. in front of coversand ridges. On higher ground, however, aeolian activity continued as indicated by the sandy character and sandy intercalations in organic deposits from this period.

Aeolian activity increased again in the later part of the Bølling (Tab. 1: phase II b) and culminated during the Older Dryas period. It is concluded that phase II b spans a longer time period from the late Bølling to 11.9 ka BP and is not strictly related to the short Older Dryas period as was previously stated for the Younger Coversand I. The Allerød period forms a gap in the aeolian record and landscape stability was complete by a closed forest cover. The short-lived cold Gerzensee oscillation did not lead to landscape instability and aeolian activity.

Phase III (c. 11–9 ka): The Younger Dryas stadial is reflected by renewed aeolian activity, but the onset of aeolian deposition is not always coinciding with the start of the Younger Dryas. It is concluded that the maximal aeolian activity occurred in the second part of the Younger Dryas after c. 10.5 ka. The Younger Dryas cooling was reflected almost immediately in the vegetation composition, but it is postulated that there was a time lag between climatic cooling and deterioration of the closed forest cover to such an extent that deflation could not occur. In addition to cooling also more intense aridity is held responsible for the opening of the vegetation cover. Phase III aeolian activity has been established in two different morphological regions. Firstly, high-lying, more drought-susceptible coversands of the previous phase II were remodelled or transformed during this phase into low dunes in the Netherlands, but new aeolian material was not supplied. Secondly, river dune fields were newly formed on the eastern banks of rivers, because of the change in channel geometry from meandering to braided at the start of the Younger Dryas.

Acknowledgments

Roel van Elsas and Peter Willekes are thanked for the pollen analysis; Wim Hoek and Sjoerd Bohncke for preparing the pollen diagram and Henry Sion for drawing the figures.

5. References

Bateman, M. D. (1995): Thermoluminescence dating of the British coversand deposits. — Quaternary Science Reviews, **14**: 791–798.

Bohncke, S., Kasse, C. & Vandenberghe, J. (1995): Climate induced environmental changes during the Vistulian Lateglacial at Żabinko, Poland. — Quaestiones Geographicae, Special Issue, **4**: 43–64.

— Vandenberghe, J. & Huijzer, A. S. (1993): Periglacial environments during the Weichselian Late Glacial in the Maas valley, the Netherlands. — Geologie en Mijnbouw, **72**: 193–210.

— Wijmstra, L., Van der Woude, J. & Sohl, H. (1988): The Late-Glacial infill of three lake successions in The Netherlands: Regional vegetational history in relation to NW European vegetational developments. — Boreas, **17**: 385–402.

Böse, M. (1991): A palaeoclimatic interpretation of frost-wedge casts and aeolian sand deposits in the lowlands between Rhine and Vistula in the Upper Pleniglacial and Late Glacial. — Z. Geomorph. N. F., Suppl.-Bd. **90**: 15–28; Berlin, Stuttgart.

Brussaard. L. & Runia, L. T. (1984): Recent and ancient traces of scarab beetle activity in sandy soils of the Netherlands. — Geoderma, **34**: 229–250.

De Gans, W. (1981): The Drentsche Aa valley system. — Thesis Vrije Universiteit Amsterdam: 132 p.; Amsterdam (Rodopi).

Dijkmans, J. W. A. (1990): Niveo-aeolian sedimentation and resulting sedimentary structures; Søndre Strømflord area, Western Greenland. — Permafrost and Periglacial Processes, **1**: 83–96.

Dücker, A. & Maarleveld, G. C. (1957): Hoch- und spätglaziale äolische Sande in Nordwestdeutschland und in den Niederlanden. — Geol. Jahrb., **73**: 215–234.

Good, T. R. & Bryant, I. D. (1985): Fluvio-aeolian sedimentation — an example from Banks Island, N. W. T., Canada. — Geografiska Annaler, **67A**: 33–46.

Goździk, J. (1991): Sedimentological record of aeolian processes from the Upper Plenivistulian and the turn of Pleni- and Late Vistulian in Central Poland. — Z. Geomorph. N. F., Suppl.-Bd. **90**: 51–60; Berlin, Stuttgart.

Hijszeler, C. C. W. J. (1957): Late-Glacial human cultures in The Netherlands. — Geologie en Mijnbouw, **19**: 288–302.

Hoek, W. (1997): Palaeogeography of Lateglacial vegetations. Aspects of Lateglacial and Early Holocene vegetation, abiotic landscape, and climate in The Netherlands. — Thesis Vrije Universiteit Amsterdam: 147 p.; Utrecht (Drukkerij Elinkwijk b.v.).

Huisink, M. (1998): Changing river styles in response to Weichselian climate changes in the eastern Netherlands. — Sedimentary Geology, submitted.

Isarin, R. F. B. & Bohncke, S. J. P. (1998): Summer temperatures during the Younger Dryas in north-western and central Europe inferred from climate indicator plant species. — Quaternary Research, in press.

— Renssen, H. & Koster, E. A. (1997): Surface wind climate during the Younger Dryas in Europe as inferred from aeolian records and model simulations. — Palaeogeography, Palaeoclimatology, Palaeoecology, **134**: 127–148.

Kasse, C. (1995): Younger Dryas climatic changes and aeolian depositional environments. — In: Troelstra, S. R., Van Hinte, J. E. & Ganssen, G. M. [eds.]: The Younger Dryas. — Koninklijke Nederlandse Akademie van Wetenschappen Verhandelingen, Afd. Natuurkunde, Eerste Reeks, **44**: 27–31.

— (1997): Cold-climate sand-sheet formation in North-Western Europe (c. 14–12.4 ka); a response to permafrost degradation and increased aridity. — Permafrost and Periglacial Processes, **8**: 295–311.

— Vandenberghe, J. & Bohncke, S. (1995): Climatic change and fluvial dynamics of the Maas during the late Weichselian and early Holocene. — In: Frenzel, B. [ed.]:

European river activity and climatic change during the Lateglacial and early Holocene. ESF Project European Palaeoclimate and Man, Special Issue 9. Paläoklimaforschung/Palaeoclimate Research, **14**: 123–150.

KOLSTRUP, E. (1980): Climate and stratigraphy in Northwestern Europe between 30.000 B.P. and 13.000 B.P., with special reference to The Netherlands. — Mededelingen Rijks Geologische Dienst, **32-15**: 181–253.

KOSTER, E. A. (1988): Ancient and modern cold-climate aeolian sand deposition: a review. — J. Quaternary Science, **3**: 69–83.

— & DIJKMANS, J. W. A. (1988): Niveo-aeolian deposits and denivation forms, with special reference to the Great Kobuk Sand Dunes, Northwestern Alaska. — Earth Surface Processes and Landforms, **13**: 153–170.

KOZARSKI, S. (1983): River channel changes in the middle reach of the Warta valley, Great Polish Lowland. — Quaternary Studies in Poland, **4**:159–169.

— (1990): Pleni and Late Vistulian aeolian phenomena in Poland: new occurrences, palaeoenvironmental and stratigraphic interpretations. — Acta Geographica Debrecina 1987–1988, **26–27**: 31-45.

— (1993): Late Plenivistulian deglaciation and the expansion of the periglacial zone in NW Poland. — Geologie en Mijnbouw, **72**: 143–157.

— & NOWACZYK, B. (1991): The late Quaternary climate and human impact on aeolian processes in Poland. — Z. Geomorph. N. F., Suppl.-Bd. **83**: 29–37; Berlin-Stuttgart.

MANIKOWSKA, B. (1991): Vistulian and Holocene aeolian activity, pedostratigraphy and relief evolution in Central Poland. — Z. Geomorph. N. F., Suppl.-Bd. **90**: 131–141; Berlin-Stuttgart.

— (1994): État des études des processus éoliens dans la région de Łódź (Pologne Centrale). — Biuletyn Peryglacjalny, **33**: 107–131.

MOL, J. (1997): Fluvial response to Weichselian climate changes in the Niederlausitz (Germany). — J. Quaternary Science, **12**: 43–60.

— & RHODES, E. J. (1997): Optical dating of quartz from Weichselian fluvial deposits in eastern Germany. — In: MOL, J. : Fluvial response to climate variations. The Last Glaciation in eastern Germany. — Thesis Vrije Universiteit Amsterdam; Enschede (Febodruk BV). — [Submitted to J. Quaternary Science].

— VANDENBERGHE, J., KASSE, K. & STEL, H. (1993): Periglacial microjointing and faulting in Weichselian fluvio-aeolian deposits. — J. Quaternary Science, **8**: 15–30.

NOWACZYK, B. (1986): The age of dunes, their textural and structural properties against atmospheric circulation pattern of Poland during the Late Vistulian and Holocene. — Adam Mickiewicz University Press, Seria Geografia, **28**: 245 p.

SCHLAAK, N. (1997): Äolische Dynamik im brandenburgischen Tiefland seit dem Weichselspätglazial. — Arbeitsberichte Geographisches Institut, Humboldt-Universität zu Berlin, **24**: 58 p.

SCHWAN, J. (1986): The origin of horizontal alternating bedding in Weichselian aeolian sands in northwestern Europe. — Sedimentary Geology, **49**: 73–108.

— (1987): Sedimentologic characteristics of a fluvial to aeolian succession in Weichselian Talsand in the Emsland. — Sedimentary Geology, **52**: 273–298.

— (1991): Palaeowetness indicators in a Weichselian Late Glacial to Holocene aeolian succession in the southwestern Netherlands. — Z. Geomorph. N. F., Suppl.-Bd. **90**: 155–169; Berlin, Stuttgart.

— & VANDENBERGHE, J. (1991): Weichselian Late Pleniglacial fluvio-aeolian deposits and cryogenic structures. — Excursion guide Symposium periglacial environments in relation to climatic change, Maastricht/Amsterdam, 3–6 May 1991, Vrije Universiteit Amsterdam: 68–77; Amsterdam.

STAPERT, D. & VEENSTRA, H. J. (1988): The section at Usselo; brief description, grain-size distributions, and some remarks on the archaeology. — Palaeohistoria, **30**: 1–28.

STARKEL, L. (1995): The place of the Vistula river valley in the late Vistulian - early Holocene evolution of the European valleys. — In: FRENZEL, B. [ed.]: European river activity and climatic change during the Lateglacial and early Holocene. — ESF Project European Palaeoclimate and Man, Special Issue 9. Paläoklimaforschung/Palaeoclimate Research, **14**: 75–88.

VAN DEN BERG, M. W. & SCHWAN, J. C. G. (1996): Millennial climatic cyclicity in Weichselian Late Pleniglacial to early Holocene fluvial deposits of the river Maas in the southern Netherlands. — In: VAN DEN BERG, M. W.: Fluvial sequences of the Maas: a 10 Ma record of neotectonics and climate change at various time-scales. — Thesis Agricultural University: 181 p.; Wageningen.

VANDENBERGHE, J. (1991): Changing conditions of aeolian sand deposition during the last deglaciation period. — Z. Geomorph. N. F., Suppl.-Bd. **90**: 193–207; Berlin, Stuttgart.

— & Krook, L. (1981): Stratigraphy and genesis of Pleistocene deposits at Alphen (southern Netherlands). - Geologie en Mijnbouw, **60**: 417–426.

— & VAN HUISSTEDEN, J. (1988): Fluvio-aeolian interaction in a region of continuous permafrost. — Proceedings V International Conference on Permafrost, Trondheim, Norway: 876–881; Trondheim.

VAN DER HAMMEN, T. (1951): Late-Glacial flora and periglacial phenomena in The Netherlands. — Thesis State University Leiden: 183 p.; Leiden (Eduard Ijdo N.V.).

— (1971): The Upper Quaternary stratigraphy of the Dinkel valley. — In: Van DER HAMMEN, T. & WIJMSTRA, T. A. [eds.]: The Upper Quaternary of the Dinkel valley (Twente, Eastern Overijssel, The Netherlands). — Mededelingen Rijks Geologische Dienst, **22**: 59–72.

— & WIJMSTRA, T. A. [eds.] (1971): The Upper Quaternary of the Dinkel valley (Twente, Eastern Overijssel, The Netherlands). — Mededelingen Rijks Geologische Dienst, **22**: 55–213.

VAN GEEL, B., BOHNCKE, S. J. P. & DEE, H. (1980/81): A palaeoecological study of an upper Late Glacial and Holocene sequence from "De Borchert", The Netherlands.

— Review of Palaeobotany and Palynology, **31**: 359–448.

— COOPE, G. R. & VAN DER HAMMEN, T. (1989): Palaeoecology and stratigraphy of the Lateglacial type section at Usselo (The Netherlands). — Review of Palaeobotany and Palynology, **60**: 25–129.

VAN HUISSTEDEN, J. (1990): Tundra rivers of the last glacial: sedimentation and geomorphological processes during the Middle Pleniglacial in Twente, Eastern Netherlands. — Mededelingen Rijks Geologische Dienst, **44**: 1–138

— VANDENBERGHE, J. & VAN GEEL, B. (1986): Late Pleistocene stratigraphy and fluvial history of the Dinkel Basin (Twente, Eastern Netherlands). — Eiszeitalter und Gegenwart, **36**: 43–59.

VINK, A. P. A. & SEVINK, J. (1971): Soils and paleosols in the Lutterzand. - In: VAN DER HAMMEN, T. & WIJMSTRA, T. A. [eds.]: The Upper Quaternary of the Dinkel valley (Twente, Eastern Overijssel, The Netherlands). — Mededelingen Rijks Geologische Dienst, **22**: 165–185.

WOO, M.-K. & WINTER, T. C. (1993): The role of permafrost and seasonal frost in the hydrology of northern wetlands in North America. — J. of Hydrology, **141**: 5–31.

ZEEBERG, J. J. (1998): The European sand belt in eastern Europe — an comparison of Late Glacial dune orientation with GCM simulation results. — Boreas, **27**: 127–139.

Address of the author:

Dr. CORNELIS KASSE, The Netherlands Centre for Geo-ecological Research, Faculty of Earth Sciences, Vrije Universiteit, De Boelelaan 1085, NL-1081 HV Amsterdam, e-mail: kask@geo.vu.nl

GeoArchaeoRhein, 3: 83–96; Münster 1999

Plenivistulian and Late Vistulian loess deposits in northwestern Poland (Western Pomerania)

KATARZYNA ISSMER

Abstract: Loess deposits from Western Pomerania represent periglacial loess and were deposited at the turn of the Upper Plenivistulian and Late Vistulian. Western Pomerania is till now the only area in Poland where Late Vistulian loess deposits have been found in small patches on different glacial and fluvioglacial landfoms. Laboratory studies were made with respect to grain size distribution, content of calcium carbonate and physical features. There were also detailed sedimentological investigations carried out on loess deposits. All these diagnostic features have been a tool for the separation of main lithofacies. Loess deposits occur there in two main lithofacies: massive loess (Lm) and laminated loess (Ll) and within laminated loess three sublithofacies: cryptolaminated (sl), laminated loess *sensu stricto* (ll) and banded loess (sm). Loess lithofacies prefer a varied topography and are distributed in end moraines, till plains and outwash plains. These lithofacies have significant connection with the periglacial zone and aeolian processes, which took place during the Vistulian in Western Pomerania.

1. Introduction

The occurrence and genesis of loess deposits in scattered position in the area of the last glaciation has not been extensively investigated to date. In the European literature articles about the occurrence of loess or loess-like deposits in scattered position within the limits of the last glaciation (Vistulian glaciation) have been published by KOLSTRUP (1991), LANG (1990) and SIEBERTZ (1988). Some Polish authors (JAHN 1950; MALICKI 1967) point out the extent of the northern limit of loess in Poland and relate it to the Saalian glaciation. According to MARUSZCZAK (1969) the northern limit of loess in western Poland is 60 km away from the maximal limits of glacial deposits of the last glaciation (loess of the Trzebnickie Hills). However, there are sites of periglacial loess in Western Pomerania found, among others, by CEGŁA & KOZARSKI (1976), ISSMER, KOZARSKI & NOWACZYK (1990), KOZARSKI & NOWACZYK (1991). The results of investigations conducted by these authors help to conclude that north of the loess limits in western Poland there are sites of loess deposits and loess-like deposits in scattered position.

2. Geomorphological description of the study area

In the area of Western Pomerania the main loess profiles are found at three research sites in Klępicz, Stare Objezierze and Żelichów, located on the Myślibórz Upland. These sites are connected directly with the marginal zone of the Pomeranian phase (16.2 ka BP) and indirectly with the Chojna phase (15.8 ka BP) (KOZARSKI 1995) of the last glaciation, formed by the lobe of the Odra (Fig. 1). The morphology of this area does not influence the occurrence of loess deposits. They lie on flat surfaces or on slopes. The Klępicz and Stare Objezierze sites are located within the till plains (Fig. 2) north of the marginal forms delimiting the maximal limits of the Pomeranian phase and formed as end moraines, consisting of boulder crash (KOZARSKI 1965, 1995). The sites in Żelichów are located directly on end moraines of the Pomeranian phase. South of the end moraines of the Pomeranian phase there are extensive areas of outwash plains, where loess patches were also found.

3. Lithofacial analysis of loess deposits

Loess deposits of Western Pomerania, which have often been researched (BIERNACKA & ISSMER 1996; BLUSZCZ et al. 1992; CEGŁA & KOZARSKI 1976; ISSMER 1988, 1995; KOZARSKI & NOWACZYK 1991, 1992), occur in different lithofacies variations. All lithofacies are connected with the periglacial environment and aeolian and slope processes occurring in this environment. Two lithofacies were identified: massive loess (Lm) and laminated loess (Ll) and three sublithofacies: cryptolaminated loess (sl), laminated loess *sensu stricto* (ll) and banded loess (sm). These lithofacies were identified on the basis of sedimentation structure, differences in the grain size, content of calcium carbonate and physical features such as: weight density, volumetric density, porosity, capillar capacity and filter coefficient.

There was no significant variability of physical features in vertical profiles, therefore statistical methods were used. All these physical features, grain size (Mz [phi] after FOLK & WARD 1956) and content of calcium carbonate were called lithophysical features. Five lithophysical groups of loess deposits, such as P_m, Ca, P_d, P_dCa and Ca_F, were delimitated by means of statistical methods, like WARD's method of hierarchical grouping and method of principal components (Fig. 5, Tab. 1).

Tab. 1: Lithophysical group of loess deposits and their connection with the main lithofacies.

Main lithofacies	Lithophysical groups	Capillar capacity P_k		$CaCO_3$ %
		P_{ko} in volume %	P_{kw} in weight %	
Massive loess (Lm)	P_d	>30	>20	0-5
Laminated loess (Ll)	P_m	0-30	0-20	5-10
Laminated loess (Ll)	Ca	0-30	0-20	>10
Laminated loess (Ll)	P_dCa	>30	>20	>10
Laminated loess (Ll)	Ca_F*)	0-30	0-20	>10

*) This group also has significant value of filter coefficient

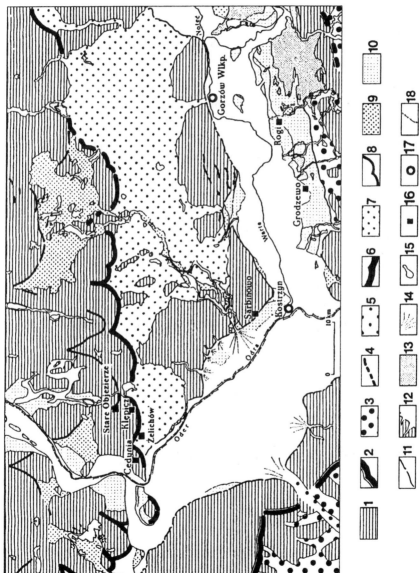

Fig. 1: Geomorphology of the Lower Warta and Lower Odra Region (Kozarski 1965). 1 – till plains, 2 – Poznań phase end moraines, 3 – Poznań phase out-washes plains, 4 – recessional end moraines, 5 – Pomeranian phase outwashes plains, 6 – Pomeranian phase end moraines, 7 – Chojna subphase out-washes plains, 8 – Chojna subphase end moraines, 9 – pradolina terraces, 10 – Late Vistulian river terraces, 11 – pradolina scarp, 12 – flood plains, 13 – dune fields, 14 – alluvial fans, 15 – lakes, 16 – sites, 17 – major towns, 18 – state boundary.

Fig. 2: Geological map (after Berendt et al. 1908, modified).
1 – loess deposits, 2 – fluvioglacial sands, 3 – boulder crash, 4 – moraine clay,
5 – marly clay, 6 – lakes and wet areas, 7 – investigated sites.

3.1 Massive loess lithofacies (Lm)

This lithofacies is characterized by the homogeneity of deposit grain size, low content of calcium carbonate (between 3.63 and 8.20 %) and lack of sedimentation structures. The thickness of this lithofacies is from 60–150 cm. It lies directly under 20–45 cm thick humus horizons, except for the Stare Objezierze 2 exposure where deposits of massive loess are covered by flow till (Fig. 3). Lithofacies of massive loess lies directly on glacial (Żelichów) or fluvioglacial base deposits (Klępicz 1, Stare Objezierze 2), as well as on deposits of laminated loess (Klępicz 2, 4).

The grain size distribution of this lithofacies varies (Fig. 4), depending on three factors: available material, which was aeolian transported, later diagenetic changes and processes related to the development of the soil profile. Dominant is the fine silt fraction, called the *loess fraction* (0.05–0.02 mm). In the massive loess lithofacies the maximum average content of sand fraction (1.0–0.1 mm) is 6.1–21.0 %, coarse silt fraction (0.1–0.05 mm) 13.1–27.1 %, loess fraction 30.8–42.1 %, clay (< 0.02 mm) 20.2–36.8 % and colloidal clay (< 0.002 mm) 9.7–12.3 %. Based on the analysis of the lithophysical features of these deposits they can be included in the P_d group (Fig. 5).

Generally massive loess has no structure. This is understood very generally since in the deposits of massive loess periglacial structures of different types are commonly found (JERSAK 1973). The loess deposits of the investigated sites have no macroscopical structures, which is confirmed by micromorphological investigation. Only in the bottom parts of the Żelichów, Stare Objezierze 2 and Klępicz 1 exposures, small sandy veins (1–5 cm) are found. In thin sections a compact uniform mass was observed which clearly had been subjected to haploidization. This process, in which the primary structure is completely obscured due to soil processes, leads to homogenization of deposits. This is evidenced by the presence of *striotubule* (= traces of earthworms) and *cutans* (= illuviated clay minerals) microstructures and considerable decalcification of this lithofacies (BIERNACKA & ISSMER 1996).

3.2 Laminated loess lithofacies (Ll)

This lithofacies is characterized by clear lamination of the deposit, visible macroscopically as a change of colours of individual laminae. Laminae reach a thickness of 1 to 5 cm. In grain size distribution it is visible as diatactic variability of particle size. Generally lighter and thicker laminae have more coarse silt (0.1–0.05 mm) and more calcium carbonate than darker and thinner laminae, which have more fine silt (0.05–0.02 mm) and less calcium carbonate. Deposits of laminated loess (Ll) contain on average 10.45 to 13.63 % of calcium carbonate. Three sublithofacies were identified in this lithofacies: cryptolaminated loess (*sl*), laminated loess *sensu stricto* (*ll*) and banded loess (*sm*).

The thickness of laminated loess lithofacies varies from 30 to 125 cm. Laminated loess lithofacies in Western Pomerania lies directly under the (20 cm) humus horizons or under other lithofacies variants of loess deposits and rests directly on fluvioglacial de-

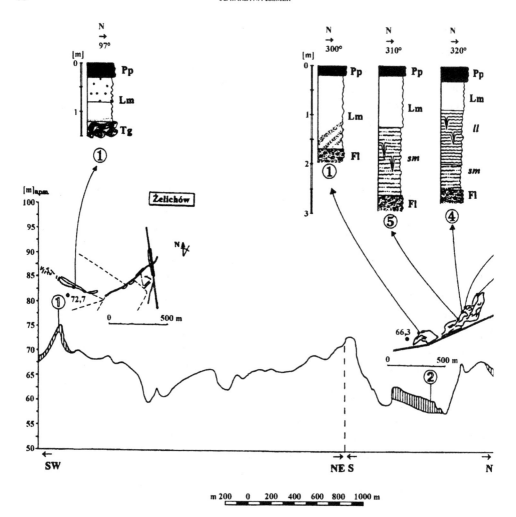

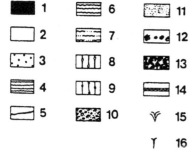

Legend for lithological profiles Żelichów, Klępicz and Stare Objezierze:
1 – humus horizons (Pp), 2 – massive loess (Lm), 3 – ferriferous horizons, 4 – crypto-laminated loess (*sl*), 5 – clay material accumulation horizons, 6 – laminated loess ss (*ll*), 7 – banded loess (*sm*), 8 – flow till (Gs), 9 – argillaceous loess (Gl), 10 – cross-bedded sand, gravel and fluvioglacial stones (Fl), 11 – structureless fluvioglacial sand (Fl), 12 – horizons of so-called weathered pebbles, 13 – boulder crash (Tg), 14 – horizons of calcium carbonate accumulation, 15 – syngenetic cracks of dessication, 16 – cracks with clay-carbonate filling.

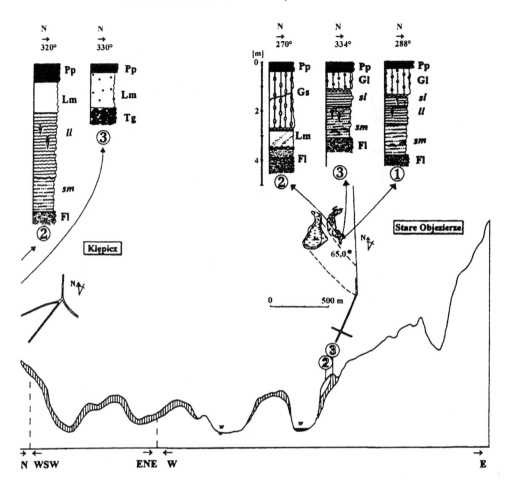

Fig. 3: Morphological profile through the moraine upland and end moraines with marked places of loess deposits and individual lithological profiles for the Żelichów, Klępicz and Stare Objezierze sites (Western Pomerania); *w* – water, N – orientation.

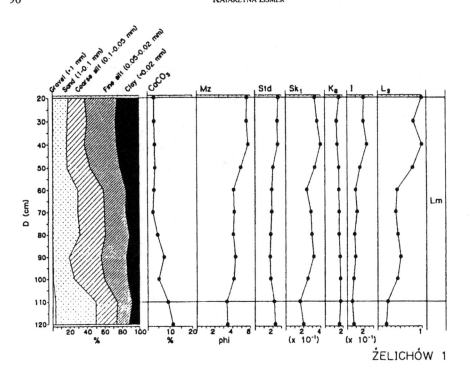

ŻELICHÓW 1

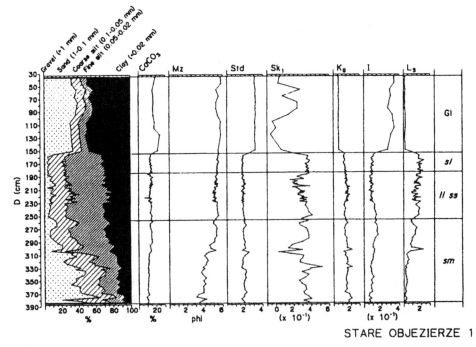

STARE OBJEZIERZE 1

(Fig. 4; compare next page)

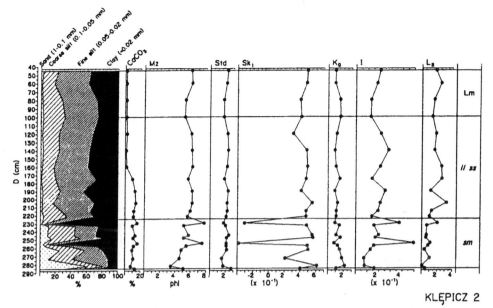

KLĘPICZ 2

Fig. 4: Grain size distribution and content of calcium carbonate of loess deposits at sites Żelichów 1, Klępicz 2 and Stare Objezierze 1.

Mz – mean size, Std – standard deviation, K_G – curtosis, Sk_1 – skewness, I – clay index, L_s – loess index.

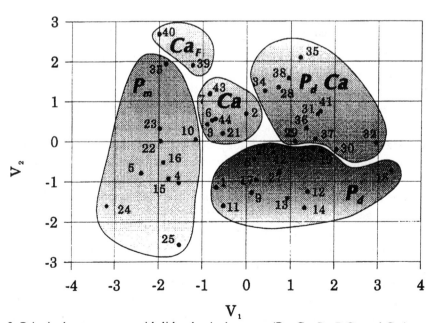

Fig. 5: Principal components with lithophysical groups (P_m, Ca, P_d, P_dCa and Ca_F).

V_1 – component of capillar capacity, V_2 – component of calcium carbonate, 1–44 no. of sample.

posits originating from the Pomeranian phase, formed as sand and gravel (Fig. 3). From the structural point of view, apart from laminae in this lithofacies one finds cracks, faults, and single plications such as inserts or lenses, consisting of a different material from the grain size point of view. These structures have many features in common with periglacial structures.

The grain size distribution of the laminated loess lithofacies varies in each sublithofacies but in all cases the loess fraction is dominant. The sublithofacies of cryptolaminated loess contains on average 6.9 % of sand (> 0.1 mm), 25.1 % of coarse silt (0.1–0.05 mm), 40.9 % of *loess fraction* (0.05–0.02 mm) and 27.0 % of clay (< 0.02 mm), 9.0 % of which is colloidal clay (< 0.002 mm). The banded loess lithofacies contains 41.9 % of sand (> 0.1 mm), 24.3 % of coarse silt (0.01–0.05 mm), 18.1 % of *loess fraction* (0.05–0.02 mm) and 15.8 % of clay (< 0.02 mm), 8.3 % of which is colloidal clay (< 0.002 mm). The change of grain size visible in the sublithofacies of banded loess is caused by the presence of single sandy inserts with lenticular bedding.

There are many explanations for the lamination in loess deposits. Some of them have been connected with slope processes such as sheet flow (MÜCHER & DE PLOEY 1977), others have emphasized the role of capillary ascent (CEGŁA 1972; LAUTRIDOU & GIRESSE 1981). GULLENTOPS et al. (1981) have mentioned fractional segregation of silt deposits in melted snow water. According to SCHWAN (1986) lamination in loess deposits is a result of deposition of silt material by snow flurries. The genesis of lamination in the loess deposits occurring in Western Pomerania should be attributed mainly to the lithological character of the alimentation areas.

4. Palaeographic significance of loess deposits in the area of the last deglaciation

Occurrence of loess deposits in Western Pomerania has diagnostic significance for the reconstruction of environmental conditions between 20 and 16.2 ka BP.

In the case of the investigated loess deposits there is a lack of fossil soil horizons or other biostratigraphic data. In order to determine the chrono-stratigraphic position of the loess deposits thermoluminescence dating was applied. Dating of Pomeranian loesses at the Klępicz site by this method did not produce satisfactory results. The dates obtained lay in the interval of 20 to 7 ka BP with two main phases of accumulation, the older one at approx. 17 ka BP and the younger one at approx. 8 ka BP. However, dates from the same horizons yielded a standard error of 165 % (BLUSZCZ et al. 1994). Consequently, the only general conclusion can be drawn that these deposits should be linked to the Late Vistulian (the Oldest Dryas).

As biostratigraphic data are lacking and the TL method proved to be unreliable, lithofacial analysis was used to determine the loess deposits.

In Western Pomerania loess deposits are formed in two basic lithofacies which lie on fluvioglacial and glacial deposits of the Pomeranian phase of the Baltic glaciation (16.2 ka BP). The basal deposits show laminated loess developed as sublithofacies of banded loess (*sm*) (Fig. 3). This sublithofacies has greater thickness in the north-eastern part of the loess patch (Stare Objezierze) and the smallest in the south-western part (Klępicz) (Fig. 3). The periglacial structure found within this sublithofacies indicate that in the first accumulation phase of Pomeranian loess permafrost had existed for many years. The presence of permafrost was confirmed by lithofacial analysis of this series of loess deposits.

Under favourable aerodynamic conditions accumulation of banded loess could be synchronous with accumulation of massive loess (site Żelichów). The relation of these structureless loesses with the periglacial zone is emphasized by the presence of pebbles in the bottom of this series on which traces of thermal contraction can be found.

Generally Pomeranian loesses in the massive facies occur in scattered position. However, in the Stare Objezierze 2 exposure they are covered by a nearly 3 metre thick flow till (Gs). Therefore these loesses can be defined as fossil loesses. The stratigraphic position of the less thick series of massive loess in the Stare Objezierze 2 exposure is significant for stratigraphic considerations of Pomeranian loess deposits (ISSMER 1995). The lithofacies of flow till (Gs) found in Stare Objezierze indicates melting of ice blocks within the ice-cored moraines present in this area (KOZARSKI 1981). The fact that this till lies directly on the deposits of massive loess proves that the loess deposits were accumulated before Allerød, i. e. the period when ice-cored moraines were melted. This is confirmed by palynological investigations carried out by KRUPIŃSKI (1992) in Chojna, north of Stare Objezierze.

The thickness of the laminated loess sublithofacies *sensu stricto* (*ll*) increases towards the south-west within the loess patch (Fig. 3). Structures such as syngenetic crack structures and a group of periglacial microstuctures, indicating the presence of periglacial climate, were also found within this series. During the accumulation of laminated loess, accumulation of massive loess on favourable surfaces continued.

The top of the laminated loess (Ll) is formed as the cryptolaminated loess sublithofacies (sl). The thickness of this sublithofacies is the greatest in the case of Pomeranian loesses in north-eastern part of the loess patch, on the Stare Objezierze-Klępicz segment. Cryptolaminated loess (sl) is a transient phase from laminated loess (Ll) to massive loess (Lm) in the case of Klępicz 2 and 4 exposures. In the case of Stare Objezierze 1 and 3 exposures it is a transient phase to argillaceous loess (Gl). Both massive loess (Lm) in the Klępicz 2 and 4 exposures and argillaceous loess (Gl) in the Stare Objezierze 1 and 3 exposure are probably synchronic deposits.

In the lithostratigraphic situation of Western Pomerania deposition of loess could start after the continental glacier receded from that area. It follows that accumulation of Pomeranian loess deposits generally occurred in the Late Vistulian. Intensification of the supply of silty material and accumulation or redeposition of loess deposits during the cooler periods was probably during presence of continuous or non-continuous permafrost, which confirms the occurrence of periglacial structures in these deposits. On the other hand, during warmer periods there was also accumulation and redeposition of loess deposits, but to a slightly limited extent. This conclusion is based on the occurrence of aeolian cover sands and dune fields in extensive areas of Western Pomerania. The origin of the dune field in the area of Sarbinowo south of this investigated loess cover is chronostratigraphically connected to the Older Dryas (KOZARSKI & NOWACZYK 1992; STANKOWSKI 1963). Likewise, west of the loess areas investigated, in the area of Cedynia, aeolian cover sands were also found. They originate in the Younger Dryas (KOZARSKI & NOWACZYK 1992). Therefore loess deposits found in areas of Western Pomerania, whose origin is connected with aeolian activity, could have developed in the same period as aeolian cover sands and dune fields, i.e. the in Late Vistulian. On the other hand, the development of the soil profiles and postdepositional diagenetic changes could contribute to the obliteration of the primary structure of these deposits.

5. Acknowledgments

I am most grateful to MIROSŁAWA LIMANÓWKA M Sc and PRZEMYSŁAW SZYMURA M Sc for helping in laboratory analysis, as well to Dr. ADAM WOJCIECHOWSKI for his valuable comments and suggestions in statistical investigations. I acknowledge also ZBIGNIEW NADSTOGA MA for the English translation of this text and native speaker Dr. JOHN CATLOW for correction of this text.

6. References

BERENDT, G., FINCKH, L., KORN, J. & SCHRODER, H. (1908): Erläuterungen zur Geologischen Karte von Preußen und benachbarten Bundesstaaten. Lieferung 81, Blatt Zehden, Gradabteilung 45, No.12; Berlin.

BIERNACKA, J. & ISSMER, K. (1996): Analiza mikrostrukturalna osadów lessowych w Klępiczu Pomorze Zachodnie (Summ.: Micromorphological analysis of loess deposits from Klępicz, Western Pomerania). — Przegląd Geologiczny, 44 (1): 43–48.

BLUSZCZ, A., KOZARSKI, S. & NOWACZYK, B. (1992): Termoluminescencyjne datowanie vistuliańskich pokryw lessowych Pomorza Zachodniego. — Zesz. Nauk. Polit. Śląskiej, Geochronometria, 10: 225–251.

CEGŁA, J. (1972): Sedymentacja lessów Polski. — Acta Universitatis Wratislaviensis, 1968: 3–72.

— & KOZARSKI, S. (1976): Osady lessopodobne na morenach czołowych stadium pomorskiego fazy zasięgu maksymalnego lobu Odry. — Sprawozdania PTPN, 91 za 1973: 38–40.

FOLK, R. & WARD, W. C. (1957): Brazos River bar: a study in the significance of grain size parameters. — Journal of Sedimentology Petrology, 27 (1): 3–26.

GULLENTOPS, F., PAULISSEN, E. & VANDENBERGHE J. (1981): Fossil periglacial phenomena in NE Belgium. — Biuletyn Peryglacjalny, 28: 345–365.

ISSMER, K. (1988): Osady lessopodobne z syngenetycznymi strukturami szczelinowymi w Klępiczu, Pomorze Zachodnie. — Maszynopis pracy magisterskiej, Zakład Geomorfologii Instytutu Badań Czwartorzędu, UAM Poznań.

— (1995): Analiza litofacjalna i litostratygrafia osadów lessowych w strefie kontaktu z osadami glacjalnymi fazy pomorskiej ostatniego zlodowacenia w Starym Objezierzu, Pomorze Zachodnie (Summ.: Lithofacies analysis and loess sequences in the contact zone with glacial deposits of the last glaciation Pomeranian phase at Stare Objezierze, Western Pomerania). — Badania Fizjograficzne nad Polską Zachodnią, **46**, Seria A, Geografia fizyczna: 63–84.

— KOZARSKI, S. & NOWACZYK, B. (1990): Late Vistulian loess on Pomeranian landforms and deposits. — In: KOZARSKI, S. & NOWACZYK, B. [eds.]: International Symposium: Late Vistulian and Holocene aeolian phenomena in Central and Northern Europe (14-18 May, 1990, Poland). Guide-Book of Excursions.

JAHN, A. (1950): Less jego pochodzenie i związek z klimatem epoki lodowej. — Acta Geologica Polonica, **1** (3): 257–310.

JERSAK, J. (1973): Litologia i stratygrafia lessu wyżyn południowej Polski. — Acta Geographica Lodziensia, **32**: 142.

KOLSTRUP, E. (1991): Danish Wechselian and Holocene aeolian deposits. — Z. Geomorphologie N.F., Suppl.-Bd., **90**: 89–97.

KOZARSKI, S. (1965): Zagadnienie drogi odpływu wód pradolinnych z zachodniej części Pradoliny Noteci - Warty. — PTPN, Prace Komisji Geogr.-Geol., **5** (1): 1–154.

— (1981): Ablation and moraines in Western Pomerania, NW Poland. — Geografiska Annaler, **631** (3-4): 169–174.

— (1995): Deglacjacja północno-zachodniej Polski: warunki środowiska i transformacja geosystemu (~20 ka → 10 ka BP). — Dokumentacja Geograficzna, **1**, PAN IGiPZ: 82.

— & NOWACZYK, B. (1991): Lithofacies variation and chronostratigraphy of Late Vistulian and Holocene aeolian phenomena in northwestern Poland. — Z. Geomorph. N.F., Suppl.-Bd. **90**: 107–122; Berlin, Stuttgart.

— & NOWACZYK, B. (1992): Późnovistuliańskie i holoceńskie zjawiska eoliczne w regionie dolnej Odry i dolnej Warty. — In: SZCZYPEK, T. [ed.]: Wybrane zagadnienia geomorfologii eolicznej. — UŚ Wydz. Nauk o Ziemi: 37–114.

KRUPIŃSKI, K. (1991): Flora późnego glacjału i holocenu z Chojnej, Polska. — In: KOSTRZEWSKI, A.[ed.]: Geneza, litologia i stratygrafia utworów czwartorzędowych, I. — Geografia, 50, UAM, Poznań: 497–510.

LANG, H. D. (1990): Der Sandlöß in der Umgebung von Bergen Krs. Celle — Verbreitung, Zusammensetzung und Entstehung. — Eiszeitalter u. Gegenwart, **40**: 97–106.

LAUTRIDOU, J. P. & GIRESSE, P. (1981): Genése et signification paléoclimatique des limons á dublets de Normandie. — Biuletyn Peryglacjalny, **28**: 149–162.

MALICKI, A. (1967): Lessy na obszarze Polski i ich związek z czwartorzędem. — In: GALON, R. & DYLIK, J. [eds.]: Czwartorzęd Polski. — PWN, Warszawa: 372–396.

MARUSZCZAK, H. (1969): Une anlyse paléogéographique de la réparation du loess polonais et ses caractéres lithologuiques directits. — Biuletyn Peryglacjalny, **20** (2): 99–133.

SCHWAN, J. (1986): The origin of horizontal alternating bedding in Weichselian aeolian sands in Northwestern Europe. — Sedimentary Geology, **49**: 73–108.

SIEBERTZ, H. (1988): Die Beziehung der äolischen Decksedimente in Nordwestdeutschland zur nördlichen Lößgrenze. — Eiszeitalter u. Gegenwart, **38**: 106–114.

STANKOWSKI, W. (1963): Rzeźba eoliczna Polski północno-zachodniej na podstawie wybranych obszarów. — PTPN, Prace Komisji Geograficzno-Geologicznej, **4** (1): 146 p.

Address of the author:

Dr. KATARZYNA ISSMER, Department of Geomorphology, Quaternary Research Institute, Adam Mickiewicz University, H. Wieniawskiego 17/19, PL-61-713 Poznań, Poland, e-mail: issmer@man.poznan.pl

GeoArchaeoRhein, **3**: 97–105; Münster 1999

Typical aeolian sand profiles and palaeosols of the Glien till plain in the northwest of Berlin

Norbert Schlaak

Abstract: The investigations in the region of the Glien have shown that the formation of the dunes mainly took place in the Late Glacial period of the Weichselian ice-age. The first phase of a thin wide-spread sedimentation of aeolian sand sheets took place prior to the complete growth of forests in the Allerød period. By its thickness between 10 and 500 cm this sand blanket caused an incredible levelling of the landscape. At the end of the Younger Dryas with the reduction of the forests due to an increasingly colder and dryer climate, a second dune phase started to build up parabolic dunes to a height of 10 metres. This was the main period of dune-formation. The main grain size is 0.1 or 0.2 mm. In the Glien area a stratigraphical separation of the two Late Glacial aeolian phases takes place through the horizon of the 'Finow soil' (Allerød age). In some locations multiple layerd Holocene sedimentation has been identified by ^{14}C-dates. The investigations show similarities to the evidences in the Eberswalde Urstromtal, in the area of the Schorfheide and the endmoraines of the Pomeranian stage.

1. Study area, points of examinations

The small till plain of the Glien within limits of the Weichselian glacial Brandenburg phase and Frankfurt phase is situated between the Berlin ice-marginal valley in the south and the Eberswalde ice-marginal valley in the north (Fig. 1). Aeolian coversands and bow-shaped dunes occupy an area of about 60 km² in the southern part of the till plain (Fig. 2). The origin of the sands, mainly transported by western winds, are the valley bottoms east of Friesack and north of Nauen ("Havelländisches Luch"). The stratigraphy of aeolian profiles has been studied in details near Perwenitz, Pausin, Neu-Vehlefanz and Wolfslake.

1.1 Neu Vehlefanz

The bow-shaped and parabolic dunes in the south of Neu Vehlefanz are open to the west and show steep eastern slopes (18°, distal) and gentle western slopes (12°, proximal), thus point to western dune-forming winds. The steep northern slopes (22–26°) and the gentle southern slopes (13°) testify a later changing wind direction from south-west. Deflation basins are not existing. The investigations in the eastern part of the Glien have shown similarities in the stratigraphy of the bow-shaped dunes with heights of about 10 m. A boring from the top of the dune in the forest-division 2103 reached the Weichselian till in

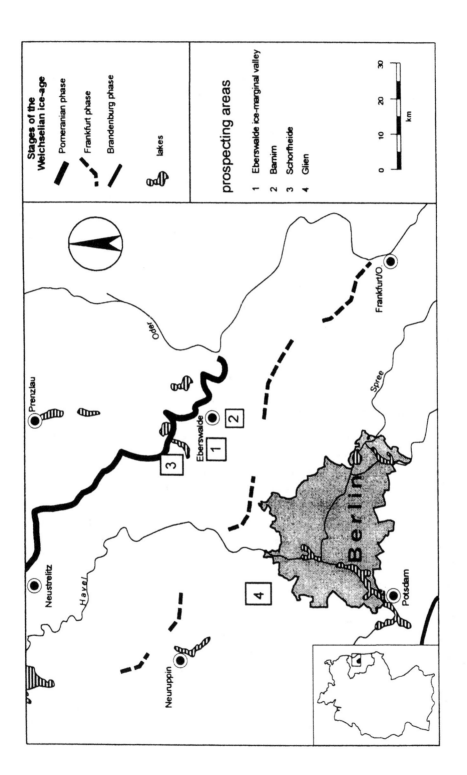

Fig. 1: Location of the prospecting areas in northern Brandenburg.

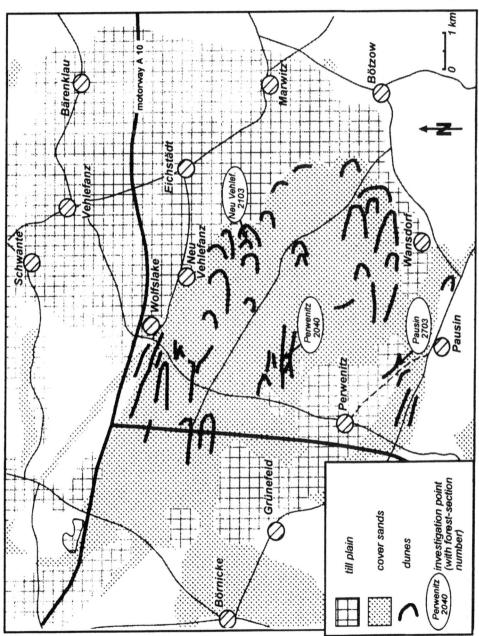

Fig. 2: Location map of the Glien till plain.

a depth of 10.8 m. The shallow decalcified till was covered by a thin aeolian sand sheet of 0.2 m thickness. 74 % of the well sorted sand range in the grain-size between 0.18 and 0.063 mm with a maximum of 0.1 mm. In the upper part the loamy brown horizon of the Finow soil has been developed. This palaeosol buried during the Younger Dryas period and well known from the dune fields of Eberswalde (SCHLAAK 1993, 1997, 1998), divides the aeolian sand profile in two series. The upper sands have a thickness of 10.6 m. Their grain-size composition is similar in all portions. A higher subdivision of the grain-size (12 classes between 0.63 and 0.063) shows two maxima (peaks) in the part between 0.2 and 0.063 mm, which is an often noticed characteristic of the Younger Dryas dune sands. Hints of a Holocene aeolian cover (palaeosols, charcoal) have not been found in that area.

1.2 Perwenitz

Longitudinal dunes with heights between 3 and 5 metres and small irregular formed dunes are typical for the wooded area 2 km north-east of Perwenitz. Stratigraphy and structure has been studied by borings and research pits (Fig. 3). On the northern slope of a longitudinal dune in forest-section 2040 five dune-sand series are developed. Five sand layers are divided by two buried palaeosols (partly relictic) and four horizons of charcoal. The Finow soil is the lowest palaeosol with a thickness of 10 cm. Charcoal pieces from the layer below that palaeosol yielded a ^{14}C age of 11,330 y BP. It may be the age of a root of an Allerød tree. The white horizontally bedded aeolian sands at the base have a thickness of 2.45 m. Borings indicate that in the south of the investigation site the surface of the till plain is in a deeper position so that the pre-Allerød coversand locally has a thickness of about 5 metres. The three upper charcoal horizons gave ^{14}C ages of 9,225 ± 80 y BP, 8,135 ± 105 y BP and 4,465 ± 95 y BP. Between the upper two charcoal horizons a podzolic soil has developed. The grain-size composition of the dune sand shows similarities to the profile of Neu Vehlefanz (Fig. 3).

1.3 Pausin

On the edge of the farmlands in some places irregular dunes were formed. A typical profile of the Pausin area is forest-section 2703. On top of the only 15 cm deep decalcified Weichselian till there is a stone layer with ventifacts (with two shaped facets at least). It is covered by a thin aeolian sand sheet in which the Finow soil is developed, similar to the profile Neu Vehlefanz. As Fig. 4 demonstrates, the silt and clay content of the Finow soil (6 %) is higher than that of the underlying older coversand (2,6 %) — a typical feature of that palaeosol. The upper part of the aeolian profile consists of two sand layers: 1. a sand sheet without charcoal pieces of 1.70 m thickness of the Younger Dryas period, with two peaks of the sieving curve at 0.2 and 0.16 mm (Fig. 4) and 2. a Holocene sand sheet of 1.60 m thickness with charcoal pieces. The sand layers are divided by a 15 cm thick charcoal horizon dated to 1,320 ± 70 y BP. It can be correlated with the regional Slavonic forest cleaning.

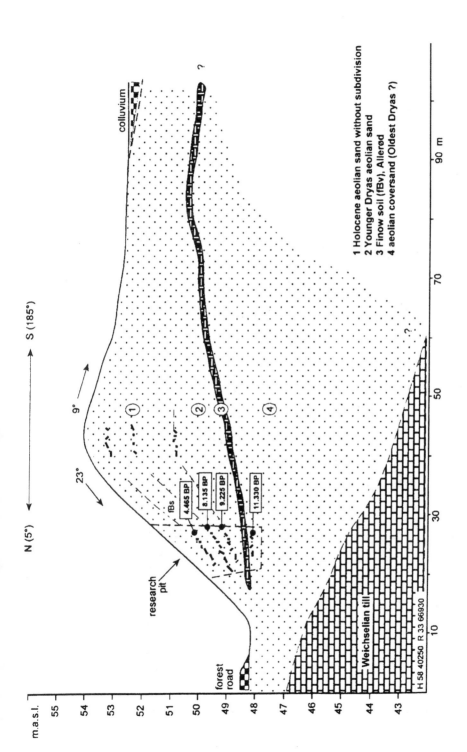

Fig. 3: Cross-section of the longitudinal dune Perwenitz 2040, Glien.

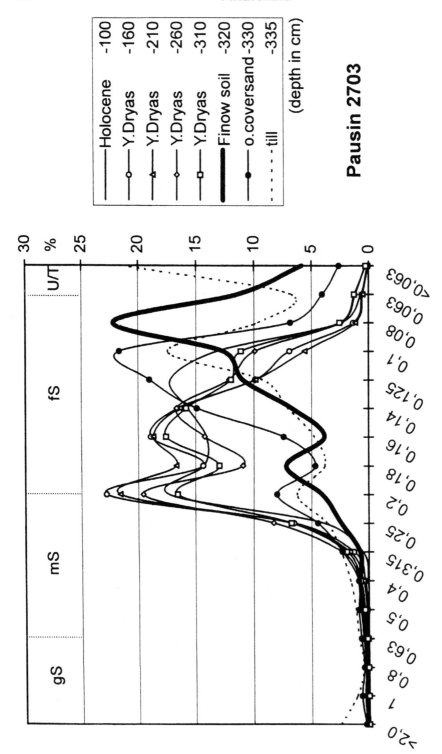

Fig. 4: Grain-size composition, Pausin.

2. Results

Against the background of similarities of the findings in the aeolian deposits in various regions of Nordbrandenburg a generalisation of the aeolian activities is possible. The Finow soil of Allerød age serves as the major regional stratigraphic marker for the older aeolian sands. Therefore a short description of its characteristics:

2.1 Finow soil

- brown earth soil, dystric cambisol
- thickness of 5–15 cm
- generally without any trace of a humus horizon on its top
- share of silt and clay is generally 5–10 % (function of water holding, high nutrient content, therefore often intensive root penetration)
- destratification to about 15 cm below the soil formation
- in some places small charcoal pieces, ^{14}C-ages between 11,330 and 10,290 y BP
- transition from the Finow soil into a peaty layer with the thin layer of pumice tuff (Laacher See tuff), ^{14}C-ages of the peaty layer: 11,400 –10,130 y BP.

2.2 Reconstruction

Reconstruction of the aeolian activity in northern Brandenburg from the Late Glacial to the Holocene (see Tab. 1):
- *Pre-Allerød phase* (Oldest Dryas/Bølling ?): wide spread sedimentation of coversand, thickness 0,1–5 m, in some areas with an incredible levelling effect, ^{14}C-date of a moss-peat layer embedded in aeolian sand (region of the Schorfheide) 12,960 y BP, cal BC 14,185–12,605), silty-banded fine sands (similarities to the Older coversand II), rarely small dunes, in an exceptional case (exposed position) a longitudinal dune with a height of 11 metres in the Eberswalde Urstromtal, in the neighbourhood of moraine plains solifluction and abluation alternating with aeolian sedimentation
- *during the Allerød*: dense vegetation, pine and birch forests, mire formation, development of the Finow soil, local forest fires
- *at the end of the Younger Dryas*: increasingly colder and dryer climate, decline of the water table, formation of big bow-shaped dunes (height 10–20 m), deep deflation
- *Preboreal-Atlantic*: dense vegetation, local forest-fires by natural impact, reactivation of dune sand, during the younger Boreal (8,200–7,800 y BP) wide-spread forest fires, sand with charcoal covering dunes
- *Subboreal-Subatlantic*: since the Neolithic age repeatedly vegetation destruction by human impact (first significant aeolian processes 4,500 y BP), recorded by aeolian sand layers with charcoal pieces, sandy peat in mires and buried soils (podzolic soils).

Tab. 1

14C-years ka BP	Chrono-stratigraphy			archaeological subdivision		Aeolian deposits in Nordbrandenburg (Barnim, Eberswalde ice-marginal valley, Schorfheide, Glien)				
						morphology processes, forms, sediments	activities (+ intensity) wide-spread / local		wind direction	14C TL Pa datings
			0,25			strong deflation on farmlands , fS-coarse sand!		●	S-W	historical references
1		Subatlantic	Younger 1,1	1,3	Slawonic age	sand with charcoal covering dunes (2 metres), fS/mS, steep slopes (lee side 30°)		●	SW, S	●●⊜ ★
2	Holocene		Older	1,6 / 2,0 Roman iron age	Migration period	local weakly sedimentation (decimetre), fS/mS with charcoal			SW, S	●
3				2,6	Pre-Roman-iron-age	local destruction of the surface by man, weakly sedimentation on lee slopes of parabolic dunes, fS/mS with charcoal	● ● ● ●			● ● ●● ●
		Subboreal	Younger	3,8	Bronze age					
4										
5			Older		Neolithic age	sand with charcoal covering dunes, reactivation by human impact, fS/mS	●		SW, S	●●●★ ⊜
5,0										⊜
6		Atlantic	Younger 6,0			local weakly sedimentation (decimetre), fS/mS with charcoal	●			●
7			Older		Mesolithic age		●			●
7,5							●			●
8		Boreal	Younger			wide-spread forest fires (natural causes), fS/mS with charcoal covering dunes from late glacial	●		SW, S	●●●● ★
9 9,0			8,5 Older			dense vegetation				
						local sand with charcoal covering dunes (natural causes)		●	SW	● ★
10 10,2			Preboreal			formation of great dune fields without charcoal (lee side 18°), deflation basins, fS, later fS/mS,	●		SW W	○ ⊜ ●●●
11 10,9		Late glacial	Younger Dryas			dense vegetation, pine and birch forests				⊜
11,75			Alleroed		Paleolithic age	brown soil (braunerde): so called „Finow soil"				●●● ● ★
12 11,95			Older Dryas			cover sands, fine-laminated with levelling-out effect, small dunes, fS/mS, silty banded sands (Older coversand II ?, solifluction and abluation alternating with aeolian sedimentation, in an exceptional case: longitudinal dune near Eberswalde (height 11 m., lee side 10°)	●	●	WSW ?	⊜ ○ ○ ○
13			Boelling							
14			Oldest Dryas							
15 15,2		Pleniglacial	Rosenthal subphase							
16			Pomeranian stage							
20			Brandenburg stage							
27										

Aeolian deposits in northern Brandenburg (incl. Glien ★) dated by 14C-, TL-measurements and pollen analysis (Pa)

3. References

SCHLAAK, N. (1993): Studie zur Landschaftsgenese im Raum Nordbarnim und Eberswalder Urstromtal. — Berliner geographische Arbeiten, **76**: 1–161; Berlin.

— (1997): Äolische Dynamik im brandenburgischen Tiefland seit dem Weichselspät-glazial. — Arbeitsberichte geogr. Institut der Humboldt-Universität zu Berlin, **24**: 58 S.; Berlin.

— (1998): Sites in the Toruń–Eberswalde ice marginal valley. — In: JÄGER, K.-D., KOWALKOWSKI, A., NOWACZYK, B. & SCHIRMER, W. [eds.]: Dunes an fossil soils of Vistulian and Holocene age between Elbe and Wisła: 27–32; Poznań (Adam Mickiewicz University, Quat. Res. Inst.).

Address of the author:

Dr. NORBERT SCHLAAK, Hochstr. 13, D-16244 Altenhof, e-mail: n.schlaak@t-online.de

GeoArchaeoRhein, **3**: 107–125; Münster 1999

Chronosequence of biogenic deposits and fossil soils in the dune near Jasień, Western Poland

ALOJZY KOWALKOWSKI, BOLESŁAW NOWACZYK & IWONA OKUNIEWSKA-NOWACZYK

Abstract: Many dunes, mainly parabolic, are found in Western Poland within the Głogów–Baruth pradolina. One of them lies on the alluvial cone of the Lubsza in Jasień. Fluvial deposits of the cone are separated from eolian sands by a thin layer of peat, radiocarbon and palynologically dated to be of Allerød and Younger Dryas age. In the distal part of the northern arm of the dune there are five arenosols with Ah finger-like horizons that separate thin series of eolian sand. In Ah horizons charcoal was found dated to 10,300 ± 190 – 9,020 ± 110 y BP. A rusty soil is lithostratigraphically, morphologically and chemically similar to the Finow soil, known from other proglacial stream valleys of the Polish-German Lowland. The main outlines of the Jasień dune were formed in the Older Dryas. In the Younger Dryas, Preboreal and Boreal the dune was remodelled.

1. Introduction

In Poland areas built of sand, including extensive pradolina, were mostly affected by eolian processes. Dunes of different size and eolian cover sands were thus formed. Under these forms biogenic deposits or fossil soil horizons are often found. In many dunes and eolian cover sands the soil horizons (sometimes there are a few of them) are composed of separate depositional units. The main layers, together with stone and ceramic artefacts found on them or sporadically in fossil humus horizons, are used to determine the chronosequence of changes occurring in the natural environment.

The age of the eolian forms occurring in the Toruń–Eberswalde and Warsaw–Berlin pradolinas (Fig. 1) has been a very frequent research topic (KOZARSKI 1962; NOWACZYK 1976a, 1976b, 1986; KOWALKOWSKI 1977a, 1977b; KRAJEWSKI 1977; NOWACZYK et al. 1985; KRAJEWSKI & BALWIERZ 1985). Dunes lying in the Głogów–Baruth pradolina, the oldest valley of the last glaciation, formed during the Leszno phase, were the last to stir the interest of researchers (NOWACZYK & OKUNIEWSKA-NOWACZYK 1996). This phase is dated by KOZARSKI (1995) at 20 ka BP and by ROTNICKI & BORÓWKA (1989) at 20.5 ka BP.

Dunes and eolian covers, which according to KOZARSKI (1995) are a record of a more moderate variation of the periglacial environment, were formed mainly in the Older and Younger Dryas. NOWACZYK (1986) ascribes higher depositional efficiency to eolian processes occurring in the Older Dryas. Soil horizons found in the eolian deposits are younger than 13,000 y BP.

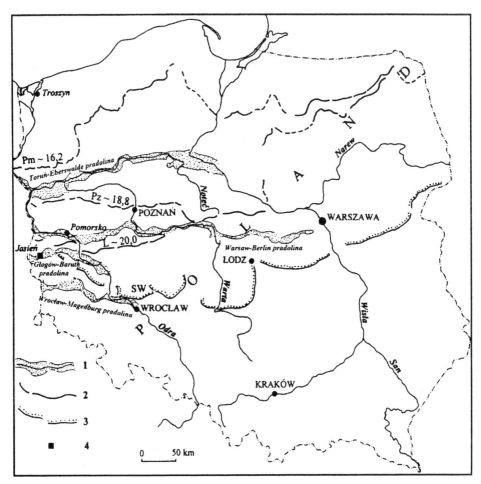

Fig. 1: Fossil soil site in Jasień.
1 – pradolina valleys, 2 – extent of Baltic glaciation phases: L – Leszno phase, Pz – Poznań phase, Pm – Pomeranian phase (numbers designate estimated age of phases in ka BP after KOZARSKI 1995), 3 – SW extent of the Warta stage, Mid-Polish glaciation.

The presence of many soils and biogenic horizons in the dunes near Jasień in the Głogów–Baruth pradolina encouraged us to start detailed investigation. The aim of the work was to determine the chronosequence of biogenic and eolian deposits and fossil soils.

2. Morphology

Dunes and eolian cover sands are often found in the Głogów–Baruth pradolina. They are marked in dune distribution maps (GALON 1958; IZMAIŁOW 1976; NOWACZYK 1986), the glaciation map of LIEDTKE (1973) and the geomorphological map of Poland (STARKEL

1980). The forms occur in complexes that form compact dune fields, or single dunes. Parabolic dunes are the most frequent genetic type.

The forms under analysis lie on extensive alluvial cones piled up by the rivers Neisse, Lubsza, Bóbr and others flowing into the proglacial stream valley from the south. The declivity, initially considerable, was levelled off, resulting in the deposition of the transported sediments. Depostion started when proglacial stream valley outflow stopped, i. e. during the Poznań phase at the latest. Alluvial cones were formed under severe climatic conditions, which is evidenced by synsedimentary frost wedges found in them.

From many dunes in the Głogów–Baruth pradolina, a geologically interesting one was selected located about one kilometer west of Jasień on the alluvial cone of the Lubsza river. It is a typical parabolic dune (Fig. 2) with secondary smaller paraboles. Its arms are opened to the west. This is proof that westerly winds contributed to the dune's morphology. The southern arm of the parabole is adjacent to the biogenic accumulation plain.

3. Lithology

Three sites were analysed in the selected dune. In its southern arm, which neighbours the biogenic accumulation plain, eolian deposits are interfingering with gyttia and peats and fossil humus horizon. In the face (Fig. 2) two fossil soils were discovered in a large exposure. These two objects have been investigated lithologically and palynologically and by radiocarbon dating (NOWACZYK & OKUNIEWSKA-NOWACZYK 1996). Likewise, in the northern arm there is a large exposure, perpendicular to the dune's morphological axis, giving insight into the sequence of deposits in the distal part of the arm. This is precisely where observations were made and samples for granulometric, physical-chemical analyses and radiocarbon datings were taken. The core of biogenic deposits under the eolian sand was analysed palynologically.

The granulation of the deposits, sampled from morphologically different soil horizons, was analysed by mesh and CASAGRANDE's areometric methods, modified by PRÓSZYŃSKI. Quartz grains rounding, 0.8–1.0 mm, were analysed on KRYGOWSKI's mechanical graniformeter (1964). C_{org} was determined by TIURIN's method and nitrogen (N) by KJELDAHL's method. Alkaline cations and cation exchange capacity were determined by KAPPEN's method. Free Fe^{3+} and Al^{3+} were determined on the basis of dithionite extracts. The pH of the soil in H_2O and KCl suspension was examined electrometrically, using combined electrode. Calcination losses were determined by burning at a temperature of 500° C. Colours were determined with the help of Munsell's table. Samples for palynological analysis were prepared in accordance with the procedure recommended by FAEGRI & IVERSEN (1975). Charcoal remnants were floated for radiocarbon dating from humus horizons. From peat layers, one centimeter thick slabs were cut out.

The base of the Jasień dune is the alluvial cone of the Lubsza, a right tributary of the Neisse. It is composed of medium and fine grained sand, most often laminated. The

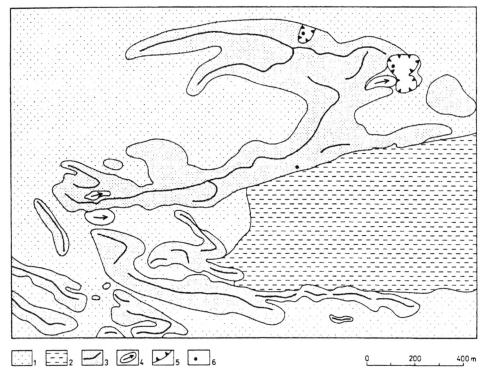

☐.₁ ⊟₂ ⊿₃ ⊘₄ ⊿₅ •₆   0   200   400 m

Fig. 2: Jasień. Geomorphological map.
1 – Lubsza alluvial cone, 2 – biogenic accumulation plain, 3 – dunes, 4 – deflation basin, 5 –
exploration exposures, 6 – research sites mentioned in the text.

presence of synsedimentary frost wedges is proof that deposition of sand occurred under
severe climatic conditions. The oldest eolian series rests on the sand of the cone; it is
part of its face and its southern arm. At the face it is covered by an Allerød fossil soil
(11,680 ± 130 y BP) and in the southern arm it lies under detritus gyttia radiocarbon
dated to 11,820 ± 140 y BP and palynologically dated to the Allerød (NOWACZYK &
OKUNIEWSKA-NOWACZYK 1996).

The sands of the cone in the part lying north of the Older Dryas cone are covered by a
thin layer of pressed peat in which horizontal fragments of wood are found (Photo 1).
The beginning of its deposition was determined in the Allerød period on the basis of the
palynological analysis (Fig. 3). The top part of the peat was dated at 10,640 ± 250 y BP
(Tab. 1) and the wood lying below at 10,870 ± 210 y BP. Above the peat there is a thin
layer of sand of eolian origin, changing towards the top into sand with bands of organic
substance; the quantity of the latter increases towards the top. On that sand one finds a
thin lamina of white-yellowish sand (see description in the next section). Based on the
examination of the exposure today, one can suppose that this thin layer spreads towards

Photo 1: Jasień. Biogenic and eolian deposits covering the Lubsza paleochannel.

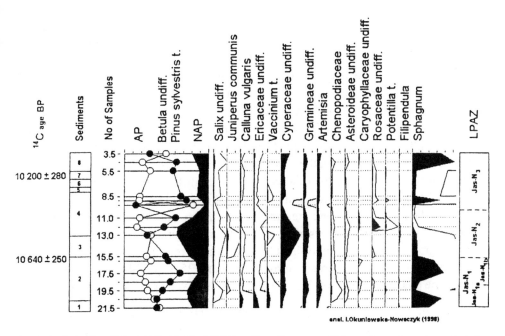

Fig. 3: Jasień. Simplified (AP+NAP=100%) pollen diagram of biogenic sediments underlying dune deposits:
1 – fluvial sand, grey; 2 – brown pressed peat; 3 – eolian sand, yellow; 4 – grey-brown sand with a lot of plant detritus; 5 – eolian sand yellow; 6 – grey-brown sand with plant detritus; 7 – brown peat, minimally sandy; 8 – grey-brown sand with plant detritus.

Tab. 1: Radiocarbon dates of fossil soil and peat horizons separating the aeolian series at Jasień.

No lab.	^{14}C date B P	Deposits
Gd-12090	10 870 ± 210	wood
Gd-10803	10 640 ± 250	peat
Gd-10807	10 200 ± 280	peat
Gd-11397	10 300 ± 190	charcoal
Gd-12085	10 150 ± 80	charcoal
Gd-11399	9 870 ± 120	charcoal
Gd-12088	9 650 ± 180	charcoal
Gd-10801	9 540 ± 270	charcoal
Gd-10797	9 390 ± 260	charcoal
Gd- 6862	11 820 ± 140	detritus gytia
Gd- 5851	11 680 ± 130	charcoal

the south, increasing its thickness. It is thus another eolian series in the dune younger than that of the Older Dryas. Its deposition occurred in the mid Younger Dryas. It is covered by peat dated to be 10,200 ± 280 y BP. The extent of these deposits is limited to an area of 33 x 18 m within the incised paleochannels of the Lubsza.

Sands deposited in the cone's top, under the peat layer, include, on average, 65.4 % of 0.10–0.25 mm fraction, 11.8 % of 0.25–0.50 mm fraction and 1.2 % of 0.50–1.00 mm fraction (Tab. 2). The percentage of the 0.10–0.02 mm fraction is quite high (about 20 %). The average grain diameter Mz (FOLK & WARD 1957) of these sands is 0.20 mm, which corresponds to the granulation of fine sand. The monomodal granulation curves of these deposits (Fig. 4 A), with dominant fraction of 0.10–0.25 mm and relatively small percentage of the 0.50–1.00 mm (Tab. 2) indicate their similarity to older eolian sands, analysed by BUSSEMER (1998) in the western part of the Głogów–Baruth pradolina in the Golssen profile. Sands lying over the peat series are differently granulated than those discussed above. The percentage of the 0.10–0.02 mm and 0.25–0.10 mm fractions is smaller. On the other hand, there are more 0.25–0.5 mm and 0.5–1.0 mm fractions. In ROTNICKI's opinion (1970), the loss of the 0.10–0.02 mm fraction is characteristic of eolian sands. The graniformametric analysis of the quartz grain rounding revealed that β grains were dominant (51.8 %), whereas γ grains constitute 25.3 % (Tab. 2). In sands above the peat type β is also dominant. However, there are fewer γ grains and more α grains.

In the part lying southwest of the paleochannels with limnic-eolian deposits, on eolian sand from the middle Younger Dryas, a humus horizon a few centimeters thick (Photo 2) with many charcoal (3) dated to 10,300 ± 190 y BP was found. Thus agewise the layer corresponds to the top lamina of the peat. At the humus horizon one finds laminated sands (2), covered with a thin humus horizon (1). It is also rich in charcoal. It was radiocarbon dated to 9,390 ± 260 y BP.

Tab. 2: Some indices of the parent rock of the soils in the dune at Jasień.

No	Mother rock	Soil horizon	Grain fractions content %				Grain rounding in percent									Wo mean	Mz mean
			grain size mm	min	max.	mean	minimum			maximum			mean				
							γ	β	α	γ	β	α	γ	β	α		
1	Fluvial-eolian sediments		0,10-0,25	64,8	66,0	65,4	17,5	51,5	18,5	29,5	52,5	31,0	25,3	51,8	22,8	1198	0,20
			0,25-0,50	9,0	14,5	11,8											
			0,50-1,00	1,0	1,5	1,3											
2	Fluvial-eolian sediments	C Ah	0,10-0,25	54,2	63,5	58,8	19,5	47,0	15,5	31,5	60,5	30,5	24,2	52,1	23,7	1172	0,22
			0,25-0,50	21,5	38,5	32,4							25,3	50,5	24,1	1179	
			0,50-1,00	2,5	5,0	3,3							23,0	53,6	23,4	1170	
3	Eolian sediments	C Ah	0,10-0,25	46,0	55,0	49,2	19,0	45,0	16,5	30,0	54,5	32,0	23,9	52,1	24,0	1178	0,25
			0,25-0,50	35,5	41,0	39,4							24,3	51,0	24,7	1170	
			0,50-1,00	3,5	7,0	5,9							23,2	53,8	23,0	1189	
4	Eolian sediments		0,10-0,25	31,5	45,0	40,0	21,0	48,5	23,0	28,0	56,0	26,5	24,3	51,3	24,3	1169	0,28
			0,25-0,50	32,5	45,0	38,2											
			0,50-1,00	7,5	18,5	11,8											

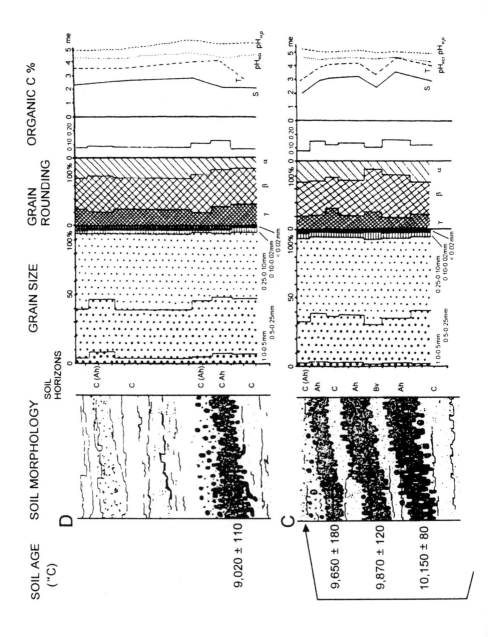

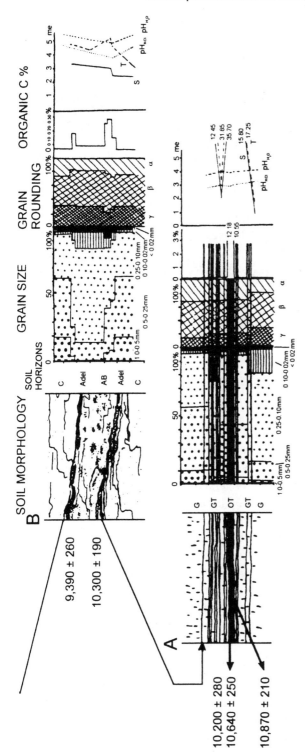

Fig. 4: Jasień. Soil morphology, granulation profile, grain rounding, content of organic C and pH.

9,390 ± 260

10,300 ± 190

Photo 2: Jasień. Eolian sand intercalated by fossil humus horizons of a rusty soil (Haplic Arenosols).

The granulation curves of the sands with terrestric series, of the litho- and autogenic fossil soils lying above the fluvio-limnic deposits reveal their differentiation in the dune's space, linked to the litho- and pedomorphogenetic processes.

Eolian deposits being part of the sequence described in the previous section are characterized by monomodal granulation curves (Fig. 4 B). They are very diversified in the vertical. In the series lying under the bottom and over the top fossil humus horizon 0.10–0.25 mm (40 % on average) and 0.25–0.50 mm (38.2 % on average) fractions are dominant. The percentage of the 0.50–1.00 mm fraction is 11.8 % and is much higher than in the sands in the top of the alluvial cone. The average grain diameter Mz is 0.28 mm, which corresponds to medium grained sand (Tab. 2). The 20–25 cm thick layer of sand between the humus horizons, strongly transformed pedogenically, has granulation similar to the sands that build the top of the alluvial cone. In this layer the dominant fraction is 0.10–0.25 mm (68.4 % on average). The percentage of the 0.25–0.50 mm fraction is 14.5 %. The 0.10–0.02 mm fraction is also considerable (14 %). In the layers described above there is only a small percentage of that fraction. The average grain diameter Mz for the layer in question is 0.17 mm. In the quartz grain rounding no significant differences between soil horizons is noticed; β grains are dominant.

East of the paleochannels with limnic-eolian deposits a few horizons of fossil soils separated with eolian series were found. Their humus horizons contained considerable amounts of charcoals which were radiocarbon dated. The lowest humus horizon (Photo 3)

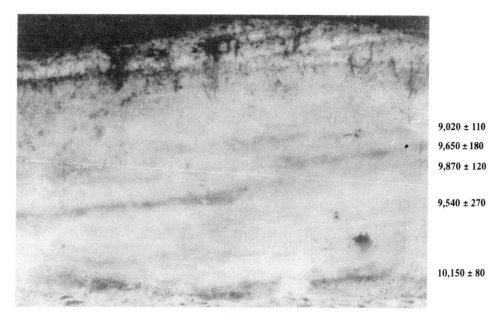

9,020 ± 110

9,650 ± 180

9,870 ± 120

9,540 ± 270

10,150 ± 80

Photo 3: Jasień. Eolian sand alternating with fossil humus horizons.

was dated to 10,150 ± 80 y BP (Tab. 1). This date is very close to that of the top layer of peat. Advanced exploitation of the sand offers the possibility to find links between these horizons. Succeding soils were dated to 9,870 ± 120, 9,650 ± 180 and 9,020 ± 110 y BP. Between the levels dated to 10,150 ± 80 and 9,870 ± 120 y BP an interrupted gray layer was found with many charcoals dated to 9,540 ± 270 y BP. The interpretation of this date is very difficult.

It was noticed in the profile that the cone building deposits are characterized by a different granulation than the series lying south west of the paleochannels with the fluvial sands being part of the alluvial cone. They are also differentiated in this profile.

Eolian sands with humus horizons dated to 10,150 ± 80 – 9,680 ± 180 y BP (Fig. 4 C) are characterized by a large percentage of the 0.10–0.25 mm fraction (58.8 %) and a lower percentage of the 0.25–0.50 mm fraction (32.4 %) on average. The percentage of the 0.50–1.00 mm fraction is very small (3.3 %). The average grain diameter Mz for this series is 0.22 mm which corresponds to fine grained sands. The rounding analysis of the quartz grains revealed the dominance of middle rounded β grains (52.1 % on average), with similar percentages of edged α grains and rounded γ grains.

Eolian sands lying under the following younger fossil humus horizon (9,020 ± 110 y BP) and above it (Fig. 4 D) are characterized by monomodal granulation curves with the maximum in the 0.10–0.25 mm fraction (49.2 % on average). The average percentage of the 0.25–0.50 mm fraction is 39.4 % and that of the larger 0.5–1.0 mm fraction is 5.9 %. Therefore the average granulation diameter Mz is 0.25 mm, which corresponds to medium grained and fine grained sands. The monomodal character of granulation and higher average grain diameter could be interpreted as an indicator of short transport, multiple redeposition and influence of pedogenetic processes (KOWALKOWSKI 1995).

4. History of flora

From the deepened paleobed of the Lubsza a core was sampled from the layer of biogenic deposits separating the sands that make up the alluvial cone from eolian sands (Photo 1). The sequence, from top to bottom, is as follows:

0.0 –   3.5 cm - eolian sand, yellow
3.5 –   5.5 cm - grey-brown sand with plant detritus
5.5 –   6.5 cm - brown peat, minimally sandy
6.5 –   7.5 cm - grey-brown sand with plant detritus
7.5 –   8.0 cm - eolian sand, yellow
8.0 – 13.0 cm - grey-brown sand with a lot of plant detritus
13.0 – 15.5 cm - eolian sand, yellow
15.5 – 20.5 cm - brown pressed peat
20.5 – 25.0 cm - fluvial sand, grey
25.0 – 30.0 cm - fluvial sand, light grey

The pollen analysis method was used to analyse 16 samples taken from the core. The samples were taken every 1–3 centimetres. Local pollen levels and sublevels were identified in this material, which posed some interpretation problems (Fig. 3):

Jas-N$_1$: *Pinus-Betula* LPAZ (16.0–21.5 cm). *Pinus* is in the range from 39.3 % – 66.9 %, *Betula* between 20.3 % and 41.9 %.

Jas-N$_{1a}$: *Pinus-Betula*-Ericaceae LPASz (19.5–21.5 cm). *Pinus* up to 45.8 %, *Betula* up to 41.9 %, Ericaceae 6.7 %, *Calluna* 4.0 %, *Vaccinium* 3.9 %. *Sphagnum* is present.

Jas-N$_{1b}$: AP-*Pinus-Betula* LPASz (16.0–18.5 cm). *Pinus* between 52.7 % and 66.9 %, *Betula* 20.3–31.8 %, *Sphagnum* up to 63.4 %.

Jas-N$_2$: *Pinus-Betula-Juniperus* LPAZ (11.0–15.5 cm). *Juniperus* is a continuous curve. *Pinus* from 27.3 % to 61.1 %, *Betula* between 15.1 % and 26.5 %. *Salix* up to 1.5 %. Cyperaceae (23.8 %) are more dominant.

Jas-N$_3$: *Pinus-Betula-Sphagnum* LPAZ (3.5–9.5 cm). *Pinus* between 14.2 % and 74.4 %, *Betula* 17.8–82.1 %. *Sphagnum* up to 105.8 %.

Deposition of pressed peat (15.5–20.5 cm) started in the Allerød and was completed at the beginning of the Younger Dryas. A phase of pine-birch forest is seen in the diagram, where initially there were favourable conditions for the development of representatives of Ericaceae. *Sphagnum* grew on the peat. In the last sample taken from this layer *Juniperus* was found, which is sufficient evidence to define the border of Allerød/Younger Dryas. This layer was radiocarbon-dated to 10,640 ± 250 y BP (Tab. 1).

A change in climate interrupted the sedimentation of biogenic deposits. A layer of sand was formed. In the younger part of Younger Dryas biogenic deposits are again deposited with some sand or with more sand than the organic substance. Periods of the expansion of Cyperaceae are noticed in the deposits, as well as periods in which representatives of Rosaceae and *Potentilla* were dominant. *Sphagnum* increased considerably prior to the destruction of the peat bog.

5. Chronosequence of paleosoils

In the northern arm of the Jasień dune one finds a chronosequence of hydrogenic soils and terrestric litho- and autogenic soils, which are characteristic of sandy deposits in pradolinas. The soil chronosequence is similar to that found in Pomorsko in the Warsaw–Berlin pradolina (NOWACZYK 1976a; KOWALKOWSKI 1977a, 1977b). However, it is different with respect to age and pedogenesis from that in the dune at the 3rd terrace level of the Oder in Troszyn near Wolin (NOWACZYK & PAZDUR 1982; KOWALKOWSKI 1995).

The age range of the lithopedostratigraphic profile of the Jasień dune from at least $10,870 \pm 210 - 9,020 \pm 110$ y BP encourages to look for similarities between the paleosoils in the dune and the Finow soil dated to $11,400 \pm 200 - 10,290 \pm 285$ y BP, described by SCHLAAK (1993, 1997) in the western part of the Toruń–Eberswalde pradolina and to the „rusty" soils with a Bv horizion dated to $9,740 \pm 100 - 8,720 \pm 80$ y BP documented by MANIKOWSKA (1977, 1998) in the eastern part of the Warsaw–Berlin pradolina. According to BUSSEMER (1998) sandy periglacial sediments with Bx and Bv horizons were deposited in the late phase of the Vistula glaciation, from 13.5 to 9.5 ka (TL). It is worth noting that the age range at which soils with Bv horizon were formed in different areas between the Elbe and Vistula covers a period of about 1,850 years, from the end of Allerød to the beginning of Boreal. The chronolithopedosequence examined in the Jasień dune was also formed at that time.

The oldest soil in the part of the Jasień dune was formed on a marshy base. It is a peaty ground-gleyic soil (Histi Umbric Gleysol) consisting of thin layers of pressed peat (0.5 to 0.7 cm) (Fig. 4 A, Photo 1) with a grey to olive black colour (5Y 2/3-4/1), interbedded by light grey eolian covers (Tab. 3). The peat layers include from 4.5 % to 21 % of poorly decomposed organic matter with lamella divisibility. It is very low in nitrogen, with the C:N ratio from 21 to 23:1 (Tab. 3). This indicates their accumulation in acid water environment. The layer of organic deposits is horizontal. Its deposition started, as is evidenced by palynological analysis, in the Allerød and continued till the end of the Younger Dryas. The biostratigraphy is confirmed by radiocarbon datings of wood samples from the bottom peat layer with $10,870 \pm 210$ y BP and from the top peat lamina $10,200 \pm 210$ y BP. It was covered severals times by sand with shiny grain surfaces originating from the fluvial underground.

In sands of the mineral-organic series, within the reach of the capillary raise of ground water, many vertical olive black streaks up to 5 cm long formed from the remains of roots and shoots of marshy plants turned into peat. This is evidence of the prolonged marshy character of the area, confirmed by the layers of gyttia and strongly pressed brown peat, dated to $11,820 \pm 140 - 8,010 \pm 60$ y BP, separated by eolian sands, found by NOWACZYK & OKUNIEWSKA-NOWACZYK (1996) at the edge of the southern arm of the dune, over 500 m from the site in question. They were accumulated in a shallow extensive water reservoir (Fig. 2).

At the distance of a few metres to southwest a poorly developed humus horizon (Photo 2) with thickness varying from 1 to 12 centimetres is found. This horizon corresponds to the initial soil (Distric Leptosol). It includes from 0.25 to 0.54 % of organic matter. The charcoal found in it was dated by ^{14}C to $10,300 \pm 190$ y BP, i. e. at the end of the Younger Dryas. This horizon is covered by eolian fine grained sand layer with a thickness of 20–25 cm (Fig. 4 B), with a higher content of the 0.10–0.02 mm fraction and a lower content of the 1.00–0.5 mm fraction and also smaller percentage of humus (Tab. 2 and 3). Its characteristic feature is a poorly expressed continuous dull yellow orange colour (10YR 7/3) with dark reddish brown humus spots. The age of this horizon of rusty initial soil (Haplic Arenosol) corresponds to rusty soils dated by MANIKOWSKA (1977, 1998) in the eastern part of the Warsaw–Berlin pradolina. The morphology and lithostratigraphy, similar to that of SCHLAAK's Finow soil (1993, 1997), also indicates this type of soil in Jasień. However, the genesis of the soil formation material is not explained. A characteristic is the framing of this soil from the bottom to the top with dark reddish brown (5YR 3/4) bands richer in humus and free Fe^{3+} and Al^{3+} than the soil itself (Tab. 3 and 4, Fig. 4 B).

In the northern distal fragment of the dune's arm there is a sequence of three initial soils - Arenosols (Fig. 4 C, Photo 3), disappearing towards the north east. Among them there are two eolian regosols (Protic Arenosols), respectively $10,150 \pm 80$ and $9,680 \pm 180$ y BP old, with C-Ah profiles and a poorly developed rusty soil (Haplic Arenosol) between them with an Ah horizon dated to $9,870 \pm 120$ y BP. The inhomogenous Ah horizons of these soils with a thickness of 20–30 cm, with very uneven finger-like passages contain 0.21–0.27 % of organic matter. They are dark yellow orange or dark yellow brown (Tab. 3). Insofar as Ah horizons are spotty, Bv and C horizons have a uniform colour. They do not exhibit sedimentation structures; they include scattered uneven small particles of charcoal. C horizons, with thickness ranging from 10 to 20 cm, contain 0.13 % to 0.24 % organic matter, which indicates the origin of their constituents — soils blown around in the direct vicinity, also at the proximal slope of the dune. Uneven and often diffusion passages from C to Ah indicate the possibility of a synsedimentary origin of the soils in question, in 200–280 year cycles, under conditions of poorly developed flora, often destroyed by fires. This genesis is also indicated by the cation exchange capacity, differentiated in the profile only to a small degree, with alkaline cation sums from 1.55 to 3.30 me and cation exchange capacity Th from 3.15 to 4.35 me/100g of soil at Ah and C horizons (Tab. 4). Note should be taken of a poorly developed but continuous Bv horizon of the rusty soil which according to ^{14}C dating could have been formed over 770 years in the Preboreal, between 10,150 ± 80 and 9,390 ± 260 y BP. It is a continuation of the soil analysed earlier (Fig 4 B). All the soils of this sedimentation facies (Fig. 4 C), compared with the complex discussed above (Fig. 4 B) contain less humus, have lower alkalic exchangeable cation sums and higher concentration of acidic exchangeable cations (Tab. 4).

In the overlying facies of eolian deposits (Fig. 4 D) there is a C-Ah horizon of arenosol (Protic Arenosols) with a divided finger-like Ah horizon, 15–20 cm thick, spotty, grey yellow brown (10YR 5/2), containing 0.20 % of organic matter. Many charcoal fragments are present in the horizon. The structureless C horizon below is grayish yellow brown (10YR 7/4) and contains 0.11 % of organic matter, twice less than the Ah horizon. Its charcoal dates to 9,020 ± 110 y BP. The Ah horizon changes directly into a poorly developed, spotty C level (Ah), 10–15 cm thick, with 0.18 % of organic matter. Its colour is grayish yellow brown (10YR 6/3). Above the Ah horizon there is eolian sand, 50–60 cm thick, with preserved remains of sedimentation structures. Its dark yellow brown colour is due to the unevenly scattered organic matter and presence of many fragments of charcoal. In the top part of these sands one finds another C-Ah arenosol, grayish yellow brown (10YR 6/3), with many fragments of black charcoal with much more humus than in the C horizon (Tab. 3). Pedogenic transformations are manifested here by a small decrease in rounded grains (Fig. 4 D). Low sums of alkalic cations, from 1.95 to 2.70 me and cation exchange capacity Th from 2.80 to 3.85 me/100 g exhibit a small pedogenic activity in this facies. Probably the soil horizons include material blown from the nearest vicinity of the dune, including older soils on which the flora was destroyed by fires. The material and soil horizons of this facies are slightly less acidic, are richer in exchangeable Ca^{2+} and Mg^{2+}, poorer in exchangeable K^+ and Fe^{3+} than in the series occurring in their floor.

Wavy and branched-off, non-continuous illuvial streaks and bands are present in the part of the Jasień dune in the entire series of the paleosoils, dating from 10,300 ± 130 to 9,020 ± 110 y BP, with their C horizons formed by sands of the fluvio-eolian and eolian facies. They are from 0.2 to 2.5 cm thick, dark brown in the bottom part of the section, brown in the middle part and light brown in the top part (Tab. 3). Their origin is pedogenic, connected with the migration of brown clayey fractions, moving iron compounds and soluble humus compounds, deeply penetrating the porous dune fine sands. The migration takes place during the periodic flows of rainwater, acidified while washing the profile of the podzols at the ground surface. There are many contradictory hypotheses about the genesis of these streaks. Their chemical composition and acidity clearly differ from the soil material and C horizons that surround them and are younger and independent of them. In the dune investigated, streaks and bands are not genetically related to the paleosoils due to age difference. It is not possible to associate their origin with the rusty paleosoils in the profile. Consequently, there is no basis to confirm PRUSINKIEWICZ et al.'s conclusion (1994) classifying sandy soils with illuvial bands as a subtype of rusty soils where they are superimposed on fossil C horizons.

6. Conclusions

The formation of the Jasień dune originated in the Older Dryas (NOWACZYK & OKUNIEWSKA-NOWACZYK 1996). Based on the present investigations one can suppose that its main outlines originated at that time. Later only some of their parts were transformed. These transformations also occurred in the northern arm of the dune. The first phase occurred in the middle of the Younger Dryas. Eolian processes in subsequent phases occurred from the end of the Younger Dryas to the beginning of the Boreal. During these phases, above the reach of the capillary rise of ground water, eolian sand was deposited for about 1,200-1,300 years with its granulation getting coarser towards the top. The pedocomplex of five poorly developed arenosols with finger-like Ah horizons and one poorly developed rusty soil with a Bv horizon and layers of eolian sand, containing humus without features of pedogenesis in situ, originating from the same time, is characterized by the decreasing frequency of recurrence of eolian activity. The comparison of ^{14}C dates in Fig. 4 helps to state that the following phases of Ah-C horizons were developed over extending time (in years): ~ 100, ~ 150, ~ 280, ~ 190, ~ 290, ~ 370. The eolian processes at the second phase were favoured by many fires, which are indicated by fragments of charcoal, found both in soil horizons and in sands of C horizons. Poorly developed flora, cyclically destroyed by fires, was not able to stabilize the dune's surface for longer periods.

The rusty Bv horizon, located in the dune, has pedostratigraphic significance. Its age is between $10,150 \pm 80$ and $9,870 \pm 120$ y BP. This evenly coloured horizon, 15–20 cm thick, coincides with SCHLAAK's Finow soil (1997) in the western part of the Toruń–Eberswalde pradolina, dated to $11,330 \pm 265 – 10,290 \pm 385$ y BP, and with rusty soils in the eastern part of the Warsaw–Berlin pradolina, dated by MANIKOWSKA (1977, 1998) to $9,740 \pm 100 – 9,380 \pm 50$ y BP. It remains to be explained whether these soils have a similar genesis, dependent on the temporal and spatial differentiation of the climate alongside the W–E axis in Central Europe in the period from the Younger Dryas to the early Boreal, or if they are soils of different genesis. Based on the results of investigations the following conclusions can be drawn concerning the distal part of the northern arm of the Jasień dune:

1. A series of peat hydrogenic deposits from Allerød and Younger Dryas occurs in the underground of the dune.
2. In the eolian deposits of the distal part of the northern arm of the dune there is a series of five Arenosols with finger-like Ah horizons, containing charcoal. They are separated by thin layers of sands originating from blown-away-soils lying on the proximal slope.
3. The rusty soil dated at the period between $10,150 \pm 80$ and $9,870 \pm 120$ y BP exhibits a lithostratigraphic, morphological and chemical similarity to the older Finow soil and younger rusty soils described earlier in the proglacial stream valleys mentioned above.

7. Acknowledgements

The authors wish to thank Dr. ANTONI SIENKIEWICZ and his team from the Chair of Forest Soil Sciences and Forest Fertilization, Agricultural Academy in Poznań, and Prof. ZYGMUNT BROGOWSKI and his team from the Chair of Soil Sciences, SGGW, Warsaw for the granulation analyses and analyses of physical and chemical properties of 26 soil samples (granulation by the areometric method, C_{org}, pH, composition of exchangeable cations). Special thanks are due to Prof. KLAUS-DIETER JÄGER from the Institute of Pre-Historic Archaeology, Martin-Luther University in Halle, for a very inspiring discussion held at the dune exposure site in Jasień.

8. References

BUSSEMER, S. (1998): Bodengenetische Untersuchungen an Braunerden und Lessive-profilen auf Sandstandorten des brandenburgischen Jungmoränengebietes. — In: BAUME, O. [ed.]: Beiträge zur quartären Relief- und Bodenbildung. — Münchener geogr. Abh., Reihe A, **149**: 27–93; München.

FAEGRI, K. & IVERSEN, J. (1975): Textbook of pollen analysis. Munksgaard. Copenhagen.

GALON, R. (1958): Z problematyki wydm śródlądowych w Polsce (Résumé: Sur les dunes continentales en Pologne). — In: GALON, R. [ed.]: Wydmy śródlądowe Pol-ski, cz. **1**: 13–31; Warszawa.

IZMAIŁOW, B. (1976): The state of researches in inland dunes in Poland. — Zeszyty Naukowe Uniwersytetu Jagiellońskiego, Prace Geograficzne, **43**: 39–63.

KOWALKOWSKI, A. (1977a): A paleopedological investigation of dunes at Pomorsko. — Quaestiones Geographicae, **4**: 7–13.

— (1977b): Dynamika rozwoju późnoplejstoceńskich i holoceńskich gleb z piasków wydmowych w Pomorsku (Summ.: Development dynamics of late Pleistocene and Holocene soils from dune sands at Pomorsko). — Soil Science Annual, **28** (3–4): 19–35.

— (1995): Chronosequence of Holocene paleosols on aeolian sands at Troszyn, NW Poland. — Quaternary Studies in Poland, **13**: 31–41.

KOZARSKI, S. (1962): Wydmy w Pradolinie Noteci koło Czarnkowa (Summ.: Dunes in the Noteć ice-marginal valley near Czarnków). — Badania Fizjograficzne nad Polską Zachodnią, **9**: 37–60.

— (1995): Deglacjacja północno-zachodniej Polski: warunki środowiska i transformacji geosystemu (~20 ka→10 ka BP) (Summ.: Deglaciation of northwestern Poland: environmental conditions and geosystem transformation, ~20 ka→10 ka BP). — Instytut Geografii i Przestrzennego Zagospodarowania PAN, Dokumentacja Geograficzna, **1**: 82 p.

KRAJEWSKI, K. (1977): Późnoplejstoceńskie i holoceńskie procesy wydmotwórcze w Pradolinie Warszawsko-Berlińskiej w widłach Warty i Neru (Summ.: Late-Pleistocene and Holocene dune-forming processes in the Warsaw–Berlin Pradolina). — Acta Geographica Lodziensia, **39**: 87 p.

— & BALWIERZ, Z. (1985): Stanowisko Bøllingu w osadach wydmowych schyłku Vistulianu w Rośłu Nowym k/Dąbia (Summ.: The site of Bølling in the dune sediments of the Vistulian decline at Rośle Nowe near Dąbie). — Acta Geographica Lodziensia, **50**: 93–109.

KRYGOWSKI, B. (1964): Graniformametria mechaniczna. Teoria, zastosowanie (Zusammenfassung: Die mechanische Graniformametrie. Theorie und Anwendung). — Poznańskie Towarzystwo Przyjaciół Nauk, Prace Komisji Geograficzno-Geologicznej, **2** (4): 112 p.

LIEDTKE, H. (1973): Die nordischen Vereisungen in Mitteleuropa. — Frankfurt am Main (Institut für Angewandte Geodäsie).

MANIKOWSKA, B. (1977): The development of the soil cover in the late pleistocene and holocene in the light of fossil soils in dunes in Central Poland. — Quaestiones Geographicae, **4**: 109–129.

— (1998): Aeolian deposits and fossil soils in dunes of Central Poland - the dune in Kamion. — In: JÄGER, K.-D., KOWALKOWSKI, A., NOWACZYK, B. & SCHIRMER, W. [eds.]: Dunes and fossil soils of Vistulian and Holocene age between Elbe and Wisła. — Guide-Book of Excursion: 92–97; Poznań.

NOWACZYK, B. (1976a): Geneza i rozwój wydm sródlądowych w zachodniej części Pradoliny Warszawsko-Berlińskiej w świetle badań struktury, uziarnienia i stratygrafii budujących je osadów (Summ.: The genesis and development of inland dunes in the western part of the Warsaw–Berlin Pradolina in the light of examinations of the structure, granulation and stratigraphy of the deposits which built them). — Poznańskie Towarzystwo Przyjaciół Nauk., Prace Komisji Geograficzno-Geologicznej, **16**: 108 p.

— (1976b): Eolian cover sands in central-west Poland. — Quaestiones Geographicae, **3**: 57–77.

— (1986): Wiek wydm, ich cechy granulometryczne i strukturalne a schemat cyrkulacji atmosferycznej w Polsce w późnym Vistulianie i Holocenie (Summ.: The age of dunes, their textural and structural properties against atmospheric circulation pattern of Poland during the Late Vistulian and Holocene). — Wydawnictwo Naukowe Uniwersytetu im. Adama Mickiewicza, Seria Geografia, **28**: 245; Poznań.

— & OKUNIEWSKA-NOWACZYK, I. (1996): Etapy rozwoju wydmy w Jasieniu w świetle datowań radiowęglowych i palinologicznych (Summ.: Development stages of the Jasień dune in light of radiocarbon and palinological dating). — In: SZCZYPEK, T. & WAGA, J. M. [eds.]: Współczesne oraz kopalne zjawiska i formy eoliczne, wybrane zagadnienia: 93–101; Sosnowiec.

PAZDUR, A., PAZDUR, M. F. & AWSIUK, R. (1985): Stratygrafia i warunki rozwoju wydmy w Pomorsku koło Sulechowa w świetle nowych badań (Summ.: Stratigraphy and conditions of dune development at Pomorsko near Sulechów-new studies). — Badania Fizjograficzne nad Polską Zachodnią, **35**, Seria A. Geografia Fizyczna: 103–127.

— & PAZDUR, M. F. (1982): Próba datowania metodą ^{14}C gleb kopalnych z wydmy w

Troszynie koło Wolina (Summ.: An attempt of dating by the ^{14}C method of fossil soils from the dune at Troszyn near Wolin). — Soil Science Annual, **33** (3–4): 145–158.

PRUSINKIEWICZ, Z., BEDNAREK, R., KOŚKO, A. & SZMYT, M. (1994): Wiek, właściwości i geneza wstęg iluwialnych w świetle badań paleopedologicznych i archeologicznych (Summ.: Age, properties and genesis of illuvial bands in the light of paleopedological and archaeological investigations). — Soil Science Annual, **45** (1/2): 5–19.

ROTNICKI, K. (1970): Główne problemy wydm śródlądowych w Polsce w świetle badań wydmy w Węglewicach (Summ.: Main problems of inland dunes in Poland based on investigations of the dune at Węglewice). — Poznańskie Towarzystwo Przyjaciół Nauk. Prace Komisji Geograficzno-Geologicznej, **11** (2): 146 p.

— & BORÓWKA, R. K. (1989): Osady górnego plenivistulianu w dolinie Prosny pod Macewem a wiek maksymalnego zasięgu ostatniego zlodowacenia podczas fazy leszczyńskiej (Summ.: Upper Pleni-Vistulian deposits in the lower Prosna valley below Macewo versus age of maximum extent of the last glaciation during the Leszno Phase). — Badania Fizjograficzne nad Polską Zachodnią, **40**, Seria A. Geografia Fizyczna: 3–20.

SCHLAAK, N. (1993): Studie zur Landschaftsgenese im Raum Nordbarnim and Eberswalder Urstromtal. — Berl. geogr. Arb., **76**: 145 p.

— (1997): Äolische Dynamik im brandenburgischen Tiefland seit dem Weichsel-spätglazial. — Arbber. Geogr. Inst. Humboldt Univ. zu Berlin, **24**: 58 p.

STARKEL, L. (1980): Przeglądowa Mapa Geomorfologiczna Polski w skali 1:500 000 [ed.] Instytut Geografii i Przestrzennego Zagospodarowania PAN.

Addresses of the authors:

Prof. Dr. ALOJZY KOWALKOWSKI, European Institute of Postgraduate Studies, Al. 1000-lecia Państwa Polskiego 7, PL-25-314 Kielce.

Prof. Dr. BOLESŁAW NOWACZYK, Institute of Quaternary Research, Adam Mickiewicz University, ul. H. Wieniawskiego 17/19, PL-61-713 Poznań, e-mail: geomorf@man.poznan.pl

Dr. IWONA OKUNIEWSKA-NOWACZYK, Institute Archaeology and Ethnology, Poznań Branch, Polish Academy of Sciences, ul. Zwierzyniecka 20, PL-60-814 Poznań.

GeoArchaeoRhein, **3**: 127–135; Münster 1999

Buried soils in dunes of Late Vistulian and Holocene age in the northern part of Central Europe

KLAUS-DIETER JÄGER & DIETRICH KOPP

Abstract: Buried soils alternating with layers of sand accumulation are frequently found in stratigraphical sequences of dunes throughout the sand belt of northern Central Europe. They reflect changing conditions of soil formation, surface shape and land use intensity in the course of Late Vistulian and Holocene. Evidence of these changes is provided by the varying occurence of soil types, by the stratigraphical subdivision of dune sequences and by included archaeological finds. The latter ones support the chronology of evidences. Some observations contradict well-known assumptions. This is examplified with reference to age and environmental conditions favouring the origin of brown earth soils in Central Europe.

1. Introduction: In the dunes of the northern part of Central Europe buried soils can be found frequently. They dominate the dune stratigraphy for they reflect periods of interrupted sand accumulation. The alternation of sandy layers and enclosed soil horizons provides a record of the manyfold dune history. Its chronology may be derived from frequent archaeological finds within these soil horizons. Moreover, the conditions of soil development during the period of pedogenesis are reflected by soil features, and the development stage of the time initiating a new sand cover has been preserved.

This is why a careful documentation and investigation of buried soils in dunes of northern Germany has been suggested and justified. Therefore, a regional inventory of sites and profile observations has been collected by the authors supported by experts, especially from archaeology and soil science. A comprising publication is in preparation.

Regardless of detailed documentation a few regionally significant results may be generalized. They concern different items, above all

1.) geomorphology and landscape development

2.) archaeology and history of settlement

as well as, last not least,

3.) soil science (especially concerning soil development and taxonomy).

The gain of knowledge is closely connected with the chance of dating buried soils mainly by means of archaeological findings. Chance for getting a differentiated dune chronology is available e. g. by luminescence dating (KOZARSKI 1990; DE BOER 1995).

2. Soil science

Regardless of all chances of precise dating a fundamental difference separates buried soils of Late Vistulian and of Holocene age. This difference may be recognized by means of the respective soil type.

The Late Vistulian is represented in the dune areas by three ones:

1. Gleyic tundra soils (e. g. Klein Müritz near Graal-Müritz, Mecklenburg-Vorpommern, cf. Fig. 1), occasionally connected laterally with layers of Late Vistulian peat.
2. Brownearth (e. g. Münchehofe near Buckow, Brandenburg, cf. Fig. 2). Occurrence above deep ground-water level only.
3. Podzolic soils in part (e. g. Jüdenberg near Bitterfeld, Sachsen-Anhalt, cf. Fig. 3). This soil type can be observed in Holocene sequences, too, but the value of the iron oxide content may be different.

Without any doubt podzolic soils are recorded from Holocene sequences, too (e. g. Midlum, district of Wesermünde, Niedersachsen: Dune site Midlum II within the dune area „Schwarzer Bär", cf. Fig. 4 and HAARNAGEL 1964: pl. 17). However, the absence of brownearth soils in Holocene sequences of unambiguous age is noticeable, the more since the supposition of Holocene datings related to this soil type is supported by the general acknowledgement of well-known theories (cf. e. g. from the current literature KUNZE, ROESCHMANN & SCHWERDTFEGER 1988). On the contrary, buried soils in Holocene sequences are either podzols (Fig. 4) or rankers (e. g. Fischbeck near Havelberg/Sachsen-Anhalt, Fig. 5). If buried soils of the brownearth type can be dated by means of archaeology the limits of Late Vistulian have not been exceeded so far. Such dating of the typical brown subsoil horizon of a brownearth may be examplified by the Münchehofe site where the covering humus horizon is dated by the Late Vistulian Swiderian (cf. Fig. 2 and, moreover, LIEBEROTH et al. 1970: 316–322).

The characteristic feature of Central European brownearth soils is the brown subsoil

---

Fig. 1: Klein Müritz (Mecklenburg-Vorpommern).
Sand-pit exposure with superficial podzolic soil and a sandy sequence below. A buried pale horizon (G_r) intercalated between sandy layers represents a gleyic tundra soil (x). The chronological position of this buried soil may be derived from the lateral transition into a peat level of Allerød age in the same level. The peat layer has been dated by means of pollen analysis.

Fig. 2: Münchehofe near Buckow (Brandenburg).
A sandy hillock in a dune field has been dissected by archaeological excavations of a Late Palaeolithic site. A buried humus horizon (bAh) may be attributed to the younger Swiderian culture due to the archaological content. The brown subsoil horizon (B_v) of a sandy brownearth soil below is separated from the humus horizon above by an intercalated wedge-shaped sandy layer (without any soil features) from left. This means a discordance between the buried soil horizons (bAh and B_v) and, moreover, a dissimilarity of age: The brown horizon (B_v) has originated before the period of the younger Swiderian in the transitional time-span between Late Vistulian and Holocene (cf. GRAMSCH, JÄGER & KOPP in LIEBEROTH et al. 1970).

(Fig. 1, explanation opposite page)

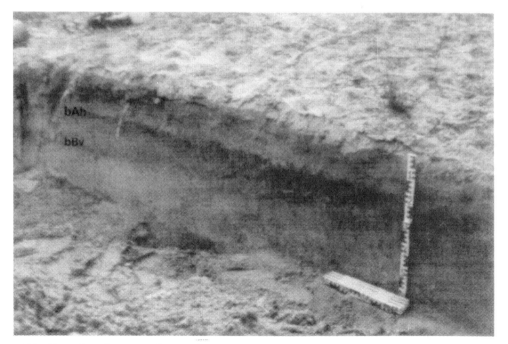

(Fig. 2, explanation opposite page)

horizon, and for that reason it is remarkable that parallels to the observations at Münchehofe are available otherwise. Comparable are datings by means of the Late Palaeolithic so-called „Federmesser" culture (represented by the Cresswellian on the British Isles) at Golßen in the Niederlausitz/Brandenburg (cf. GRAMSCH 1969).

These and other comparable field observations require new considerations concerning the correctness of usual theories related to age and environmental conditions leading to the origin of brownearth soils (a.o. KOPP 1969; JÄGER & KOPP 1969; KOPP & JÄGER 1972: 79–80; JÄGER 1997: 7–8).

3. Geomorphology and landscape development

Numerous buried soils of Holocene age in dune sequences prove without any doubt that the shape of dune areas in northern Central Europa is anything but the exclusive result of Late Vistulian open grounds. Moreover, their development did not end within the limits of that period.

On the other hand, eolian redeposition and accumulation within dense woodland is hard to believe.

During the Holocene open grounds which are independent from natural environmental factors as climate or, locally, substrate are due to anthropogenic land use. An increasing significance of anthropogenic effects was the inevitable consequence of the introduction of agriculture during the Neolithic period. Varying courses of way and intensity on sandy substrates in the northern regions of central Europe are recorded by the stratigraphy of dunes. The evidence is given by the alternation of aeolian sand layers and intercalated buried soils (e. g. in the case of the Fischbeck site, cf. Fig. 3 and additionally with reference to the detailed description of local findings and datings by RICHTER 1961).

This is why a local differentiation of dune stratigraphy has been expected, due to the local differentiation of settlement according to course and intensity. However, this view may require some corrections since KOZARSKI (1990) could recognize far-reaching correspondences of stratigraphical observations and their datings in northern Poland. There periods of rather high settlement density correspond with significant reactivations of eolian accumulation, for instance during the Neolithic the Funnel beaker and during the Bronze Age the Lusatian culture (KOZARSKI 1990: Tab. 2). The reason is an intensification of agrarian land use during these periods causing a deterioration of the vegetation cover and in part destruction of the highly vulnerable dune surface.

4. Archaeology and history of settlement

Due to the conditions mentioned just before during Holocence soil formation in dunes has been dependent on the regional course of settlement history. Oscillations of natural environmental conditions, such as climate, have been of less significance. A consequence is a remarkable high frequency of archaeological sites in dune areas. Another one can be derived from likewise frequent sections with buried soils in stratigraphic superposition.

(Fig. 3, explanation next page)

(Fig. 4, explanation next page)

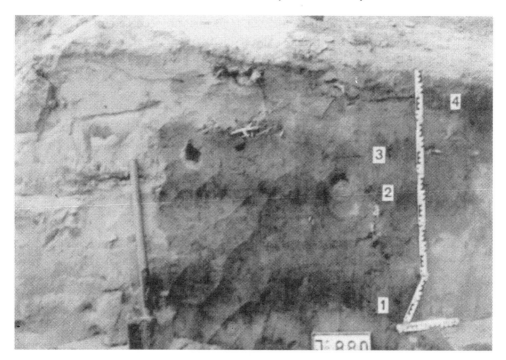

Fig. 5: Fischbeck near Havelberg (Sachsen-Anhalt).
Dune section of a sandy sequence with alternation of sandy layers with buried humus horizons (1-4), i. e. buried soils of ranker type. They are all dated by means of archaeology. From bottom to top they represent the late Neolithic time (Schönfeld culture: 1), the late Bronze Age (so called Urnfield period: 2), and the early Iron Age (Jastorf culture: 3). The surficial humus soil (4) contains scattered sherds of Slavonic Medieval pottery (cf. RICHTER 1961).

Fig. 3: Jüdenberg near Bitterfeld (Sachsen-Anhalt).
Dune exposure with truncated buried podzolic profile. The subsoil horizon of the buried podzolic soil is panthered. Kryoturbations in the sandy layers above prove a Late Vistulian soil formation, evidently before the melting of last glacial permafrost.

Fig. 4: Midlum, district of Wesermuende (Niedersachsen).
Dune exposure on occasion of archaeological excavations. In the section two buried podzolic soils in stratigraphical superposition. Archaeological datings from both of these soils give proof that the whole sequence was deposited within a few centuries (cf. HAARNAGEL 1964: Tab. 17b: Site Midlum II).

There the oscillations of changing settlement intensities are recorded by the alternation of sandy layers and buried soils (Fig. 3). Frequently their precise chronology can be derived from archaeological finds, such as fragments of pottery, objects of stone etcetera. Sometimes in consequence of stratigraphical superposition several buried soils are situated in the same exposure, one above the other, and occasionally such sequences enable other pedogenetical conclusions due to the precise archaeological datings, for instance concerning the timespan of soil formation. A surprising example is presented by the dune profile of Midlum near the coast of Niedersachsen (Fig. 4), where — according to archaeological settlement datings — two fully developed podzolic soil profiles, one above the other, have originated during less than two centuries (HAARNAGEL 1964: Tab. 17).

5. Resuming conclusions

Altogether buried soils in dune exposures of the lowlands in northern Central Europe provide experiences of fundamental significance, some of them in contrast with usual theoretical concepts of the respective scientific disciplines. Special consequences relate to soil science, geomorphology, and (prehistoric) archaeology. New conceptions require critical examination with the purpose of verification or rejection. The aim is a sufficient legitimation of additional intensive observation and investigation of dune exposures in the area in question and elsewhere.

6. References

DE BOER, W. M. (1995): Äolische Prozesse und Landschaftsformen im mittleren Baruther Urstromtal seit dem Hochglazial der Weichselkaltzeit . — Berliner geographische Arbeiten, **84**: 216 p.; Berlin.

GRAMSCH, B. (1969): Ein Lagerplatz der Federmessergruppe bei Golßen, Kr. Luckau. — Ausgrabungen und Funde, **14** (3): 121–128; Berlin.

HAARNAGEL, W. (1964): Die spätlatène- und kaiserzeitlichen Siedlungen am westlichen Geestrande der Hohen Lieth im Wesergebiet zwischen den Ortschaften Midlum und Langen, Kr. Wesermünde. — Varia Archaeologica — Wilhelm Unverzagt zum 70. Geburtstag dargebracht: 111–147, pl. 16–19; Berlin.

JÄGER, K.-D. (1997): Böden und Bodensedimente als historische Quellen. — Archäologie in Sachsen-Anhalt, **7**: 4–12; Halle/Saale.

— & KOPP, D. (1969): Zur archäologischen Aussage von Profilaufschlüssen norddeutscher Sandböden. — Ausgrabungen und Funde, **14** (3): 111–121; Berlin.

KOPP, D. (1969): Die Standorte des Tieflandes. — In: KOPP, D. et al.: Ergebnisse der forstlichen Standortserkundung in der Deutschen Demokratischen Republik, **I** (Die Waldstandorte des Tieflandes), 1: 16–142; Potsdam.

— & JÄGER, K.-D. (1972): Das Perstruktions- und Horizontprofil als Trennmerkmal periglaziärer und extraperiglaziärer Oberflächen im nordmitteleuropäischen Tiefland. — Wissenschaftliche Zeitschrift der Ernst-Moritz-Arndt-Universität Greifswald, Mathematisch-Naturwissenschaftliche Reihe, **21** (1): 77–84; Greifswald.

KOZARSKI, S. (1990): Geomorphic history of the Western part of Torun–Eberswalde Pradolina and adjacent areas to the Polish-German border. — In: KOZARSKI, S. & NOWACZYK, B. [eds.]: Late Vistulian and Holocene aeolian phenomena in Central and Northern Europe. — Int. Symp., 14–18 May, 1990, Poland, Guide-Book of Excursions: 2–6, Tab. 2; Poznań.

KUNTZE, H., ROESCHMANN, G. & SCHWERDTFEGER, G. (1988): Bodenkunde. — 4. Aufl.: 568 p.; Stuttgart.

LIEBEROTH, I., EHWALD, E., KOPP, D., GONDEK, H., JÄGER, K.-D. & GRAMSCH, B. (1970): Exkursion III am 14.10.1967 in die Umgebung von Berlin. — In: Tagungsbericht der Deutschen Akademie der Landwirtschaftswissenschaften zu Berlin, **102**: 306–322; Berlin.

RICHTER, G. (1961): Eine Dünengrabung in der Elbniederung bei Fischbeck, Kr. Havelberg. — Ausgrabungen und Funde, **6** (1): 13–15; Berlin.

Addresses of the authors:

Prof. Dr. KLAUS-DIETER JÄGER, Martin-Luther-Universität Halle-Wittenberg, Institut für Prähistorische Archäologie, Brandbergweg 23, D-06099 Halle (Saale).

Dr. habil. DIETRICH KOPP, Dömitzer Str. 20, D-19303 Tewswoos.

GeoArchaeoRhein, **3**: 137–146; Münster 1999

Holocene dunes in southern Poland

Renata Dulias

Abstract: Dunes formed in Holocene only are extremely rare. Recently, a dune complex formed as a whole in the Holocene has been investigated in Southern Poland (Częstochowa Upland). The radiocarbon dates as well as the analysis of the structure of the dunes indicate that dune-forming phases took place in the following periods: Atlantic, Subboreal and Subatlantic. These ages of the dunes may have been caused by specific local conditions. Moreover, this means that human interference in geographical environment may create conditions for the development of aeolian processes, which have visible morphogenetic effects even in the conditions of moderate climate.

Key words: Holocene dunes, Southern Poland, fossil soils.

It is generally agreed that in Holocene, aeolian processes were characterised by low intensity, and that they consisted in the transformation of already existing dunes. In many dunes investigated so far, Holocene series have been found. However, dunes formed entirely in Holocene are extremely rare. There exist only a few examples in Poland (Krajewski 1977; Nowaczyk & Pazdur 1982; Jaśkowski 1985; Nowaczyk 1986). Recently, a dune complex formed in the Holocene only has been investigated in southern Poland (Dulias 1997). This is an unusual phenomenon for the country and, apart from coastal dunes, the only one that has been described so far. It is their unique age that makes these forms remarkable.

The complex of Holocene dunes studied is located in the southern part of Częstochowa Upland (Fig. 1). A characteristic feature of the upland relief is the occurrence of two types of planations — upper summit planation corresponding to the karstic surface of planation, and lower sub-cuesta flat areas in the form of fossil poljes, namely Ryczówek Depression and Huciska Basin. These two horizons are separated by (up to 100 metres) high structural-denudational thresholds, to which correspond: Świniuszka Hills, Ryczów Cuesta and Ruskie Mountains (Fig. 2). On both the upper and lower planations the sequence of sediments is basically similar. On Tertiary clay with limestone debris covering Upper Jurassic limestones, occur Quaternary sandy deposits. At the bottom, there are rhythmically laminated deposits formed as result of rill-wash and congelifluction. In the upper layer, there are aeolian sands. On lower planations, aeolian series are of Holocene origin. They form quite large dunes. On the other hand, on the summit, aeolian sands appear mainly in the form of coverbeds because intensive activity of wind in that area hindered the preservation of dunes (Szczypek 1986). The author quoted above dated them to Older and Younger Dryas, which means that they are covers of Late

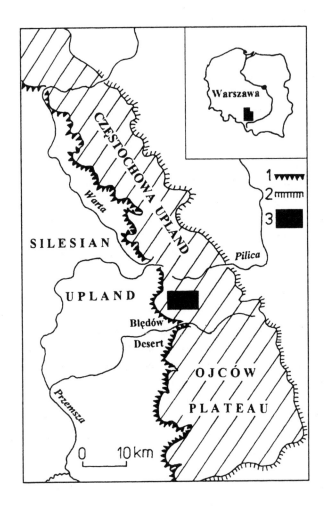

Fig. 1:
Location of the study area.
1 – course of Upper Jurassic
cuesta, 2 – other thresholds
and edges of different origin,
3 – investigated area.

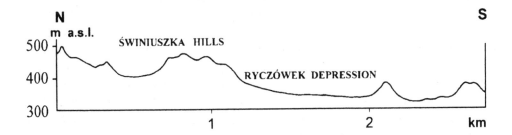

Fig. 2: Morphological cross-section through the southern part of the Częstochowa Upland.

Glacial not Holocene age, as it is on sub-cuesta flat areas.

The author of this work assumes that in this part of Częstochowa Upland, the differences in age of the dune-forming phases in two different hypsometric horizons — summits and valleys — may have been caused by water conditions. In Late Glacial times in summer, over-permafrost water was stored above the upper layer of permafrost (at the bottom of molisol). This enabled aeolian redeposition of the dried upper sand layers. On the other hand, in the depressions of the valleys situated tens of metres beneath, the whole amount of permafrost water flowing down slopes was stored. The effect was that the substratum was too wet to initiate dune-forming processes. Therefore, only after the total decay of permafrost and erosion in river valleys at the turn of Late Glacial and Holocene, the groundwater level could decrease enough to activate dune-forming processes on sub-cuesta areas. Such hypothetical course of events may as yet be applied to only one, relatively small part of the upland. The situation may be an exception. Nevertheless, it proves great influence of local conditions on morphogenetic processes.

The main complex of dunes is situated in the eastern and central part of the Huciska Basin (Fig. 3). The most splendid form (10 metres high) is Dune I closing the valley from NE by "blocking" the outlet of the large valley. This form consists of three aeolian series (Fig. 4). On sandy-rubbly substratum, a fossil soil occurs horizontally. Charcoal from this soil has been dated by means of the ^{14}C method to 8,250 ± 150 y BP. On top of the lower aeolian series lies another fossil soil ^{14}C-dated to 5,820 ± 150 y BP. A fossil soil horizon in the upper layer of the middle aeolian series has not been dated yet. Dates quoted above let us presume that the described dune was formed in Holocene. Obviously, we cannot exclude the possibility that inside the dune, the oldest soil appears in the upper layer of Late Glacial aeolian series. Even if it were so, it would be a series forming just a hillock hardly relevant for the relief. Nor would this change the fact that the dune is of Holocene age in its substantial mass.

Dune II, in morphological terms, has a longitudinal form pointing from west to east (Fig. 3). In the substratum of the form, on rhythmically laminated horizontally bedded sands, a fossil soil appears which has not been dated yet. As regards the charcoal from the upper layer of the lower aeolian series, it has been dated to 5,250 ± 150 y BP. This radiocarbon data is very similar to the date obtained for the middle fossil soil of Dune I. In both forms, 3 fossil soils have been distinguished; in each dune the lowest soil lies on the deposits of the substratum. Therefore, we may assume that the bottom soil from Dune II is similar in age to the lower soil from Dune I, that is about eight thousand years BP. This is highly probable also because the geomorphological situation shows clearly that Dune I was the first to originate in the area investigated. Hence, Dune II must also be regarded as Holocene.

Dune III is a parabolic dune situated farthest to the west (Fig. 3). Within its southern arm, on the slope facing south, nine aeolian series have been counted. They are separated by fossil soil horizons. The scarcity of charcoal in the lowest fossil soil horizon made it impossible to date it by means of ^{14}C. Nevertheless, charcoal from a higher soil horizon has been dated to 4,810 ± 140 y BP. The date indicates that the substantial mass

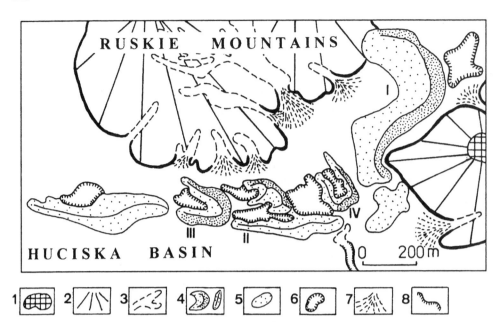

Fig. 3: Geomorphological sketch-map of the Huciska Basin (eastern and central part).
1 – karstic-denudational relict hills, 2 – slopes, 3 – small erosive-denudation valleys, 4 – dunes, 5 – aeolian coversands, 6 – blow-outs and closed depressions, 7 – alluvial fans, 8 – erosional scarps.

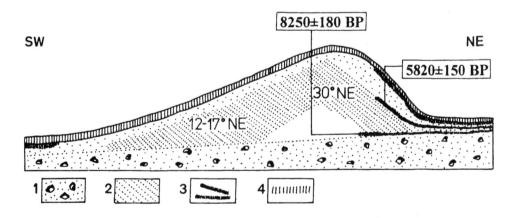

Fig. 4: Scheme of the geological composition of Dune I (Huciska Basin).
1 – sandy-rubbly deposits, 2 – diagonally laminated aeolian sands, 3 – fossil soils, 4 – contemporary soil horizon.

of deposits forming the southern arm of the dune originates in the younger Holocene. One of the lowest dunes in the Huciska Basin is form IV (2.5 metres high) (Fig. 3). About 80 m away, east of the dune, a very well developed fossil soil (3,790 ± 120 y BP old) has been discovered on the underlying sandy-rubbly deposits. A lower, thin series of aeolian sand is covered by another fossil soil in which many fragments of clay pots were found. The archaeologists estimate that these come from the late Middle Ages. Above this soil horizon appear three more series of yellow and grey aeolian sands separated by thin horizons of organic accumulation (Fig. 5).

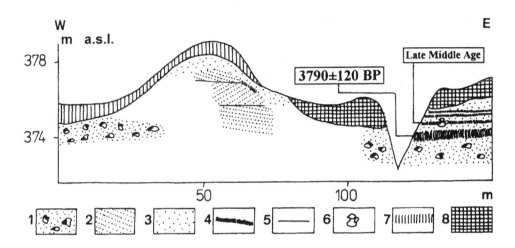

Fig. 5: Geological cross-section through Dune IV (Huciska basin).
1 – sandy-rubbly deposits, 2 – diagonally laminated aeolian sands, 3 – structureless aeolian sands, 4 – fossil soils, 5 – surfaces of discordance, 6 – fragments of the Late Middle Ages pots, 7 – contemporary soil horizon, 8 – anthropogenic changed soil.

Another dune complex is situated in the so-called Ryczówek Depression, which is, like the Huciska Basin, a fossil polje (Fig. 6). One of the investigated dunes (V), having a nearly ideal shape of a parabola, consists of two aeolian series separated by a fossil soil dated by ^{14}C method to 3,130 ± 120 y BP (Fig. 7). Detailed investigation of the area shows that the lower aeolian series lies on rhythmically laminated sand which is crowned by a fossil soil of 6,330 ± 150 y BP. Thus, we may assume that the older aeolian series was formed within the period of time mentioned above. Further evidence for the Holocene origin of dunes in the analysed area is a geomorphological situation of little dunes on the western bank of the Minożka river (Fig. 6). These are underlain by a fossil soil dated to 2,500 ± 130 y BP (^{14}C). Everything points to the fact that they were formed after a knick point recession of the Minożka river. The recession caused a considerable decrease in groundwater level, and by drying the sands it enabled them to form dunes. The knick

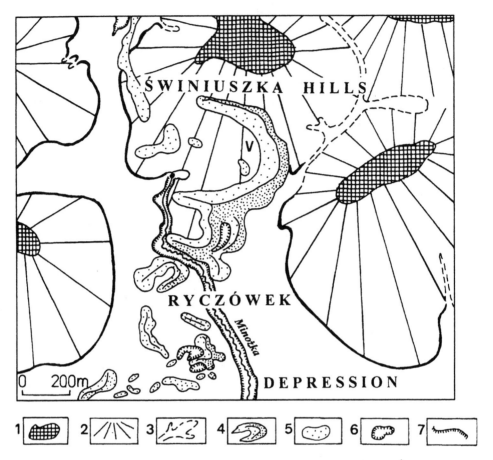

Fig. 6: Geomorphological sketch-map of the Ryczówek Depression and the Świniuszka Hills.
1 – karstic-denudational relict hills, 2 – slopes, 3 – small erosive denudation valleys, 4 –
dunes, 5 – aeolian coversand, 6 – deflation basins and depressions between dunes, 7 – erosional scarps.

point recession could not have happened before because the dunes in the eastern part of
the valley would not have been formed then. These dunes are (at least in their lower
parts) older than the dunes in the western part.
To sum up the results of investigation of aeolian sands in the southern part of the
Częstochowa Upland, we should emphasize that none of the radiocarbon dates obtained
for fossil soil horizons overlaps the Late Glacial period, and that all forms studied are of
Holocene age. The radiocarbon dates as well as the analysis of the structure of the dunes
indicate that dune-forming processes took place in the following periods: Atlantic,
Subboreal and Subatlantic. We might presume that the first onset was older than those
mentioned above only in the forming of Dune I. This does not mean that the redeposition

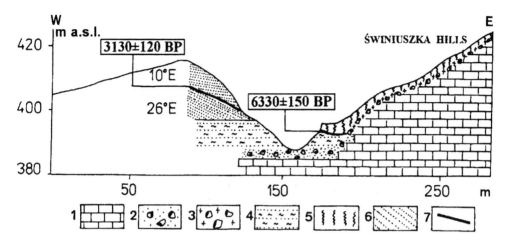

Fig. 7: Geological cross-section through Dune V (Ryczówek Depression).
1 – limestones, 2 – calcareous rubble in sand, 3 – calcareous rubble in clay, 4 – rhythmically laminated sand with thin laminae of silt, 5 – dust and dusty sand deluvia, 6 – diagonally laminated aeolian sand, 7 – fossil soils.

of the substratum by wind did not occur in former times. Some tiny forms possibly existed, but those were blown away during later dune-forming phases essential to the area. The chances are that in the Huciska Basin this phase occurred in the Atlantic period and in the Ryczówek Depression, at the turn of Atlantic and Subboreal periods. Dunes of the right bank of the Minożka began to form towards the end of Subboreal period. At the same time, dunes in the Huciska Basin were redeposited by wind. The distribution of dated aeolian series along a W–E line indicates that younger and younger series appear towards the west. This confirms the conclusion drawn on the grounds of the analysis of relief and structural measurement that Dune I, located in the eastern part of the Huciska Basin, was the first to originate. Younger and younger dunes grew by its side gradually.

The lack of Late Glacial dunes in the area studied has its cause in local conditions, which was indicated before. The influence of individual features of the environment on morphogenetic processes has been emphasized in many paleogeographical theses. The features may not only determine the type of processes but also affect their intensity. The delay in aeolian processes in the depressions of the southern part of the Częstochowa Upland, when compared with its summit areas and obviously with other regions in Poland, was connected with specific water conditions in this well-sculptured karstic massif. On the other hand, morphogenetic activity of wind during the Atlantic climatic optimum was associated with considerable deforestation caused either by natural fires, or human activity.

Dunes from the area of Smoleń, several kilometres NE of the Huciska Basin are in a very similar geomorphological situation (DULIAS 1996). On the summit, there are small dunes consisting of two aeolian series separated by a fossil soil. The age of the soil is difficult to establish unequivocally as there are no ^{14}C datings. However, its characteristic macroscopic features suggest that it originated in the Allerød period. Thus, it would be another site confirming that Late Glacial aeolian series occur on the summit, whereas a dune and a hillock of aeolian sand occur at the bottom of the valley 100 m deep. In each of the forms there is one series of aeolian sand deposited on sandy-silty deluvia. Aeolian sand raised the former bottom of the valley up to several metres. At present, it is divided by the Sączenica river, which has its source here. The age of the dune is hard to establish but the hillock presumably originated in the Holocene. That is because it consists of not very compact, in fact, almost loose material.

From outside the Częstochowa Upland IzMAIŁOW & NALEPKA (1994) also report the presence of a Holocene dune in southern Poland. The authors examined a dune in Przeryty Bór on the Tarnów Plateau. This dune was formed on an erosive-denudational plain running parallel to the Dąbrówka valley. This plain is covered by sandy till deposits of the South Polish glaciation (Mindel). The dune has a form of an embankment running across the valley, with its southern end descending directly to the Holocene terrace of Dąbrówka. It contains two aeolian series of different age separated by a fossil soil whose age was established as being Subatlantic. The older dune-forming phase, also of Holocene age according to the authors, was completed in the Subboreal period at the latest, and the second starting of aeolian processes on the dune took place in the Subatlantic period as a result of deforestation caused by man's economic activities. The amount of sand heaped up at that time (up to 4 m) is bigger than the amount of deposition during the former phase. The research shows that in the second dune-forming phase the primary form grew in size, became partly mobile and changed its shape. This proves that aeolian processes were very effective at that time.

We cannot doubt the relatively high effectiveness of the Subatlantic phase when taking into account that we know the case of a modern dune 4.4 m high, which arose in 15 years (SZCZYPEK & WACH 1991). It is a scarp dune in Bukowno (Silesian Upland) formed at the edge of a vast sandpit. The speed of aeolian accumulation observed by the authors is extremely high — the average increase in thickness of the cover per year amounts to 10–30 cm. The dune is anthropogenic in that man has created the possibility for the wind to uncover the sandy substratum.

Holocene dunes were formed throughout centuries in the Błędów Desert, a vast area in the Silesian Upland (Fig. 1), deforested in the Middle Ages for the needs of developing silver and lead ore mining, and later zinc ore mining (SZCZYPEK, WACH & WIKA 1994). It should be emphasised that in some investigated dunes, whose substantial mass was formed during the Late Glacial, we find series that undoubtedly are of Holocene age although they are several metres thick, for instance in Rabsztyn on the Ojców Plateau (NOWACZYK, PAZDUR & SZCZYPEK 1982) or in Siedlec Janowski on the Częstochowa Upland (SZCZYPEK 1992).

To conclude: In southern Poland, like in the rest of the country, dunes are connected mainly with Late Glacial dune-forming phases. However in the areas characterised by specific local conditions, not only Holocene aeolian series but also Holocene dunes could be formed. This means that human interference in geographical environment may create conditions for the development of aeolian processes, which have visible morphogenetic effects even under conditions of the moderate climate.

Acknowledgements

The author would like to thank GABRIELA CICHY for a translation of the text from Polish into English.

References

DULIAS, R. (1996): Wydmy okolic Smolenia na Wyżynie Częstochowskiej (Dunes in the vicinity of Smoleń on the Częstochowa Upland). — In: SZCZYPEK, T. & WAGA, J. M. [eds.]: Współczesne oraz kopalne zjawiska i formy eoliczne. Wybrane zagadnienia. UO, PK "CKKRW": 39–46; SGP Sosnowiec.

— (1997): Późnoglacjalny i holoceński rozwój pokryw pyłowo-piaszczystych w południowej części Wyżyny Częstochowskiej (The Late-Glacial and Holocene development of dusty-sandy covers in the southern part of Częstochowa Upland). — Geographia. Studia et dissertationes, **21**: 7–100; UŚ Katowice.

IZMAIŁOW, B. & NALEPKA, D. (1994): Wiek i efektywność najmłodszej fazy rozwoju wydmy w Przerytym Borze na Wysoczyźnie Tarnowskiej (Age and effectiveness of the youngest development phase of the dune in Przeryty Bór on the Tarnów Plateau). — In: NOWACZYK, B. & SZCZYPEK, T. [eds.]: Vistuliańsko-Holoceńskie zjawiska i formy eoliczne (wybrane zagadnienia): 33–45; SGP Poznań.

JAŚKOWSKI, B. (1985): Wydmy Niecki Włoszczowskiej (Dunes of the Włoszczowa Basin). — Dokumentacja Geograficzna, **7**; IGiPZ PAN Warszawa.

KRAJEWSKI, K. (1977): Późnoplejstoceńskie i holoceńskie procesy wydmotwórcze w Pradolinie Warszawsko–Berlińskiej w widłach Warty i Neru (Late-Pleistocene and Holocene dune-forming processes in the Warsaw–Berlin Pradolina). — Acta Geographica Lodziensia, **39**: 1–87; Łódź.

NOWACZYK, B. (1986): Wiek wydm, ich cechy granulometryczne i strukturalne a schemat cyrkulacji atmosferycznej w Polsce w późnym Vistulianie i holocenie. (The age of dunes, their textural and structural properties against atmospheric circulation pattern of Poland during the Late Vistulian and Holocene). — UAM, Ser. Geografia, **28**: 245 p.; Poznań.

— & PAZDUR, M. F. (1982): Próba datowania metodą C-14 gleb kopalnych z wydmy w Troszynie koło Wolina (An attempt of dating by the C-14 method of fossil soils from the dune at Troszyn near Wolin). — Roczniki Gleboznawcze, **33** (3-4): 145–158.

— PAZDUR, M. F. & SZCZYPEK, T. (1982): Wiek eolicznych przekształceń wydm w północno-zachodniej części Płaskowyżu Ojcowskiego (The age of aeolian transformations of the dunes in the north-west part of Ojców Plateau). — Geographia. Studia et dissertationes, **6**: 34–49; UŚ Katowice.

SZCZYPEK, T. (1986): Procesy wydmotwórcze w środkowej części Wyżyny Krakowsko-Wieluńskiej na tle obszarów przyległych (Dune forming processes in the middle part of the Cracow–Wieluń Upland against a background of the neighbouring area). — 183 p.; UŚ Katowice.

— (1992): Wydmy północnej części Płaskowyżu Częstochowskiego w okolicach Siedlca Janowskiego (Dunes in the northern part of the Częstochowa Plateau near Siedlec Janowski (Southern Poland)). — In: SZCZYPEK, T. [ed.]: Wybrane zagadnienia geomorfologii eolicznej: 141–154; WNoZ UŚ Sosnowiec.

— & WACH, J. (1991): Rozwój współczesnej wydmy w warunkach silnej antropopresji (Development of the modern dune in the strong human impact conditions). — 79 p.; UŚ Katowice.

— WACH, J.& WIKA, S. (1994): Zmiany krajobrazów Pustyni Błędowskiej (Changes of landscapes in the Błędów Desert (Silesian Upland–Southern Poland)). — 87 p.; UŚ WNoZ Sosnowiec.

Address of the author:

Dr. RENATA DULIAS, Faculty of Earth Sciences, University of Silesia, Będzińska 60, PL-41-200 Sosnowiec, Poland, e-mail: kgf@ultra.cto.us.edu.pl

GeoArchaeoRhein, **3**: 147–161; Münster 1999

The Bliesendorf soil and aeolian sand transport in the Potsdam area

ARTHUR BRANDE, MARGOT BÖSE, MARION MÜLLER, MICHAEL FACKLAM
& STEFFEN WOLTERS

Abstract: The Glindow till plain belongs to the Zauche (dry land) landscape and is partly covered by sand dunes. In a sand pit WSW of Bliesendorf a fossil soil occurs on top of kame deposits and beneath aeolian sands. This Bliesendorf podzolic brown soil is of Late Weichselian to Holocene age, excluding the last 700 to 800 years. No further soil of Late Glacial age, especially of Allerød time, exists in this section; Younger Dryas aeolian sands are absent. Fossilisation of the soil occurred in high to late mediaeval time and was triggered by woodland clearance connected with the foundation of the Lehnin monastery and the corresponding onset of intensive and large-scale land use. Mire stratigraphy in an adjacent part of the Zauche area as well as in Berlin reveals the same processes of mediaeval landscape change. At both sites peat deposits are covered by several metres of wind-blown sands, whereas Younger Dryas sand layers are missing in those geomorphological positions.

1. Sand dunes of the Zauche

The investigation area is part of the Zauche landscape situated between Potsdam, Brandenburg and Belzig (Fig. 1). The Slavic/Polabic meaning of Zauche is dry land. The Zauche consists of several topographic units including till plains — the investigation site is situated on the Glindower Platte (Glindow till plain) —, terminal moraines of the Weichselian maximum phase, outwash plains, the distinct outwash fan of the Beelitzer Sander as well as marginal meltwater valleys.

The Glindower Platte is bounded by the Havel valley to the N and NE, and by the Kaniner Tal (meltwater valley) at the SE and SW. This meltwater valley (Fig. 2) was formed by the retreating ice, when the outwash cone of the Beelitzer Sander was no longer active. The beginning of the Kaniner Tal at the southwestern margin of Lake Schwielow is characterized by some deep channels, filled with mud and peat (mire type a, Fig. 2). The southeastern adjacent area to this part of the Kaniner Tal has a dead ice topography formed by a subglacial, SE-oriented channel system, feeding the outwash fan of the Beelitzer Sander at the maximum phase. This dead ice landscape is rich in kettle holes which contain Late Weichselian and Holocene organic sediments up to 14 m thick (mire type b), e. g. Großes Moor. In the transition between the Kaniner Tal and the dead ice landscape the mire known as Langes Fenn forms an intermediate type (mire type c, Fig. 2 and 6) with an elongated and branched shape. It was obviously part of the subglacial channel system and was preserved by dead ice from meltwater infill during

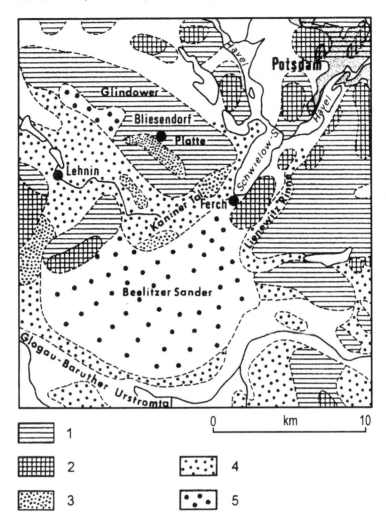

Fig. 1: The Zauche landscape south of Potsdam (adapted from Scholz & Wandrey 1969).
1 – till plain, 2 – end moraine and kame, 3 – dune area, 4 – glaciofluvial channel, 5 – outwash cone and plain.

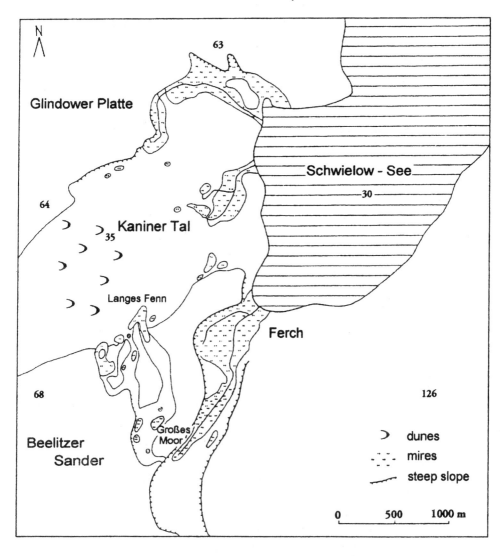

Fig. 2: Geomorphological situation of the Kaniner Tal and adjacent areas (simplified from FRANZ 1961).

the subaerial meltwater flow in the Kaniner Tal, and came morphologically into existence during the Bølling/Older Dryas chronozone, according to palynological results of the entire 8 m sequence (W<small>OLTERS</small> 1996).

The bottom of the Kaniner Tal (40 m) is now partly occupied by aeolian coversands as well as by dune fields with some parabolic dune forms. A perfect dune form is displayed by the nearby Renneberge (77 m), extending from the meltwater valley to the SW fringe of the Glindower Platte. A third dune area is in an untypical situation in the landscape, located on the till plain (about 60 m a. s. l.). These dunes are not of parabolic shape but show irregular forms. The highest points are the Kirchenberg (77 m) and the Krummahdberg (78 m).

A sand pit is situated in this third dune area, WSW of the village of Bliesendorf. The pit is about 50 m broad, its surface is slightly domed, and its highest part lies about 8 m above the bottom. The site shows the following sequence from the top:

– aeolian sand with an initial podzolic brown soil on top,
– sandy layered kame deposits overlain by a fossil brown soil containing charcoal in its upper horizon,
– a till underlying the sands (Fig. 3).

The whole profile shows only two soils: a fossil Late Weichselian to Holocene soil, and the modern initial soil.

2. Land use history

The Glindower Platte shows almost no evidence of prehistoric settlements. One high mediaeval Slavic village (12th and early 13th century) was located close to Lake Kolpin, 4 km west of Bliesendorf, already situated on the upper terrace of the Kaniner Tal. In A. D. 1180, Markgraf Otto I of Brandenburg founded the Cistercian monastery of Lehnin (Fig. 1) close to a channel lake in the meltwater valley. Shortly before A. D. 1200, several other villages in the vicinity such as Göhlsdorf, Plötzin, Netzen, Rädel, Schwina and Michelsdorf were founded. Some of them were abandoned already in the 13th century. Bliesendorf was probably also founded in the late 12th century as it is first mentioned in the proper name of Wilhelmus de Blisendorp in 1236. This village did not belong to the monastery of Lehnin.

Large-scale woodland clearance since the second half of the 12th century as well as man induced fires triggered deflation. The sand of the dune area close to Bliesendorf was deflated mainly from the terrace of the meltwater valley by westerly winds. Kames on the till plain captured the sands, and an aeolian relief was superimposed on the glaciofluvial sands. The now fossil soil on top of the kame sands shows no signs of ploughing, being probably too steep, dry and poor for agriculture, but pasture close to the village is very likely. Reforestation measures since the second half of the 18th century were mainly associated with the sandy areas, whereas the till areas remained under agricultural cultivation.

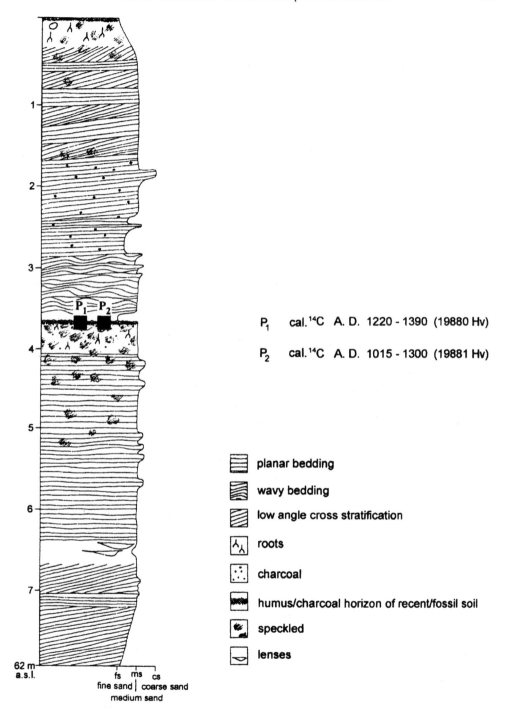

P_1 cal. ^{14}C A. D. 1220 - 1390 (19880 Hv)

P_2 cal. ^{14}C A. D. 1015 - 1300 (19881 Hv)

planar bedding

wavy bedding

low angle cross stratification

roots

charcoal

humus/charcoal horizon of recent/fossil soil

speckled

lenses

Fig. 3: The Bliesendorf section.

3. Soil analyses
3.1 The modern soil

The soil on top of the upper sands represents an initial podzolic brown soil with the following horizons: Ah / Ahe / Ahe+B(s)v / B(s)v / Bv / Cv (AG Boden 1994). The Ahe+B(s)v horizon results from disturbance by ploughing during reforestation with pine about 25 years ago.

The soil development is only of low to medium depth. The humus horizons have pH-values of about 3, exceeding 4 only at a depth of 1 m and more. The dithionite-soluble iron contents show a slight impoverishment in the Ahe horizon and an enrichment in the Ahe+B(s)v horizon. A substantial displacement of aluminium can be deduced from the distribution of the oxalate-soluble Al (Tab. 1).

3.2 The fossil soil

The base of the upper sands consists of medium-sandy fine sands. Besides some charcoal particles, the lower 11 cm show a significantly higher proportion of organic carbon owing to a mixture with the underlying fossil Ah-horizon.

A fossil soil shows the following horizons: fAh / fBsv / fBv / fCv. The fAh horizon is about 6 cm thick. The transition to this horizon is distinct, although somewhat frayed at the cm-scale. Granulometric analyses show clear differences to those of the upper sands; the sorting of the samples is moderate, and the grain-size distribution is bimodal (BÖSE et al., in preparation).

The fine-sandy-medium sands of this horizon have a dark colour owing to an organic carbon content of 13.4 g/kg. Fragments and specks of charcoal have been found repeatedly in this horizon at the entire site. Round, more or less bleached spots with diameters of 1 to several cm are clearly visible. Some of them display rust spots at their margins, similar to those found sporadically in the substratum.

The boundary to the following fBsv horizon is distinct, and the thickness of this horizon varies from 20 to 30 cm. It also consists of fine-sandy medium sands with a downwardly increasing content of coarse sand; layering is absent. The fBsv horizon is marked by a clear brownish colour. Bleached round spots, similar to those in the fAh horizon, occur here as well, giving a marbled look. Occasional specks of charcoal have been found here, too. There is a diffuse transition from the fBsv horizon to a fBv horizon, about 15 cm thick. The colour is brighter, and besides a faint marbling some bleached former root passages occur, measuring several cm in diameter. The fBv horizon is followed by the Cv horizon, also consisting of fine-sandy medium sands.

The pH-values of these horizons vary between 4.7 and 4.9, but show no vertical trend. The high values and low amplitude result from an adjustment of the equilibrium of the proton concentration of the seepage water and the soil matrix. The presumably originally lower pH-value is thus transformed. The organic content decreases from the fAh to the fBsv to the fBv horizon. It has not been tested whether the organic content is identical with humus or to charcoal. The highest content of dithionite- and oxalate-soluble iron is

Tab. 1: Analytical data of the Bliesendorf soils.

Depth below surface (cm)	Horizon	Texture	Bulk density g/ccm	C org g/kg	pH CaCl₂	Fe (d) mg/kg	Fe (o) mg/kg	Fe (o)/Fe(d)	Al (o) mg/kg
modern soil									
0 - 2	Ah	fSms	n.b.	28.4	2.79	n.b.	n.b.	n.b.	n.b.
2 - 4	Ahe	fSms	n.b.	5.9	3.23	560	200	0.35	177
4 - 9 - 20	Ahe+B(s)v	fSms	n.b.	3.9	3.43	720	285	0.39	190
20 - 50	B(s)v	fSms	1.601	<1	3.91	615	198	0.32	340
50 - 100	Bv	fSms	1.585	n.b.	4.09	620	185	0.29	361
> 100	C	fSms	1.527	n.b.	4.13	653	165	0.25	335
dune basis									
> 354	C	fSms	1.555	0.4	4.80	553	270	0.49	485
354 - 365	C	fSms	1.550	0.8	4.88	635	253	0.40	550
fossil soil									
365 - 371	f Ah	mSfs	1.534	13.4	4.86	1090	668	0.61	600
371 - 400	f Bsv	mSfs	1.515	2.4	4.74	1375	870	0.63	1828
400 - 415	f Bv	mSfs	1.586	1.1	4.88	845	348	0.41	1136
415 - >465	f Cv	mSfs	1.602	0.3	4.82	445	173	0.39	380

in the fAh and fBsv horizon, the maximum value being in the latter. Macroscopic studies reveal a redistribution of the iron in the fAh horizon by the dissolution of the iron coating of the sand grains and the concentration of the iron in coproform aggregates (Blume 1981). Like in the modern profile, the oxalate-soluble aluminium fraction shows a distinct impoverishment in the fAh horizon and a correlated enrichment in the fBsv and fBv horizon. A faint displacement of iron and a distinct displacement of aluminium point to podzolisation. Consequently, the fossil soil was originally a podzolic brown soil. Therefore a shortening of the profile including the Ae and possibly parts of the Bsv horizon is likely. On account of the iron budget, max. 25 cm have been eroded.

4. Pollen analysis

Pollen analysis of dry sandy soils in a subcontinental region is in general unsatisfactory, largely owing to corrosion and partly to percolation. Accordingly, in the Bliesendorf fossil brown soil the pollen content is low and pollen preservation is poor. Nevertheless, a pollen spectrum with quite clear results was obtained (Tab. 2). It can be dated and correlated with two complete Late Weichselian and Holocene pollen diagrams in the adjacent sand dune area of the Kaniner Tal and the dead ice landscape 7 km southeast of Bliesendorf. A simplified version of those two diagrams is given in Figs. 4 and 5, comprising the whole Subatlantic period, i. e. the last 2700 years.

Tab. 2: Pollen and spore spectrum of the Bliesendorf fossil soil. % of 297 pollen and spore grains exclusive mosses (*Sphagnum*). AP: arboreal pollen, NAP: non aboreal pollen.

Pinus	20.2	*Dianthus* type	0.3
Betula	4.7	*Lychnis* type	0.3
Alnus	11.5	Caryophyllaceae p. p.	0.3
Quercus	8.4	Geraniaceae	0.3
Ulnus	0.3	*Ranunculus acris* type	0.3
Tilia	0.3	Rubiaceae	0.3
Fagus	0.7	Apiaceae	0.7
Carpinus	0.3	Poaceae p. p.	3.4
Corylus	0.7	Cyperaceae	0.7
AP	**47.1**	*Pteridium*	5.1
		Polypodiaceae p. p.	14.1
Calluna	1.0	*Botrychium*	1.4
Cerealia p. p.	1.0	*Lycopodium clavatum* type	0.7
Cerealia cf.	1.7	Varia	0.3
Secale cf.	1.4	Indeterminata	13.1
Artemisia	1.0	**NAP**	**52.8**
Asteroideae p. p.	0.7		
Cichorioideae	4.7	*Sphagnum*	7.7

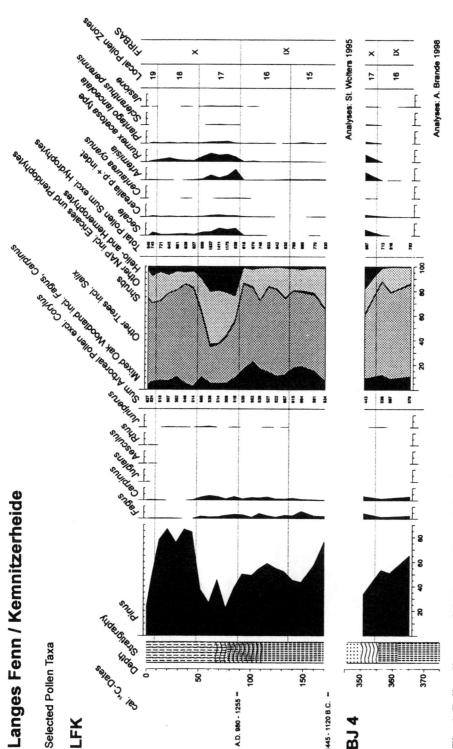

Fig. 4: Pollen diagram of the Langes Fenn. Selected taxa of the Subatlantic chronozone (adapted from BRANDE & WOLTERS 1997). Location of LFK and BJ4 see Figs. 2 and 6.

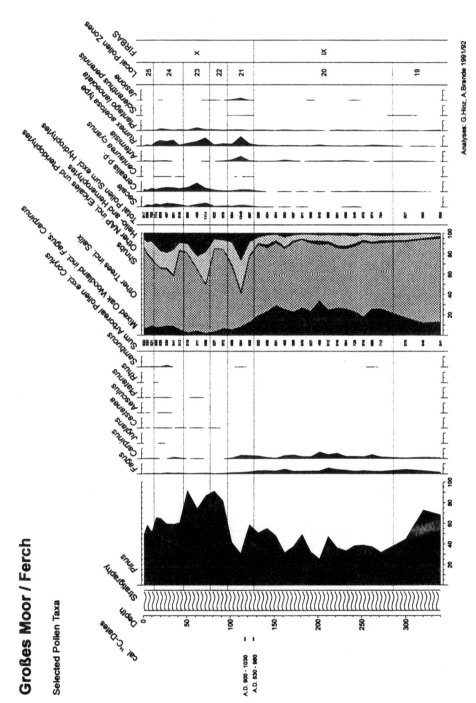

Fig. 5: Pollen diagram of the Großes Moor. Selected taxa of the Subatlantic chronozone (adapted from Brande & Wolters 1997). Location see Fig. 2.

The presence and percentages of beech (*Fagus*), hornbeam (*Carpinus*) and cereals including probably rye (*Secale*) date the Bliesendorf spectrum to the beginning of the Younger Subatlantic period. This is confirmed by correlation not only with the two pollen diagrams, but also with many others in the Berlin and Potsdam region.

Typical elements from wet-to-moist and dry soils in the vicinity are alder (*Alnus*) and birch (*Betula*), and among the mosses, ferns and dwarf shrubs *Sphagnum* from the mires, bracken (*Pteridium*) and heather (*Calluna*).

The spectrum represents the pollen composition during the shortening of the soil profile and its beginning fossilisation: Oak (*Quercus*) and pine (*Pinus*) are the dominant trees on this soil before aeolian activity. The fAh horizon is rich in charcoal of deciduous trees (mainly oak). They have been cut and burnt for timber and fuel and, in the plain, to obtain arable and grass land. The pollen of other trees and shrubs on these poor soils is typically very rare, e. g. elm (*Ulmus*), lime (*Tilia*) and hazel (*Corylus*).

Elements of the sandy dry grassland on the dune are absent, i. e. *Scleranthus perennis* and *Jasione*, which either first appear or increase in the two pollen diagrams just after woodland clearance (Fig. 4 and 5). This confirms the dating of the pollen spectrum to the very time of devastation on the kame, and moreover it excludes pollen percolation from the sand dune vegetation cover.

These results are precisely supported by pollen spectra from the upper peat of the Langes Fenn (Fig. 4). In its western part, the mire is covered by aeolian sands of the Kaniner Tal (Fig. 6). Very soon after the beginning of the high mediaeval intensive woodland clearance (cal. [14]C A. D. 980–1255), linked with the appearance or increase of *Secale, Artemisia, Rumex, Plantago, Scleranthus* and *Jasione,* the formation of *Sphagnum* and fen peat stops immediately in this topographic position, but continues up to the 20th century in the central part of the mire. The radiocarbon dates are in accordance with those from the fAh horizon of the Bliesendorf fossil soil (cal. [14]C A. D. 1015–1390). By contrast, the kettle hole mire of Großes Moor, situated in the dead ice landscape 400 m southeast of the Langes Fenn, contains only little blown sand in the contemporaneous *Sphagnum* peat (Fig. 5), although anthropogenic influence in the forests of the surrounding steep sandy slopes starts earlier (cal. [14]C A. D. 830–1030) and is more dynamic than in the Langes Fenn.

5. Discussion

The fossilisation of the Bliesendorf soil by aeolian sands has been dated independently by three different methods: the pollen spectrum of the fAh + fBsv horizon, the radiocarbon dates of the charcoal from the fAh horizon, and the history of land use, especially the beginning of the German colonisation of the Slavic territory, closely linked with the foundation of the Cistercian monastery Lehnin at the end of the 12th century (A. D. 1180).

In the Berlin and Potsdam region three chronological phases of sand dune formation are known:

- Old dunes: Late Weichselian dunes of pre-Allerød time with a remobilisation during the Younger Dryas and with poor or no reactivation in mediaeval and modern times,
- Young dunes: Holocene dunes of high mediaeval origin without a Late Weichselian sand core. Sand dunes of early to mid Holocene origin or remobilisation have not yet been found.
- Old and young dunes combined.

The formation of the Bliesendorf fossil soil comprises the Late Weichselian and Holocene excluding the last 700–800 years. No separate Late Weichselian soil, e. g. of Allerød age like the Finow soil (Schlaak 1997 and in this volume), was found. The preservation of those soils is linked to the superimposition by Younger Dryas aeolian sands. Such a situation prevails on the margins of peat-filled hollows like in the catena of the Postdüne (Schlaak 1997) or in the Teufelsfenn (Böse 1991; Brande 1995). The sediment sequences of the Langes Fenn do not include any Younger Dryas sand layers in the centre or at the western margin of the mire, where the young dune sands superimpose the peat (Fig. 6). It is not surprising that the situation is similar for the 14 m thick sediment sequence of the Großes Moor (Böse, Brande & Rowinsky 1993), although the Late Weichselian incline of the kettle hole slope was 36 %.

In the Berlin area, data from the kettle hole mire Alter Hof support the results obtained at the Langes Fenn and Bliesendorf. In that mire a Younger Dryas sand layer is also absent, but about one third of the mire is covered by young aeolian sand of up to 5 m thickness. The latest date of the peat formation below this sand is the 12th/13th century according to pollen analysis, and cal. A. D. 1210–1420 according to radiocarbon dating (Böse & Brande 1986).

Thus at all these sites the young dune formation which started in high mediaeval time at the earliest, is an additional argument for the geomorphological and pedological processes in the Bliesendorf site. During the long Late Weichselian and Holocene time span, a podzolic brown soil developed on the kame deposits, whereas on the surrounding till plain, lessivés came into existence and have been used for agricultural purposes since the 12th/13th century.

6. Acknowlegments

We thank Prof. Dr. Mebus A. Geyh, Niedersächsisches Landesamt für Bodenforschung /Hannover for radiocarbon dating of the Bliesendorf and Langes Fenn samples, Dipl.-Geogr. Holger Kampmann for field work in the Bliesendorf sand pit, and the participants of the INQUA-excursion during the symposium "Dunes and Fossil Soils between Elbe and Wisła" in August 1998 for discussion, especially Prof. Dr. K.-D. Jäger, Dr. habil. D. Kopp and Prof. Dr. A. Kowalkowski.

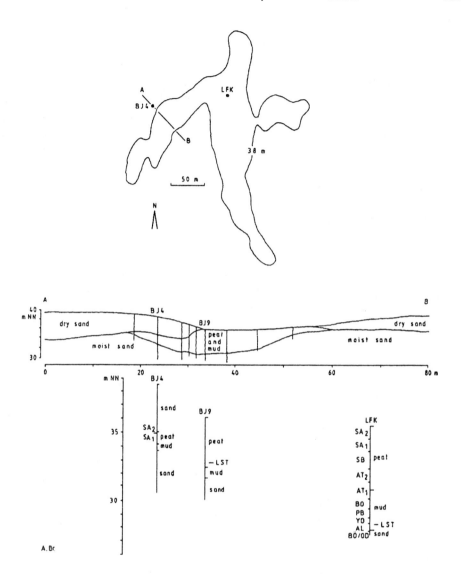

Fig. 6: Shape and chronostratigraphy of the Langes Fenn (Geoelectrical and stratigraphical section A–B from MÜLLER et al. 1998, chronozones of the LFK from WOLTERS 1996).

7. References

AG Boden 1994: Bodenkundliche Kartieranleitung. — 4. Aufl.; Hannover.

BLUME, H.-P. [red.] (1981): Typische Böden Berlins. — Mitteilungen der Deutschen Bodenkundlichen Gesellschaft, **31**; Göttingen.

BÖSE, M. (1991): A palaeoclimatic interpretation of frost wedge casts and aeolian sand deposits in the lowlands between Rhine and Vistula in the Upper Pleniglacial and Late Glacial. — In: KOZARSKI, S. [ed.]: Late Vistulian (= Weichselian) and Holocene Aeolian Phenomena in Central and Northern Europe. — Z. Geomorph. N. F., Suppl.-Bd. **90**: 15–28; Berlin, Stuttgart.

—   & BRANDE, A. (1986): Zur Entwicklungsgeschichte des Moores "Alter Hof" am Havelufer (Berliner Forst Düppel). — Berlin-Forschungen, **1**: 11–42; Berlin.

—   BRANDE, A. & ROWINSKY, V. (1993): Zur Beckenentwicklung und Paläoökologie eines Kesselmoores am Rande des Beelitzer Sanders. — Berliner Geographische Arbeiten, **78**: 35–53; Berlin.

—   MÜLLER, M., BRANDE, A. & FACKLAM, M. (in prep.): Zur Jungdünenproblematik in Brandenburg. — Brandenburgische Geowissenschaftliche Beiträge.

BRANDE, A. (1995): Moorgeschichtliche Untersuchungen im Spandauer Forst (Berlin). — Schriftenreihe für Vegetationskunde, **27** (Sukopp-Festschrift): 249–255; Bonn-Bad Godesberg.

—   & WOLTERS, S. (1997): Zur Vegetationsgeschichte des Potsdamer Raumes. — 7. Jahrestreffen Arbeitskreis Vegetationsgeschichte der Reinhold-Tüxen-Gesellschaft, Kurzfassung der Vorträge und Poster: 21; Graz.

FRANZ, H.-J. (1961): Morphogenese der Glaziallandschaft südlich von Potsdam. — Geographische Berichte, **20/21** (3/4): 214–231; Berlin.

MÜLLER, M., BAETGE, J., YARAMANCI, U. & BÖSE, M. (1998): Geoelektrische Sektionsmessungen in quartären Sedimenten am Beispiel des Moorstandortes "Langes Fenn" südwestlich Potsdam. — Geo-Berlin '98, Terra Nostra, Schriften der Alfred-Wegener-Stiftung, **98** (3): 128–129; Köln.

SCHLAAK, N. (1997): Äolische Dynamik im brandenburgischen Tiefland seit dem Weichselspätglazial. — Arbeitsberichte Geographisches Institut Humboldt-Universität Berlin, **24**: 58 p.; Berlin.

SCHOLZ, E. & WANDREY, E. (1969): Geomorphologische Übersichtskarte der Bezirke Potsdam, Frankfurt/O. und Cottbus 1 : 500 000. — In: KRAMM, H.-J.: Geographische Exkursionen im Bezirk Potsdam. Kartenbeilage; Potsdam.

WOLTERS, S. (1996): Palynologische Untersuchung zur Vegetationsgeschichte im Bereich der Fercher Berge südwestlich von Potsdam (Langes Fenn bei Kemnitzerheide). — Diplomarbeit Universität Potsdam: 121 p.; Potsdam.

Addresses of the authors:

Dr. ARTHUR BRANDE, Insitut für Ökologie und Biologie, Fachgebiet Ökosystemkunde/Pflanzenökologie, Technische Universität Berlin, Schmidt-Ott-Str. 1, D-12165 Berlin.

Prof. Dr. MARGOT BÖSE und Dipl.-Geogr. MARION MÜLLER, Institut für Geographische Wissenschaften, Fachrichtung Physische Geographie, Freie Universität Berlin, Malteserstr. 74–100, Haus H, D-12249 Berlin, e-mail: mboese@mercator.geog.fu-berlin.de

Dipl.-Ing. MICHAEL FACKLAM, Institut für Ökologie und Biologie, Fachgebiet Bodenkunde, Technische Universität Berlin, Salzufer 11–12, D-10587 Berlin.

Dipl.-Biol. STEFFEN WOLTERS, Institut für Systematik und Didaktik der Biologie, Universität Potsdam, Maulbeerallee 1, D-14469 Potsdam.

GeoArchaeoRhein, **3**: 163–176; Münster 1999

Influence of wind and older relief on the character of sandy deposits in the Starczynów "Desert" (southern Poland)

JOLANTA PEŁKA-GOŚCINIAK

Abstract: The paper presents textural features of aeolian sand in the Starczynów "Desert" as well as the estimation of both wind and older relief influence on the grain size distribution and quartz grain abrasion. The character of the analysed material depends on anemological conditions. The aeolian sand is characterized by the following tendencies of changes according to dune-forming wind direction: coarsening, worsening of sorting, improvement of quartz grain abrasion, increasing share of garnet and decreasing content of feldspar. Therefore, the textural features connected with grain size distribution behave in a different way from the typical aeolian environment. The reason therefore is the existence of older relief in a form of the Upper Jurassic cuesta, which makes a barrier on the route of wind. Valleys of rivers as well as cuestas, which represent the older relief, influenced not only the morphological direction of the dune axes but also the character of textural features of the aeolian deposits. The clear zonality of the relief (deflative —accumulative) as well as the textural features of aeolian sand (redeposition —deposition, well abraded —worse abraded) is observed in an area of the Starczynów "Desert". Considering the textural features of the analysed material it is possible to say that dune sands are very similar to aeolian cover sands.

Key words: aeolian sands, grain size distribution, quartz grain abrasion, Silesian Upland, Southern Poland.

1. Introduction

The influence of wind on the substratum material is not only documented by changes in share of quartz in the sandy fraction, sorting degree, small content of dusty particles, degree of quartz grains abrasion and frosting, micromorphology of grains, transported in the aeolian environment, content of heavy minerals etc., but also in a form of segregation in space, i. e. territorial, according to wind direction, proper distribution of this material in respect of fraction (grain size), sorting, shape, degree of mechanical abrasion. Wind is characterised by a specific dynamic force, so the material should struggle with gravitation force during transport, even under the conditions of rather gentle airflow. Therefore, the clear differentiation of these deposits within whole sandy fields as well as in selected aeolian forms has been studied.

Research on aeolian deposits and forms allows to distinguish the factors, which influence aeolian processes. They can be reduced to the following groups: connected with climate (the influence of wind velocity and direction, air temperature and humidity), connected with the character of topographic surface and mineral substratum (the influence of surface variety degree, terrain cover, grain size distribution, petrographic composition, humidity of surface material, existence of vegetation etc.) (e. g. PETTIJOHN, POTTER & SIEVER 1972).

The aim of this paper is to present, how some factors influence the formation of sandy deposits textural features in the so-called Starczynów "Desert" in the Silesian Upland.

2. Methods of investigation

To solve the problems mentioned above, a detailed field study was carried out during which 900 sand samples were collected from aeolian coversands and selected dunes by using a series of knot points of a square net.

The whole material was subjected to laboratory investigation, which included standard analyses of grain size distribution according to equations of FOLK & WARD (1957), quartz grain abrasion 1–0.8 mm, applying methods of morphoscopy by CAILLEUX (1942) and mechanical graniformametry by KRYGOWSKI (1964). Also the content of heavy minerals and feldspars was analysed.

The statistics compilation of data allowed to map the textural parameter trends as well as spatial distribution. These data were also the base to make a complex estimation of these parameter anomalies. For a set of particular parameters smoothed by a movable mean, average values and their confidence intervals (at $\alpha = 0.05$) were calculated. It was assumed, that parameters within this interval characterise the average conditions of the analysed sand, while those beyond the intervals (positive or negative anomalies) indicate a relative predominance of deposition (accumulation) or redeposition (deflation) processes. It was estimated that redeposition is described by positive anomalies of Mz (mm), δ, K_G and negative anomalies of Sk, while the opposite anomalies of these parameters indicate deposition.

3. Area of investigation

The Starczynów "Desert" is situated in the eastern part of the Silesian Upland (Southern Poland). It occupies an area located within the following geomorphological units: Mitręga Basin, backward of the Middle Triassic cuesta and in front of the Upper Jurassic cuesta (GILEWSKA 1972). It forms part of the widely understood "Large Błędów Desert" (KOZIOŁ 1952) (Fig. 1).

The desert studied is a compact area of aeolian sand, which until the 60s was intensively blown out. It has a flat surface sloping from the east to the west, varied by numerous different dunes in form of clear parallel belts. They extend from the western part of the desert to about 3/4 of the whole length. In the vicinity of the cuesta, owing to readjustment of aeolian relief to this older element of relief, it changes its character and forms small irregular dunes of general meridional course. Aeolian coversands show changing thickness within the whole desert. They form a monotonous, slightly waved area of little

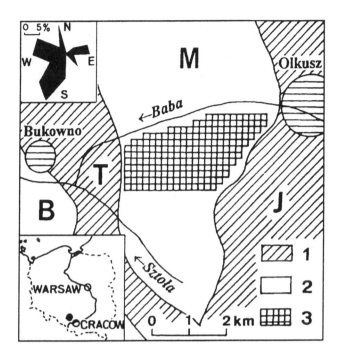

Fig. 1: Location of the investigated area: 1 – cuestas: T – Middle Triassic, J – Upper Jurassic,
2 – tectonic basins: M – Mitręga, B – Bór Biskupi, 3 – investigated area.

inclination (in the majority 0–2°) with weakly marked slopes and relative heights (compare NOWACZYK 1976; CASTEL, KOSTER & SLOTBOOM 1989). Their surface is varied by small hillocks and flat, rather irregular depressions without drainage, where in some places signs of rill- and sheet wash occur (PEŁKA-GOŚCINIAK 1995) (Fig. 2).
This desert is not a typical climatic dry area, but it is a result of human impact on the natural environment. The wind activity in the area investigated in the Late Vistulian and Holocene caused the transformation of sand features and the formation of numerous accumulative forms. Till the early Middle Ages this area was covered with dense forests. Tree cutting and uncovering of sandy substratum was a consequence of wood demand to heat in the contemporary lead and silver ironworks, which were located near Olkusz (SZCZYPEK & WACH 1991a). Due to uncovering of the dune area, the hitherto fixed sand was removed and the remodelling of the earlier relief followed. The transformation of aeolian relief is still going on.
The origin of the sand of the Silesian Upland, later transformed into dunes, was subject of many investigations. The majority of authors connect the time of their formation with the Middle Polish Glaciation (e. g. KOZIOŁ 1952; KRZYŻKIEWICZ 1952; GILEWSKA 1972). Recent research by LEWANDOWSKI & ZIELIŃSKI (1990) connects the age of deposits of the

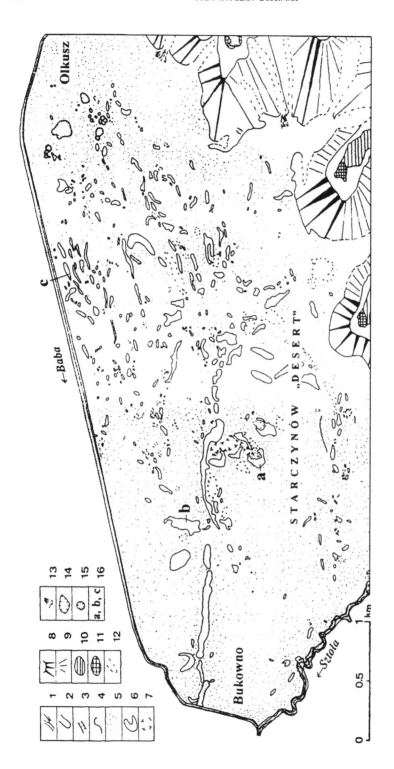

Fig. 2: Geomorphological sketch of the Starczynów "Desert": 1 – rivers, 2 – valleys, 3 – concreted river channel, 4 – erosional scarps, 5 – aeolian cover sands, 6 – dunes, 7 – depressions without drainage, 8 – Upper Jurassic cuesta, 9 – slopes, 10 – flat-topped surfaces of slopes, 11 – karstic relict hills, 12 – erosional-denudational valleys, 13 – alluvial fans, 14 – excavations, 15 –collapse cones, 16 – dunes analysed: a – barkhan-like, b – transverse, c – longitudinal.

Biała Przemsza valley with three glaciations: Oder, Warthe (Middle Polish) and Weichselian. The genesis of sands in the eastern part of the Silesian Upland was either fluvioglacial (e.g. LEWIŃSKI 1914; KOZIOŁ 1952; GILEWSKA & KLIMEK 1967), fluvial-proluvial (e. g. KRZYŻKIEWICZ 1952; RÓŻYCKI 1960, 1972; LEWANDOWSKI 1982, 1987; SZCZYPEK & WACH 1989; LEWANDOWSKI & ZIELIŃSKI 1990), fluvial or proluvial-deluvial (SENDOBRY & SZCZYPEK 1991). It is assumed that the deposits located in the eastern part of the Starczynów "Desert" are of fluvial-proluvial origin (SZCZYPEK, WACH & WIKA 1994). The thickness of the Quaternary deposits in the investigated area varies. The maximum height is 27.4 m. Fine and medium sand predominates. It is also possible to observe some gravels and boulders. The degree of quartz grains abrasion is rather good.

Taking into account the lack of possibilities to estimate the age of forms and deposits and the time of defined processes activity, one should assume that dunes and aeolian coversands are of the same age which is younger than 480 ± 50 BP (SENDOBRY & SZCZYPEK 1991). Therefore, it is possible to state that the development of lead, zinc and silver ore mining and metallurgy in the investigated area caused the movement of the aeolian sand by south-westerly winds.

4. Anemological conditions of the investigated area

The anemological conditions of the investigated area were analysed by means of data supplied by the Institute of Meteorology and Water Management in Katowice from the nearest meteorological stations in Olewin, Ząbkowice and Sławków for the period 1961–1990.

These data indicate that in the last 30 years winds from widely understood western sector (about 44 % of cases) clearly predominate. Winds from these directions are also characterised by the largest mean velocities from 3 to 3.6 m/sec.

On the base of data mentioned above, the rose of morphological effectiveness of winds in Fig. 1 has been constructed. According to rules by BORÓWKA (1980) the winds blow with a velocity ≥ 4 ms^{-1}. Such a rose informs about potential morpho-forming possibilities of winds blowing from the defined directions. The shape of the rose for the station in Sławków indicates predominant westerly winds (Fig. 1).

Taking into account the results of field measurements, i. e. observations of morphological axes and internal structure of aeolian forms selected and wind-shaped trees in the Starczynów "Desert" it can be stated, that under real conditions the westerly winds predominated in the investigated area (PEŁKA 1994).

5. Textural and mineralogical features of aeolian sands in the Starczynów Desert

5.1. Aeolian coversands

Aeolian coversands in the Starczynów "Desert"exhibit a thickness of 1.5 m in the central and eastern parts to 2.5 m in the western part. Below thin series of structureless sand (30–50 cm), laminated sand deposits occur. Their laminae dip generally in eastern

or north-eastern direction at an angle of 6–8°. The substratum sand shows horizontal stratification. Tab. 1 presents the basic textural features of the analysed sand.
The predominant medium-grained fraction (0.5–0.25 mm) amounts approximately to 56.4 %. The content of the fraction > 0.8 mm is rather small: 1.89 %. The addition of dusty fraction is characterised by similar content and it amounts to 1.47 %. The value of mean grain diameter Mz reaches 0.316 mm. The sorting of the sands is moderate, the value of standard deviation δ equals 0.599. The deposits analysed are characterised by good mechanical abrasion with the majority of well-rounded grains of γ type — on average 42.1 %. Medium rounded grains of β type and angular grains of α type sum up to 40.3 % and 17.6 %. A high share of mat-rounded grains of RM type shows up to 44.7 %, the value of abrasion degree parameter Wo amounts on average to 1376 (Tab. 1).
In the composition of aeolian covers 1.5–2 % heavy minerals are present, among them garnet makes about 32 % of the transparent fraction mass. The small amount of feldspars (about 2 %) was also noticed.

Tab. 1: Values of grains size distribution and quartz grains abrasion parameters for aeolian coversand in the Starczynów "Desert".

Parameters	Minimal value	Mean value	Maximal value
Mz (mean grain diameter in mm)	0.228	0.316	0.454
δ (standard deviation –sorting degree)	0.29	0.599	0.96
Sk (graphic skewness)	-0.17	0.074	0.44
K_G (kurtosis)	0.85	1.07	1.60
Wo (abrasion degree)	1130	1376	1571
α (angular grains in %)	3.2	17.6	33.3
β (medium rounded grains in %)	20.0	40.3	67.5
γ (well rounded grains in %)	22.06	42.1	62.2
RM (mat rounded grains in %)	16.07	44.47	80.0
EL (polished rounded grains in %)	0.0	1.40	9.48
NU (non abraded grains in %)	0.0	1.66	8.7

5.2. Dune sand

For the study of the textural parameters of dune sand, material from dunes (barkhan-like, transverse and longitudinal) was collected. The results are presented in Tab. 2.
From the observation of the basic textural features of aeolian sand on Starczynów "Desert" results that materials which build aeolian coversands and dunes are very similar. It refers to grain size distribution as well as to quartz grain abrasion because the material which builds dunes is medium-grained (on average 59 %), the value of Mz = 0.315 mm. The share of fraction > 0.8 mm amounts to 1.52 %. It contains about 2.5 % of additional dusty fraction. Dune sands are characterised by moderate sorting (δ = 0.56), they are also well abraded, grains of γ type is about 41.9 %, β 32.08 % and α 26 %. The value of Wo amounts on average to 1311.

Tab. 2: Values of more important parameters of grain size distribution and quartz grain abrasion for sands of particular types of dunes.

Parameters	Windward side	Crest line	Leeward side
Barkhan-like dune			
Mz [mm]	0.36	0.21	0.20
δ	0.70	0.44	0.47
Wo	1243	1109	1192
γ [%]	35.5	26.0	25.5
Transverse dune			
Mz [mm]	0.28	0.28	0.36
δ	0.53	0.45	0.54
Wo	1406	1324	1576
γ [%]	48.7	43.0	63.4
Longitudinal dune			
Parameters	South-west part	Middle part	North-east part
Mz [mm]	0.36	0.31	0.32
δ	0.64	0.55	0.41
Wo	1526	1229	1278
γ [%]	56.1	39.3	38.1

6. The influence of wind and older relief on the character of sandy deposits in the Starczynów Desert

The analysis of the aeolian coversands and dunes allows to state that even in relatively small areas and within rather small forms, a clear spatial segregation of sand is observed (compare SZCZYPEK & WACH 1991, 1993). First of all, the influence of wind on the character of aeolian sands on Starczynów "Desert" is reflected in the coarsening of sandy material, evident by the increase in Mz (in mm) value and the decrease in Sk value, less sorting as the Upper Jurassic cuesta comes near (the increase in δ values), the decrease in values of K_G, which means the pulsatory changes in the environment energetics during deposition and the improvement of the abrasion degree by the increase in values of both Wo and the content of well-rounded grains of γ type. The decrease of RM grains together with the direction of dune-forming wind is also typical of the analysed area. The aeolian deposits are also characterised by the increasing share of garnets and the decreasing content of feldspars from west to east. Considering the tendencies of changes in the spatial distribution of dunes, it is evident that the barkhan-like and longitudinal dunes are very similar, because their material becomes finer, better sorted and worse abraded. The transverse dune presents the opposite trend.

Another characteristic feature of aeolian sands occurring in the Starczynów "Desert", which results from the influence of wind on the texture of the deposits, is the clear zonality of areas with deposits in the phase of redeposition (deflative areas) and deposition (accumulative ones). This zonality of textural features is observed in both grain size distribution (Fig. 3) and quartz grain abrasion (Fig. 4). It is very interesting that at the dune "shadow" there follows the clear change in character of deposit features from accumulative into deflative as well as from better to weaker abraded. It is also interesting that when we approach the Upper Jurassic cuesta, the sandy material obtains the features which betoken the growing lithodynamical activity. SZCZYPEK (1986) explains such tendency of changes by the existence of an older relief in the form of a cuesta, being an obstacle to the route of wind. On one hand, the situation observed can be explained by the decrease in the velocity of the air stream, which overcomes an obstacle. There — in the place of contact with the barrier — the increase of surface friction as well as the decrease in wind transport energy forces the coarser sand to accumulate. On the other hand, it can be explained by the increase in velocity of air stream which overcomes the barrier and which is connected with the larger share of coarser material, transported by dragging. The size of grains decreases upward slope. Over the barrier only finer material is transported. The author mentioned above explains the decrease in sorting by pulsatory wind character, which sometimes occurs in a form of air whirls, being of great relief-forming importance. Another influence of older relief on sandy material textural features is observed in the vicinity of river valleys. At rivers which arc natural barriers to the further development of wind transport as well as sand translocation, accumulation prevails.

The southern part of the "desert" is the area, where less abraded grains predominate. This can be easily explained, because the area is widespread and monotonous here and therefore wind can freely reflect its activity. Thus, the sandy deposit obtains features of increased aeolization.

Comparing maps of differentiation of grain size distribution and quartz grain abrasion it is concluded that areas with sands in the phase of redeposition (deflative) are characterised by the occurrence of material of a weaker degree of abrasion, but the areas with the tendency to deposition by better abraded one.

To estimate the dune-forming wind force on Starczynów "Desert" the diagrams by BAGNOLD (1941) and PERNAROWSKI (1962) were applied. Range transport velocities are as follows: $V_{tB} = 0.32-0.45$ m· s⁻¹, $V_{tP} = 7.5-11$ m· s⁻¹. On the base of the diagram, proposed by NOWACZYK (1986) the velocity, which initiates sand movement, was estimated to $V_N = 4.8-7.8$ m· s⁻¹. The last-mentioned initiating velocity was already considered by KOZARSKI (1962) as the most proper in the estimation of the aeolian environment dynamics.

7. Recapitulation

Results of research presented in this paper allow some summarising remarks:

- The most typical elements of relief of the Starczynów "Desert" are aeolian coversands and dunes. Dune forms of different shape and size occur here. Their morphology very often was strongly conditioned by different elements of the older relief, i. e. the occurrence of cuestas and river valleys. The area of the "desert" is rather flat and

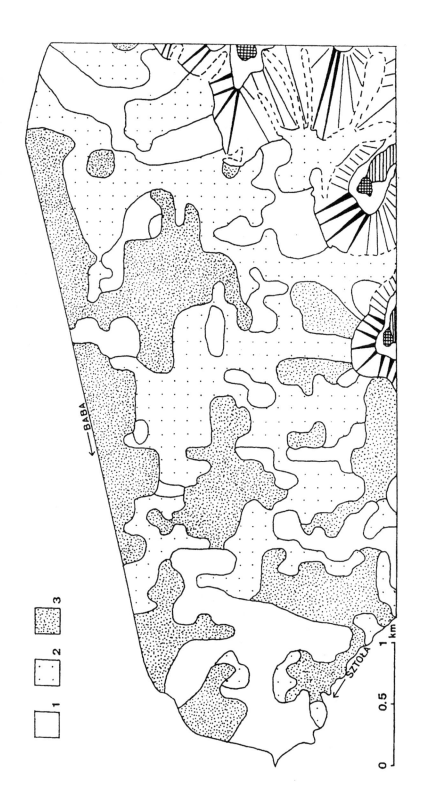

Fig. 3: Differentiation of areas in respect of grain size distribution in the Starczynów "Desert": 1 – areas with sands in phase of redeposition (deflative), 2 – transition areas, 3 – areas with sands in phase of deposition (accumulative), elements of relief as in Fig. 2.

172

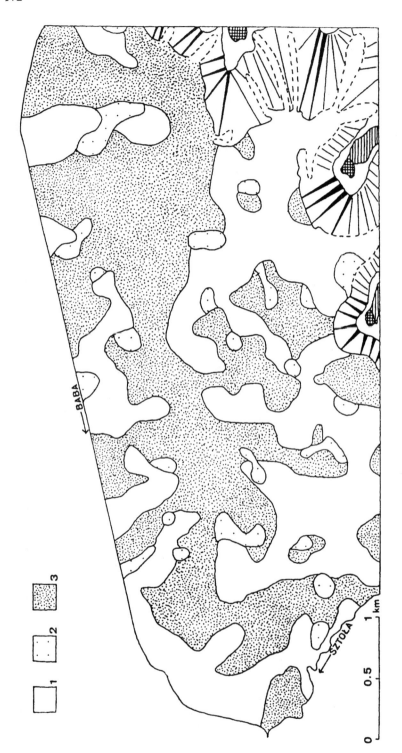

Fig. 4: Differentiation of areas in respect of quartz grain abrasion in the Starczynów "Desert": 1 – areas with weakly abraded sands, 2 – transition areas, 3 – areas with better abraded sands, elements of relief as in Fig. 2.

located at the back of the Middle Triassic cuesta part along the Baba Valley and at the front of the Upper Jurassic cuesta. The Middle Triassic cuesta is morphologically not effective here, so it did not make any obstacle for the prevailing westerly winds. Therefore, in the investigated area the arrangement of dunes is approximately W–E. The Baba valley was of certain importance for deviation of the wind direction, visible by the axes of dunes located in its vicinity. Near the Upper Jurassic cuesta dunes have also changed the meridional arrangement. The substratum of aeolian covers and dunes are probably created by fluvial-proluvial deposits of Oder, Warthe and Weichselian glaciations. The aeolian sands and dunes are built of material, which originate from the transformation of older aeolian series and it is probably very similar to the substratum material.

- On the base of the analysis of anemological conditions it is most certain that in the studied area winds from widely understood west sector predominated. This is also confirmed by the rose of morphological wind effectiveness and dune-forming wind directions, which has been reconstructed thanks to the observation of morphological axes of both dunes and wind-shaped trees. Westerly winds were also characterised by the largest velocity — from 3 to 3.6 m/sec. Wind velocities, reconstructed from diagrams of BAGNOLD, PERNAROWSKI and NOWACZYK (1986) amounted relatively to 0.29–0.45 m· s^{-1}, 6.8–11 m· s^{-1} and 4.7–8.4 m· s^{-1}.

- Considering the lack of possibilities to determine the age of forms and deposits, one only can assume that the dunes and the aeolian coversands are of the same age which is younger than 480 ± 50 BP.

- The influence of anemological conditions on the character of sandy deposits on the Starczynów "Desert" was observed. The aeolian sands are characterised by the following tendencies of changes according to the dune-forming wind direction: coarsening, decrease in sorting, improvement of quartz grain abrasion, increasing share of garnets and decreasing content of feldspars. Therefore, the textural features connected with grain size distribution behave in a different way from the typical aeolian environment. The reason is the existence of an older relief in the form of the Upper Jurassic cuesta, which is a barrier on the route of wind. On one hand such a situation can be explained by the fact that wind, which blows over the obstacle decreases its velocity, creating the conditions for coarser material to accumulate. But on the other hand it is characterized by the increase in air stream velocity, when it overcomes the barrier. It seems that the latter factor is of larger importance in the distribution of textural features of material in the vicinity of a cuesta slope.

- Considering textural features of material it is possible to say that dune sands are very similar to aeolian coversands. Very important in both forms is the direction of changes in space.

- Valleys of the Sztoła and Baba as well as cuestas, which represent the older relief, influenced not only the direction of the dunes' morphological axes but also the character of the textural features of aeolian deposits.

• The dynamics of both transport and accumulation processes of material in the analysed area were changing in space. The Starczynów "Desert" presents clear zonality of the relief (deflative — accumulative) as well as of the textural features of the aeolian sand (redeposition — deposition, better abraded — weakly abraded).

8. References

BAGNOLD, R. A. (1941): The physics of blown sand and desert dunes. — 265 p.; London (Chapman and Hall LTD).

BORÓWKA, K. R. (1980): Współczesne procesy transportu i sedymentacji piasków eolicznych oraz ich uwarunkowania i skutki na obszarze wydm nadmorskich (Present-day transport and sedimentation processes of eolian sands – controlling them factors and resulting phenomena on a coastal dune area). — PTPN, Prace Kom. Geogr.-Geol., **20**: 126 p.; Warszawa-Poznań (PWN).

CAILLEUX, A. (1942): Les actions éoliennes périglaciaires en Europe. — Mem. Soc. Geol. France, **21**, 46: 176 p.

CASTEL, I, KOSTER, E. & SLOTBOOM, R. (1989): Morphogenetic aspects and age of Late Holocene eolian drift sands in Northwest Europe. — Z. Geomorph. N. F., **33** (1): 1–26; Berlin, Stuttgart.

FOLK, R. L. & WARD, W. C. (1957): Brazor river bar: a study in the significance of grain size parameters. — Journal. Sed. Petrol., **27** (1): 3–26.

GILEWSKA, S. (1972): Wyżyny Śląsko-Małopolskie, Geomorfologia Polski, **1**: 232–339 [ed. KLIMASZEWSKI, M.], PWN; Warszawa.

— & KLIMEK, K. (1967): Czwartorzęd Wyżyny Śląskiej, Czwartorzęd Polski: 498–527, PWN; Warszawa.

KOZARSKI, S. (1962): Wydmy w Pradolinie Noteci koło Czarnkowa (Dunes in the Noteć ice-marginal valley near Czarnków). — Bad. Fizjograficzne nad Polską Zach., **9**: 37–60.

KOZIOŁ, S. (1952): Budowa geologiczna Pustyni Błędowskiej (Geological structure of the Błędów Desert). — Z badań czwartorzędu w Polsce, **1**, Biuletyn PIG, **65**: 383–416; Warszawa.

KRYGOWSKI, B. (1964): Graniformametria mechaniczna. Teoria, zastosowanie (Die mechanische Graniformametrie – Theorie und Anwendung). — PTPN, Prace Komisji Geograf.-Geolog., **2** (4): 112 p.; Poznań.

KRZYŻKIEWICZ, J. (1952): Czwartorzęd doliny Białej Przemszy pod Golczowicami (The Quaternary of the Biała Przemsza valley near Golczowice). — Z badań czwartorzędu w Polsce, **4**, Biuletyn PIG, **68**: 275–318.

LEWANDOWSKI, J. (1982): Zasięg lądolodu zlodowacenia środkowopolskiego na Wyżynie Śląskiej (Extent of ice sheet of Middle-Polish glaciation in the Silesian Upland). — Z badań czwartorzędu w Polsce, **26**, Biuletyn IG, **357**: 115–142; Warszawa.

— (1987): Zlodowacenie odry na Wyżynie Śląskiej (Odra glaciation in the Silesian

Upland). — Biuletyn Geol. UW, **31**: 247–312.

— & ZIELIŃSKI, T.(1990): Wiek i geneza osadów kopalnej doliny Białej Przemszy (Wyżyna Śląska) (Age and origin of fossil valley-fill deposits the Błędów Formation, Quaternary, Southern Poland). — Biuletyn PIG, **364**: 97–126.

LEWIŃSKI, J. (1914): Utwory dyluwialne i ukształtowanie powierzchni przedlodowcowej dorzecza Przemszy (Die diluvialen Ablagerungen und die präglaziale Oberflächengestaltung des Przemszagebietes). — Prace Towarzystwa Naukowego Warszawskiego, **7**: 159 p.; Warszawa.

NOWACZYK, B. (1976): Eolian coversands in Central-West Poland. — Quaestiones Geographicae, **3**: 57–77, UAM; Poznań.

— (1986): Wiek wydm, ich cechy granulometryczne i strukturalne a schemat cyrkulacji atmosferycznej w Polsce w późnym vistulianie i holocenie (The age of dunes, their textural and structural properties against atmospheric circulation pattern of Poland during the Late Vistulian and Holocene). — Ser. Geografia, **28**: 245 p., UAM; Poznań.

PEŁKA, J. (1994): Rekonstrukcja lokalnych warunków anemologicznych we wschodniej części Wyżyny Śląskiej na podstawowe analizy eolicznych form terenu i drzew sztandarowych (Reconstruction of local anemological conditions in the eastern part of the Silesian Upland on the ground of both aeolian landforms and wind-shaped trees analysis). — Vistuliańsko-holoceńskie zjawiska i formy eoliczne (wybrane zagadnienia): 57–67, SGP; Poznań.

PEŁKA-GOŚCINIAK, J. (1995): Zarys geomorfologii Pustyni Starczynowskiej, Procesy geomorfologiczne. — Zapis w rzeźbie i osadach, WNoZ, SGP, Materiały 3 Zjazdu Geomorfologów Polskich: 62–63.

PERNAROWSKI, L. (1962): O procesach wydmotwórczych w świetle badań utrwalonych form wydmowych Dolnego Śląska (The processes of dune formation in view of conditions in Lower Silesia). — Czasopismo Geograficzne, **33** (2): 175–197; Warszawa, Wrocław.

PETTIJOHN, F. J., POTTER, P. E. & SIEVER, R. (1972): Sand and sandstone. — 618 p.; Berlin (Springer).

RÓŻYCKI, S. Z. (1960): Czwartorzęd regionu Jury Częstochowskiej i sąsiadujących z nią obszarów. — Przegląd Geologiczny, **8**: 424–429.

— (1972): Plejstocen Polski Środkowej na tle przeszłości w górnym trzeciorzędzie. — 315 p.; PWN; Warszawa.

SENDOBRY, K. & SZCZYPEK, T. (1991): Geneza i wiek podkuestowych osadów piaszczystych w okolicach Olkusza (Origin and age of sub-cuesta sandy deposits near Olkusz). — Geographia, studia et dissertationes, **15**: 88–104; UŚ Katowice.

SZCZYPEK, T. (1986): Procesy wydmotwórcze w środkowej części Wyżyny Krakowsko-Wieluńskiej na tle obszarów przyległych (Dune forming processes in the middle part of the Cracow-Wieluń Upland against a background of the neighbouring area). — 183 p.; UŚ Katowice.

— & WACH, J. (1989): Accumulation phases of the Quaternary deposits in the Błędów Desert based on lithological studies. — Quaestiones Geographicae, SI, **2**: 137–145; UAM Poznań.

— & WACH, J. (1991): Rozwój współczesnej wydmy w warunkach silnej antropopresji (Development of the modern dune in the strong human impact conditions). — 79 p.; UŚ Katowice.

— & WACH, J. (1991a): Human impact and intensity of aeolian processes in the Silesian-Cracow Upland (southern Poland). — Z. Geomorph. N.F., Suppl.-Bd. **90**: 171–177; Berlin, Stuttgart.

— & WACH, J. (1993): Antropogeniczna wydma krawędziowa na Wyżynie Śląskiej w latach 1989–1993 (Anthropogenic scarp dune at Bukowno on the Silesian Upland in the period 1989–1993). — 52 p.; UŚ Katowice.

— WACH, J. & WIKA, S. (1994): Zmiany krajobrazów Pustyni Błędowskiej (Changes of landscapes in the Błędów Desert/Silesian Upland – Southern Poland). — 87 p.; UŚ, WNoZ, Sosnowiec.

Address of the author:

Dr. JOLANTA PEŁKA-GOŚCINIAK, University of Silesia, Faculty of Earth Sciences, PL-41-200 Sosnowiec, Będzińska 60, Poland, e-mail: pelka@usctoux1.cto.us.edu.pl

GeoArchaeoRhein, **3**: 177–186; Münster 1999

Human impact and development of a modern scarp dune

TADEUSZ SZCZYPEK & JERZY WACH

Abstract: The paper presents the morphological development of a modern dune, which has been created on the scarp of an excavation pit due to joint action of both human impact and natural geomorphological processes. The conditions of dune formation change during the period 1986–1993 and allow to describe the dune from its genesis through main stages of its development (Fig. 5).

Key words: scarp dune, human impact, geomorphological processes, sandpit, Silesian Upland.

1. Introduction

Economic activity of human beings leads not only to the pollution of atmosphere and water but to the poisoning of the soil, qualitative and quantitative destruction of the vegetation cover as well as to the intensive transformation of the Earth's face relief. This is demonstrated by the creation of new concave and convex landforms that do not occur under natural conditions and results from specific economic needs. A human creature can, being unaware of this, contribute to the development of different forms and natural processes. One of the examples of human activity is to promote morphogenetic wind activity. It took place in the past and we can find the evidences for this in the internal composition of many stabilised dunes; this happens also nowadays.

The aim of this study is to present the morphological development of a dune that was created on top of the scarp of one of the sandpits on the Silesian Upland (southern Poland). It is an evident example of human impact on the course of natural processes. The development of this dune had been studied for seven years (1986–1993), by taking annual geodetic surveys. On the basis of them the assessment of the interval changeability of this form was done. There were additional observations to find out the reasons for that changeability.

2. The conditions of dune development

Resulting from industrial sand exploitation there was built a large opencast pit within an area of 27 km² and of several metres in depth. The pine forest was cut off and the substratum was completely exposed (Fig. 1 A). This substratum is built of a number of sand series but on the bottom there appear extraglacial fluvial deposits of Vistulian age. Above them five series of aeolian sand of Late Vistulian and Holocene age lie in superposition divided by dated horizons of fossil soils (SZCZYPEK 1988; SZCZYPEK & WACH 1991). The

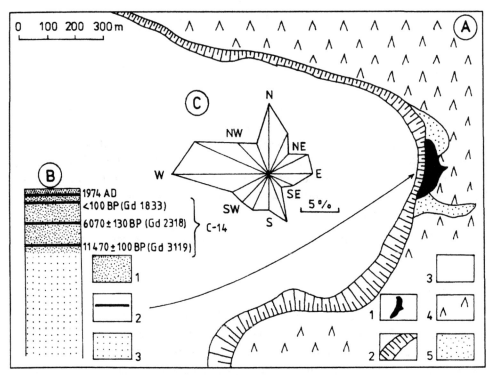

Fig. 1: Location of the investigated dune (A), schematic geological profile of the deposits with dated soil horizons (B) and a wind rose showing the morphological effectiveness (C).
A: 1 – dune, 2 – wall of the open-work, 3 – bottom of the sandpit, 4 – pine forest, 5 – forest clearings; B: 1 – Late Vistulian and Holocene aeolian sand, 2 – fossil soil horizons, 3 – Plenivistulian fluvial extraglacial deposits.

youngest aeolian series are modern deposits of the present dune (Fig. 1B). There occur medium grained sands with little content of dust particles characterised by good mechanical abrasion of quartz grains. It is shown by the content of rounded grains that reaches up to 38 % on average and value of abrasion index Wo, according to the mechanical method by KRYGOWSKI (1964), reaching up to 1200 on the average. These features are typical both for aeolian sands (the youngest inclusive) and for extraglacial fluvial deposits (SZCZYPEK 1988; SZCZYPEK & WACH 1991; PEŁKA 1992).
The dry (as a result of the appearance of a cone of depression) exposed sandy material of fluvial and aeolian origin having specific granulometric features was easily set in motion by modern dominant west and south-western winds (PEŁKA 1994). Those winds are characterised by the highest morphogenetic effectiveness of 23.5 %. The wind rose drawn in Fig. 1 C concerns the weather station placed nearby the sand-pit but not the sand-pit itself. The results of the wind impact on the substratum was the draught of sand both at the bottom of the sandpit and on the slopes of its. It led to appearance of a little transverse dune on the east scarp of the opencast pit. Its development had started in

1974 and the research was done from 1986–1993. Then the dune area equalled about 1 ha and the thickness of deposits grew up to 4.40 m (1.50 m on average).

3. Changes of the shape and the range of the dune during the research

The presented dune was created as a result of the west and south-western wind influence. Those winds were perpendicular or slanting to the slope of the opencast pit (Fig. 1 A; SZCZYPEK & WACH 1991). During the research, it was developing under both natural aeolian factor and human impact. The last one was marked off by (1) shifting toward east as a result of industrial sand exploitation at the slopes of the sandpit, (2) cutting off the leeward slope for the sand scooping by local population and (3) attempts of planting *Salix acutifolia* bushes at the foot and the top of the slope of the opencast pit to limit deflation processes. All those anthropogenic processes modified the development of the dune visibly contributing mainly to decrease its area and mass, however this did not stop the development.

Fig. 2 shows that generally the dune form shifted toward east covering partly a pine forest in front of it. The greatest superficial and morphological changes on the surface

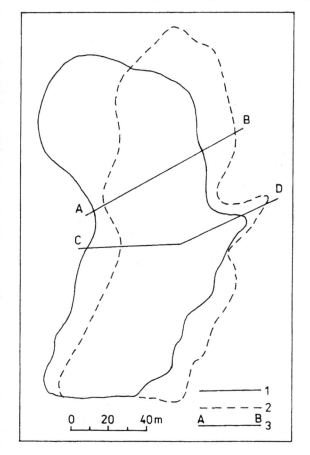

Fig. 2: Changes in location of a dune in 1986–1993.
1 – range of the dune in 1986,
2 – range of the dune in 1993,
3 – morphological profile lines (cf. Fig. 4).

of the dune always took place after heavy winds that appeared several times a year.
In 1986, the beginning of research, the dune area equalled 1.25 ha and the volume of
sands of the dune equalled 19.2 thousand cubic metres. Within time the morphology of
the dune surface was diversified (Fig. 3A). Deflation forms cut the dune into a southern
and a northern part. The cut was a result of a gap in the pine forest that was filled by a
sandy tongue located east of the dune. The gap promoted the concentration of air stream
and the increase of its velocity what led to the intensive sand deflation in the middle part
of the form. The southern and northern parts of the dune consisted of well-developed
leeward slopes with an angle of 30–31° (Photo 1). The characteristic transit slope
(according to STANKOWSKI 1963) existed only in the NW part.
In 1993, at the end of research, the dune area equalled 1.20 ha (SZCZYPEK & WACH
1993) and its morphology was simplified (Fig. 3B). The subdivision into a southern and
northern part had disappeared. Windward and leeward slopes together with transit slopes

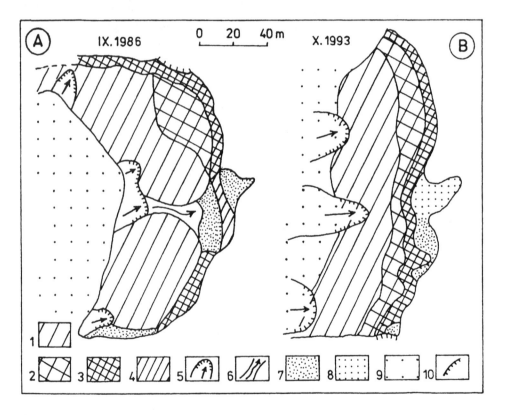

Fig. 3: Surface relief of the investigated dune in 1986 (A) and in 1993 (B).
1 – windward slope, 2 – transit slope, 3 – leeward slope, 4 – secondary leeward slope, 5 –
deflation basins, 6 – deflation trench, 7 – aeolian accumulation cover, 8 – dead aeolian
accumulation cover, 9 – slope of the sandpit, 10 – anthropogenic undercuts.

Photo 1: Investigated dune burying the pine forest — July, 1993 (Photo by T. SZCZYPEK).

Photo 2: Deflation basins on the sandpit slope and windward slope of the dune — July, 1993 (Photo by T. SZCZYPEK).

were uniformed in the whole dune area. Distinct deflation basins existed only at the foot of the windward slope (Photo 2).

During seven years of observation, the relief of the analysed dune was changing and shifting toward east. The amount of sand dislocation is shown by two cross sections (A–B and C–D in Figs. 2 and 4). It shows that the face of the dune shifted 22 m toward NE (A–B) but only 16 m toward E. The maximum shift (north of A–B) was 27 m. The dune area lessened to about 3.9 %. Comparatively little shift of the dune resulted from the pine forest being an obstacle for the wind activity.

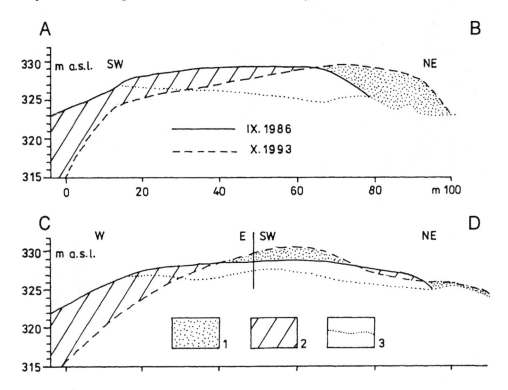

Fig. 4: Changeability of dune surface in 1986–1993 along the profiles A–B and C–D (cf. Fig. 2). 1 – increase, 2 – decrease, 3 – substratum.

4. Genesis and main stages of the dune development

The observations in the sandpit on the Silesian Upland allow to describe the origin and the main stages of the dune development.

No doubt, the factor initiating the creation and triggering the development of the dune was ignorant human activity that started a big and deep opencast pit thus exposing large surfaces of loose sandy deposits. In the pretty narrow sandpit the increased force of wind caused a dune as the result of air concentration. This dune should be undoubtedly numbered among the scarp forms. It was created as a result of blowing-off the material both from the bottom and from the slopes of the sandpit on top of the upper scarp of the opencast pit. It is consistent with the theory of KEILHACK (PRUSINKIEWICZ 1971). The material of the dune consists of sandy extraglacial fluvial deposits of Plenivistulian age and sands of four aeolian series of Late Vistulian and Holocene age. The average pace of vertical mass increase of the dune equalled 10–30 cm · year $^{-1}$. The similar range of values, 30–50 cm, was mentioned by KLUCHAREV (1969) when describing the development of aeolian cover on the scarp of Kuybyshev reservoir on the Volga river. But REINHARD's (1953–1954) calculation concerning the development of the scarp dune on Hiddensee Island and PRUSINKIEWICZ's (1971) calculation concerning an aeolian scarp cover on the Wolin island shows that those forms grew definitely slower (≈ 0.5–1.0 cm · year $^{-1}$). The intensive increase of sandy mass of the dune on the Silesian Upland occurred under influence of heavy winds blowing in summer and winter. KLUCHAREV (1969) and PRUSINKIEWICZ (1971) show that the main importance for development of the dune forms described by them were winds in winter.

Main stages of creation of the scarp dune in the Silesian Upland are drawn in Fig. 5. Stage A is a primeval area covered with pine forest. The forest protected the substratum against deflation and therefore morphogenetic aeolian activity could not take place. In 1974 resulting from industrial sand exploitation a steep face of an opencast pit was created (stage B). There around the forest was grabbed out in the proximity of several meters exposing the modern podzolic soil. Since then intensive influence of western and south-western winds started (stage C). A first sandy aeolian cover wandered over the bottom and the slopes of the opencast pit soothed by deflation and landslides. At the same time on the scarp of the sandpit, the wind started depositing a thin cover built from sandy pieces blown-out off the bottom and the slope. Nowadays the growth of sand on top of the scarp can be observed in many places of the sandpit (SZCZYPEK 1994) (stage D). Its face is moving off the edge of the opencast pit. The maximum thickness of deposits still occurs near to the scarp (cf. KLUCHAREV 1969), whereas the face of the cover is thin. At first, the slow shifting of the cover is linked with adjustment of the structure of deposits to the relief of the substratum (several metres from the sandpit there existed a visible linear depression in the substratum leading to SW–NE). The internal structure shows easy inclination of laminae according to the direction of the movement. In stage E the face of the cover reaches the thick pine forest and continues to move burying the first line of trees (stage F). The tree fragments sticking out of the sand surface were broken down by wind and then removed by man. In stages F and G the movement of the cover face was clearly stopped by the forest. The constant delivery of sandy material causes only minimal movement of the dune's face, but the increase of its height at the same time. This causes the creation of a high leeward slope with the corresponding structure of material and laminae that descents backward. Thus the aeolian cover is transformed into a dune. In stage H (1987) a sudden human impact took place by cutting off the base and moving away the wall of the opencast pit together with the proximal part of the dune form. The dune was cut off from its alimentation source. The

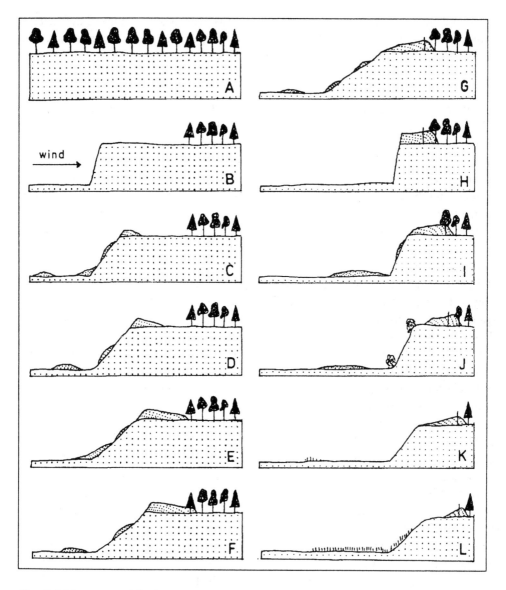

Fig. 5: Main stages of the investigated dune formation (A–L — explanation in the text).

lack of material supply caused increased deflation at the windward slope of the dune that became lower and lower in favour of increasing the height of the dune face. From time to time as a result of the sand exploitation the bases of some other parts of the leeward slope were cut. It caused interference in the process of development of this part of the dune. In stage I, the slope of the pit is soothed among others by deflation. New wandering of sand covers started. The windward side of the dune is still being blown out. In stage J (1989) willow bushes (*Salix acutifolia*) are planted at the foot of the sandpit wall and on scarps. Because of the lack of fresh material, blowing-out of the windward slope and separation of the dune from the scarp of the sandpit continues. In stage K at the bottom and slope of the opencast blowing-out of sand starts anew and triggers wandering of the dune towards east. It was possible due to destruction of the willow bushes by wind and man. Stage L (1992 and 1993) shows the gradual degradation of the dune. This is caused by natural stabilisation of the sand at the bottom and partly the slope of the openwork by herbaceous plants (*Corynephorus canescens* and *Koeleria glauca*). So once again the sand supply was stopped. The dune retreats from the scarp of the sandpit and its width and extent decreases but the height of its face grows. Tendency to gradual destruction of the scarp dune starts.

5. Final remarks

The above-described dune was created consequently from development of natural geomorphological processes induced by man. It occurred in an area where, without human impact in the present climate, it could not have come into existence. The morphological development of this dune as well as the intensity of natural processes were up to a certain degree due to human impact which changed the form in shape and range. Natural segregation of sand material properties both on the surface and in the internal composition took place.

In early spring of 1994 the scarp dune finished its existence as a result of anthropogenic flattening of the walls of the sandpit and of the whole dune. Inside this newly created and artificial form a nucleus consisting of sand was preserved raised by naturally influencing aeolian factor. Man caused the intensive development of the dune and man led to its sudden disappearance. It is the evident example of visible and fast human impact on the modern refief of the Earth's crust in industrial regions.

6. Acknowledgements

The authors would like to thank Miss AGNIESZKA SZOTEK for translation of this paper from Polish into English.

7. References

KLUCHAREV, N. I. (1969): Eolovye processy na levoberezh'e Kuybyshevskogo vodokhranilishcha u g. Tolyatti. Izv. AN SSSR, ser. geogr., 5: 76–78.

KRYGOWSKI, B. (1964): Graniformametria mechaniczna. Teoria, zastosowanie (Zusam.: Die mechanische Graniformametrie — Theorie und Anwendung). — PTPN, Prace Kom. Geogr.-Geol., 2 (4): 112 p.; Poznań.

PEŁKA, J. (1992): Rola wiatru w kształtowaniu cech osadów piaszczystych w Kotlinie Biskupiego Boru (Summ.: Influence of wind activity on character of sandy deposits in the Biskupi Bór Basin). — In: SZCZYPEK, T. [ed.]: Wybrane zagadnienia geomorfologii eolicznej. — WNoZ UŚ, SGP Sosnowiec: 129–140.

— (1994): Rekonstrukcja lokalnych warunków anemologicznych we wschodniej części Wyżyny Śląskiej na podstawie analizy eolicznych form terenu i drzew sztandarowych (Summ.: Reconstruction on local anemological conditions in the eastern part of Silesian Upland on the ground of both aeolian landforms and wind-shaped trees analysis). — In: NOWACZYK, B. & SZCZYPEK, T. [eds.]: Vistuliańsko-holoceńskie zjawiska i formy eoliczne — wybrane zagadnienia. — SGP Poznań: 57–67.

PRUSINKIEWICZ, Z. (1971): Naspy przyklifowe — nowy typ gleb morskiego pobrzeża (Summ.: Cliff naspas — a new type of soils on marine coast). — Zesz. Nauk. UMK, Geografia, **8**: 133–157; Toruń.

REINHARD, H. (1953-1954): Kliffranddünen und Brandungshöhlen der Insel Hiddensee. — Wiss. Z. Univ. Greifswald, **3**, Mat.-Naturwiss., **8**: 595–605.

STANKOWSKI, W. (1963): Rzeźba eoliczna Polski północno-zachodniej na podstawie wybranych obszarów (Summ.: Eolian relief of North-West Poland on the ground of chosen regions). — PTPN, Prace Kom. Geogr.-Geol., **4** (1): 147 p.; Poznań.

SZCZYPEK, T. (1988): Działalność eoliczna we wschodniej części Wyżyny Śląskiej na przykładzie okolic Bukowna (Summ.: Aeolian activity in the eastern part of the Silesian Upland on the example of the Bukowno vicinity). — Geographia, studia et dissertationes, **11**: 7–22; UŚ Katowice.

— (1994): Pasowość rzeźby deflacyjno-akumulacyjnej — na przykładzie piaskowni w Bukownie na Wyżynie Śląskiej (Summ.: Deflation-accumulative relief zonality — with the sandpit at Bukowno on the Silesian Upland as an example). — In: NOWACZYK, B. & SZCZYPEK, T. [eds.]: Vistuliańsko-holoceńskie zjawiska i formy eoliczne — wybrane zagadnienia. — SGP Poznań: 77–88.

— & WACH, J. (1991): Rozwój współczesnej wydmy w warunkach silnej antropopresji (Summ.: Development of the modern dune in the strong human impact conditions). — UŚ Katowice: 79 p.

— & WACH, J. (1993): Antropogeniczna wydma krawędziowa w Bukownie na Wyżynie Śląskiej w latach 1989-1993 (Summ.: Anthropogenic scarp dune at Bukowno on the Silesian Upland in the period 1989-1993). — UŚ Katowice: 52 p.

Address of the author:

Prof. Dr. TADEUSZ SZCZYPEK, University of Silesia, Dep. Physical Geography, Będzińska str. 60, PL-41-200 Sosnowiec, Poland, e-mail: kgf@ultra.cto.us.edu.pl

Dr. JERZY WACH, University of Silesia, Dep. Physical Geography, Będzińska str. 60, PL-41-200 Sosnowiec, Poland, e-mail: kgf@ultra.cto.us.edu.pl

GeoArchaeoRhein, **3**: 187–190; Münster 1999

Definitions concerning coversand, fossil soil and paleosol

Wolfgang Schirmer

The following definitions are proposals. They partly contrast to other definitions.

Eolian coversand

Eolian coversand is eolian sand spread in a blanket-like form or veneer over the bedrock. Its surface is flat or undulating, its inner fabric laminated or bedded or homogeneous. It differs from dunes by lack of typical dune forms and inner dune structures.

The additional adjective eolian is essential in contrast to other sandy coverbeds that prevalently occur in sandstone or sand areas as sand blankets of glacial, fluvial or colluvial (deluvial) origin. Therefore in the German earth science language the differentiation between Decksand = coversand (a lithological term only) and Flugdeck-sand = eolian coversand (lithological as well as genetical term) is a long and useful tradition (e. g. DÜCKER & MAARLEVELD 1957).

Eolian coversand is a morphological as well as lithological body and thus completely independent from any stratigraphical definition.

Contrast to different definitions:

The restriction of the term coversand to only Weichselian deposits — as recommended by KOSTER (1982: 122) — is considered not useful. Coversand as well as eolian coversand as a lithofacies should be free to occur through the whole earth history. The fact that we are aware of typical coversand deposition during the late Upper Weichselian before the Allerød period is an interesting result of investigation but no reason to restrict this lithological body to that period. In case this late Upper Weichselian coversand shows typical features to be identified, e. g. for mapping purposes, it is possible to add a local name like Veluwe coversand. This latter term could then be restricted within certain stratigraphic boundaries.

Fossil soil

A fossil or buried soil is covered by a deposit of any thickness that separates it visibly and by measurable soil properties from the present soil.

A fossil or buried soil is covered by a deposit thick enough that the recent soil formation does not essentially affect it or incorporate it into the recent surface soil (Fig. 1).

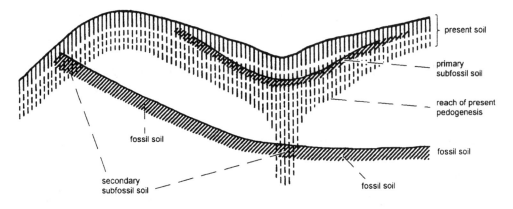

Fig. 1: Illustration demonstrating the terms fossil soil, primary subfossil and secondary subfossil soil.

Subunits:

Subfossil soil

A subfossil soil is a fossil soil covered by a deposit thin enough or with porosity high
enough (e. g. dune sand, pumice tephra, coarse debris) that the recent soil formation
affects the fossil soil, or the fossil soil is being incorporated into the present soil formation.
The subfossil soil is a subunit of the polygenetic soil in which a fossil soil becomes
amalgamated (welded) with the present soil.

Genetically the subfossil soil can be subdivided into two major groups:

Primary subfossil soil

A surface soil that has been covered by a deposit thin enough or with porosity high
enough that the present soil formation affects it or is being incorporating it.

Secondary subfossil soil

A fossil soil the cover of which has been removed enough that it becomes encroached by
the present soil formation.

Comment

The term „subfossil soil" is a term to designate the reach in which the present soil
formation encroaches a buried soil, respectively the interfingering section of a buried
and the present soil. In other words it may be only a question of time until this
interfingering section is fully incorporated into the recent soil formation.

The difference between the primary and the secondary subfossil soil is: The primary subfossil soil, once covered, is affected by the new soil formation almost from the first day on, actually with the downward arrival of the first rain drop, earthworm or root end. The secondary subfossil soil has been fossil without being affected by later soil formation prior to its subfossil status.

The term subfossil soil may be used to point to the fact of welding between a fossil soil and the present soil. The terms primary and secondary subfossil soil may be used to point to the history and genesis of the fossil soil welded with the present soil. By ranging these terms as subunits — subfossil as subunit of fossil, primary and secondary as subunits of subfossil — it remains arbitrary whether the subunit terms are used or not. It should depend on the topic treated whether it is of interest to point out the fossil soil being a secondary subfossil soil or a mere fossil soil.

Other definitions handle the interfingering space by defining distinct depths to determine what has to be called present soil and fossil soil. The Soil Survey Staff (1992: 1) establishes more than 50 cm (under distinct conditions more than 30 cm) distance between the deeper lying soil and the recent soil to separate the deeper lying soil from the recent soil as buried soil.

The Handbuch für Bodenkunde (FELIX-HENNINGSEN & BLEICH 1996) defines to designate a soil as fossil soil covered by deposits of 7 dm or more in thickness.

By using the definition of a subfossil soil given above, the delimitation of depth for designating a soil buried becomes superfluous. For it depends on the properties of the present soil and that of the substratum, whether the present soil regime encroaches more or less deeply downwards.

Paleosol

A paleosol is a soil formed prior to about 12,700 radiocarbon years BP. This age is the first onset of soil formation of most of the present surface soils. It is the beginning of the Late Glacial embracing the Meiendorf, Bølling and Allerød Interstadials. In the course of the decline of the last glaciation from the Meiendorf Interstadial on, continuous vegetational cover is proved for wide areas of the temperate northern hemisphere. Likewise this vegetational onset can be linked with the onset of the soil formation of the present soils (SCHIRMER 1996).

Other definitions use the Pleistocene/Holocene boundary (FELIX-HENNINGSEN & BLEICH 1996: 5) respectively the mark 10,000 BP (WG Paleopedology 1994). These definitions include the Late Glacial period into the time of forming paleosols and they exclude the roots of formation of most of the present soils from the term present soil. Consequently most of the present soils would embrace a certain paleosol component. This does not hit the core of the matter.

References

DÜCKER, A. & MAARLEVELD, G. C. (1957): Hoch- und spätglaziale äolische Sande in Nord-westdeutschland und in den Niederlanden. — Geol. Jb., **73**: 215–234; Hannover.

FELIX-HENNINGSEN, P. & BLEICH, K. E. (1996): Böden und Bodenmerkmale unterschiedlichen Alters. — In: BLUME, H., FELIX-HENNINGSEN, P., FISCHER W. R., FREDE, H.-G., HORN, R. & STAHR, K.: Handbuch der Bodenkunde, Kap. 4.5.1: 1–9; Landsberg (Ecomed).

KOSTER, E. A. (1982): Terminology and lithostratigraphic division of (surficial) sandy eolian deposits in The Netherlands: An evaluation. — Geologie en Mijnbouw, **61**: 121–129.

SCHIRMER, W. (1996): Spätglaziale Böden unter Laacher See-Tephra. — In: Landesamt für Natur und Umwelt des Landes Schleswig-Holstein [Hrsg.]: Böden als Zeugen der Landschaftsentwicklung: 49–58; Kiel (L.-A. Natur u. Umwelt SH).

Soil Survey Staff (1992): Keys to soil taxonomy. — 5. edition, Soil Management Support Services (SMSS) technical monograph, **19**: 541 p.; Blacksburg, Virginia (Pocahontas).

WG on definitions used in Paleopedology (1994): Paleopedology glossary. — INQUA/ISSS Paleopedology Commission Newsletter, **14** (1997): 13–14.

Address of the author:

Prof. Dr. WOLFGANG SCHIRMER, Abt. Geologie, Heinrich-Heine-Universität, Universitätsstr. 1, D-40225 Düsseldorf, e-mail: schirmer@uni-duesseldorf.de

GEOARCHAEORHEIN

Herausgeber: Wolfgang Schirmer
Wissenschaftlicher Beirat: Brigitta Ammann (Bern),
Wolfgang Andres (Frankfurt a. M.),
Henk Berendsen (Utrecht), Wolfgang Boenigk (Köln),
Gerhard Bosinski (Monrepos),
Sierd Cloetingh (Amsterdam), Wilfried Haeberli (Zürich),
Alexander Ikinger (Düsseldorf),
Wighart von Koenigswald (Bonn), Thomas Litt (Bonn),
Christian Schlüchter (Bern),
Jef Vandenberghe (Amsterdam)

Eva-Maria Ikinger
Der endeiszeitliche Rückenspitzen-Kreis Mitteleuropas
In der Endphase der letzten Eiszeit kam es in weiten Teilen Europas und darüber hinaus zur Ausbreitung von charakteristischen Pfeilspitzen mit gestumpftem Rücken, den sogenannten Rückenspitzen. Europäische Fundinventare mit entsprechenden steinernen Projektilen können zum endpaläolithischen Rückenspitzen-Kreis gestellt werden, der zwar regional gewisse Eigenheiten aufweist, insgesamt jedoch in seinen archäologischen Zeugnissen, wie den Artefakten, der Kunst und dem Siedlungswesen recht einheitlich ist.
Mit vorliegender Arbeit wird für das Gebiet Mitteleuropas erstmals eine umfangreiche Zusammenstellung und Auswertung entsprechender Funde vorgenommen. Schwerpunkte liegen dabei in der Herausarbeitung von Entwicklungstendenzen der Pfeilspitzenmorphologie, welche ein Gerüst zur Datierung von Rückenspitzen-Inventaren bildet. Vergleiche mit Vorkommen in West- und Osteuropa zeichnen darüber hinaus ein differenziertes Bild von regionalen Sonderentwicklungen sowie von komplexen Ausbreitungs- und Rückzugsbewegungen des Rückenspitzen-Kreises innerhalb Europas.
Bd. 1, 1999, 600 S., 59,80 DM, br., ISBN 3-8258-3628-2

Alexander Ikinger (Hrsg.)
Festschrift Wolfgang Schirmer
Geschichte aus der Erde
Anlaß für die Zusammenstellung dieser Festschrift war der 60. Geburtstag von Prof. Dr. Wolfgang Schirmer, dessen engagiertes Wirken als Forscher und Lehrer in der Geologie auf diese Weise gewürdigt werden sollte. Aus der Vielfältigkeit seiner Arbeitsgebiete ergab sich die vorliegende Zusammenstellung der Beiträge von Kollegen und Schülern aus der Geologie und Nachbarwissenschaften.
Zeitlich umfassen die Aufsätze das Quartär. Inhaltliche Schwerpunkte sind Flußgeschichte und Lößstratigraphie Mitteleuropas. Hierbei liegt der Rhein mit angrenzenden Flußgebieten im Zentrum der Betrachtung. Darüber hinaus sind ausgewählte Beispiele aus Flußgebieten Nordamerikas und Kleinasiens aufgenommen. Die Beiträge umfassen Arbeiten zur Stratigraphie (Beiträge W. Boenigk; A. Semmel; J. Klostermann), zur Flußgeschichte (H. Jerz; M. C. Roberts & O. R. Morningstar; H. Strunk; V. Loùek; B. Schröder), zur Glazialmorphologie (L. Feldmann; O. Keller & E. Krayss), zu Fragen absoluter Datierungsmethoden (M. A. Geyh & Ch. Schlüchter; F. Heller et al.), zur Vegetationsgeschichte (U. Schirmer; G. Waldmann), zur Bodenentwicklung (G. Schellmann), zur Archäologie und Geologie (M. Frechen & A. Justus; A. Ikinger & E.-M. Ikinger; R. Gerlach) und zur Forschungsgeschichte der Geologie (R. Streit).
Bd. 2, 1998, 272 S., 68,80 DM, gb., ISBN 3-8258-3629-0

Wirtschaftsgeographie

herausgegeben von Prof. Dr. Wolf Gaebe,
Prof. Dr. R. Grotz, Prof. Dr. Helmuth Nuhn,
Prof. Dr. Ludwig Schätzl
und Prof. Dr. Eike W. Schamp

Wolf Gaebe; Eike W. Schamp (Hrsg.)
Gateways to the European market: Case studies from the Netherlands and Germany
Three major forces determine the kind of access to the European market: two political events, namely the creation of the European Single Market and the collapse of the socialist block, and the restructuring of economic organizations in search of flexibility. The gateway concept – both in functional and in geographical terms – proves to be useful for the analysis of the spatial consequences. This book focuses on the development of seaports on the one hand and on investments in manufacturing on the other. Distribution and production are thus combined in a broader understanding of the gatecay concept. Case studies are taken from the core region of European production and its major gateway region, i. e. Germany and the Netherlands.
Bd. 4, 2., unv. Aufl. 1995, 150 S., 48,80 DM, br., ISBN 3-89473-986-x

Simone Strambach
Wissensintensive unternehmensorientierte Dienstleistungen: Netzwerke und Interaktion – am Beispiel des Rhein-

LIT Verlag Münster – Hamburg – London
Bestellungen über:
Grevener Str. 179 48159 Münster
Tel.: 0251 – 23 50 91 – Fax: 0251 – 23 19 72
e-Mail: lit@lit-verlag.de – http://www.lit-verlag.de
Preise: unverbindliche Preisempfehlung

Neckar-Raumes

Wissensintensive unternehmensorientierte Dienstleistungen gewinnen zunehmende strategische Bedeutung im sozioökonomischen Strukturwandel. Zum einen durch ihr dynamisches Wachstum, zum anderen durch die indirekten Effekte, Innovationsimpulse und positiven Rückkopplungswirkungen, die von ihnen als einer Quelle externen Wissenstransfers für die Nachfrageseite ausgehen können.

Entscheidend sowohl für ihre Wachstumsdynamik, als auch für die Entstehung von Multiplikator-Effekten sind die Interaktion und die Interdependenzen zu anderen ökonomischen Aktivitäten.

Die Arbeit setzt auf drei Ebenen mit der Analyse an. Auf der Makroebene wird die Entwicklung dieser Dienstleistungen in Deutschland herausgearbeitet und auf der regionalen Ebene, soweit amtliche Daten es zulassen, weiter differenziert.

Im Vordergrund der mikroanalytischen Ebene steht die Interaktion, die mit Hilfe des theoretischen Netzwerkkonzeptes der institutionellen Ökonomie untersucht wird.

Die Ergebnisse zeigen, daß Netzwerkbeziehungen eine Schlüsselfunktion erfüllen im Interaktionsprozeß zwischen Anbietern wissensintensiver Dienstleistungen und deren Nachfragern. Außerdem wird die Bedeutung von Netzwerkstrukturen auch speziell für die Anbieter sichtbar. Die Nutzung interorganisationaler Netzwerkstrukturen bietet wissensintensiven Dienstleistungsunternehmen, die in besonderem Maße dem Innovations-, Zeit- und Qualitätswettbewerb ausgesetzt sind, Flexibilitätspotentiale zur Anpassung an die sich schnell verändernde Organisationsumwelt.

Bd. 6, 1995, 170 S., 48,80 DM, br., ISBN 3-89473-984-3

Rolf Sternberg

Technologiepolitik und High-Tech Regionen – ein internationaler Vergleich

Seit den 1980er Jahren werden in allen Industriestaaten technologiepolitische Programme implementiert, um auf der lokalen, der regionalen und der nationalen Ebene ökonomische und technologische Ziele zu erreichen. Regionale Ziele werden hingegen insbesondere von der nationalen Technologiepolitik nur selten in expliziter Form verfolgt, obgleich deren regionale Wirkungen offensichtlich sind. Die zentrale Frage der Habilitationsschrift lautet: Welchen Einfluß haben die verschiedenen Facetten der Technologiepolitik auf die Entstehung von High-Tech Regionen?

Untersuchungsobjekt sind sieben Regionen in vier Industriestaaten: München (Deutschland), "Silicon Valley"/CA, Greater Boston/MA und "Research Triangle"/NC (USA), Kyushu (Japan) sowie der "Western Crescent" und Cambridgeshire (Großbritannien). Für jede dieser Regionen werden Indikatoren des Entwicklungsstandes und der -dynamik diskutiert und die Ursachen des Aufstiegs zur High-Tech Region unter besonderer Berücksichtigung technologiepolitischer Einflüsse bewertet. Diese Fallstudien werden ergänzt um länderspezifische Querschnittanalysen zur Bewertung der Bestimmungsfaktoren der High-Tech Intensitäten in allen Teilregionen der vier Staaten (Korrelations- und Regressionsanalysen).

Die Studie bestätigt für alle vier Staaten die Eingangsthese. Demzufolge hatten und haben die verschiedenen impliziten und expliziten Technologiepolitiken der Nationalregierungen einen signifikanten, gleichwohl nicht intendierten Einfluß auf die Entstehung von High-Tech Regionen. Die räumlichen Effekte staatlicher Technologiepolitik begünstigen diesen Regionstyp stärker als andere Regionen; allerdings ist dieser Einfluß primär impliziter, d. h. nicht intendierter Natur. Dies bedeutet, daß die regionalen Wirkungen der impliziten Technologiepolitik größer sind als jene der expliziten Technologiepolitik mit regionalen Zielen.

Bd. 7, 2. Aufl., 1998, 384 S., 48,80 DM, br., ISBN 3-8258-2339-3

Andreas Stamm

Strukturanpassung im Agrarsektor von Costa Rica – neue Perspektiven für die Entwicklung ländlicher Räume?

Bd. 8, 1997, 312 S., 48,80 DM, br., ISBN 3-8258-2496-9

Stephanie Pfützer

Strategische Allianzen in der Elektronikindustrie

Organisation und Standortstruktur

Seit Beginn der 80er Jahre gewinnen strategische Allianzen zunehmend an Bedeutung. Die Elektronikindustrie gehört zu den Branchen, die von dieser Entwicklung besonders betroffen sind. Die Arbeit untersucht, wie strategische Allianzen die Arbeitsteilung und damit die Standortstruktur der beteiligten Unternehmen verändern. Zunächst werden verschiedene theoretische Konzepte daraufhin geprüft, inwieweit sie erklären können, warum Unternehmen arbeitsteilige Aktiväten in Form strategischer Allianzen koordinieren. Die Ergebnisse werden in ein standorttheoretisches Konzept integriert und Hypothesen über die organisatorischen und räumlichen Auswirkungen strategischer Allianzen entwickelt. Nach einem kurzen Überblick über Entwicklungen der Weltelektronikindustrie auf der Basis sekundärstatistischer Materials werden die Hypothesen anhand von Fallbeispielen aus verschiedenen Elektronikbereichen empirisch

LIT Verlag Münster – Hamburg – London
Bestellungen über:
Grevener Str. 179 48159 Münster
Tel.: 0251 – 23 50 91 – Fax: 0251 – 23 19 72
e-Mail: lit@lit-verlag.de – http://www.lit-verlag.de
Preise: unverbindliche Preisempfehlung

überprüft.
Bd. 9, 1995, 268 S., 48,80 DM, br., ISBN 3-8258-2621-X

Christine Tamásy
**Technologie und Gründerzentren
in Ostdeutschland – eine
regionalwirtschaftliche Analyse**
Technologie- und Gründerzentren (TGZ) gehören
in Ostdeutschland seit der deutschen Vereinigung
zu den populärsten Instrumenten insbesondere
der kommunalen Innovationspolitik. Ungeachtet
einer Vielzahl eröffneter Einrichtungen und einer
unbekannten Anzahl weiterer Projekte, die sich
im Planungsstadium befinden, fehlen bisher aus-
reichend theoretisch sowie empirisch fundierte
Untersuchungen zu den Wirkungen der TGZ und
ihrer Determinanten.
Hauptziel der Arbeit ist es, die TGZ in Ostdeutschland im Rahmen einer regionalwirtschaftlichen Analyse und anhand der von den TGZ-
Managern selbst formulierten Zielsetzungen zu be-
werten. In einem theoretisch-konzeptionellen Teil
werden zunächst die grundlegenden Wirkungszu-
sammenhänge erläutert, die für eine regionalwirtschaftliche Beurteilung der TGZ notwendig sind.
Die anschließende Literaturanalyse der Stand-
ortvoraussetzungen innovativer Unternehmen in
Ostdeutschland berücksichtigt besonders regional-
und gründungsspezifische Auswirkungen der Systemtransformation. Im empirisch-analytischen
Hauptteil, der auf umfangreichen Erhebungen in
36 TGZ und 272 Unternehmen beruht, werden
die Konzeption und Struktur der ostdeutschen
TGZ sowie die darin ansässigen Unternehmen
untersucht (u.a. Motive der Standortwahl, In-
anspruchnahme des Leistungsangebots in TGZ,
Beschäftigungseffekte, Innovationsorientierung).
Die Arbeit leitet abschließend politische Hand-
lungsempfehlungen ab und gibt Anregungen für
zukünftige Forschungsarbeiten.
Bd. 10, 1996, 240 S., 48,80 DM, br., ISBN 3-89473-884-7

Rolf Schlunze
**Japanese Investment in Germany: a spatial
perspective**
Bd. 11, 1996, 176 S., 58,80 DM, br., ISBN 3-8258-3149-3

Britta Klagge
**Internationalisierung des Bankwesens in
Osteuropa**
Die ausländische Direktinvestitionstätigkeit
im ungarischen und tschechischen Bankensektor im Spannungsfeld zwischen nationalen
Bedingungen und der internationalen Nieder-
lassungspolitik multinationaler Banken
Für die zukünftige wirtschaftliche Entwicklung in
den Transformationsstaaten Osteuropas sind die
ausländischen Direktinvestitionen im Bankwesen
von besonderer Bedeutung. Die vorliegende Studie
analysiert
die ökonomischen und rechtlichen Rahmenbedingungen für die Entwicklung des Bankwesens in
Ungarn und Tschechien,
die ausländischen Direktinvestitionen im ungarischen und tschechischen Bankensektor und die in
diesen Ländern verfolgten Unternehmensstrategien
sowie
unternehmensinterne regionale Netzwerkstrategien
in multinationalen Banken.
Die Analysen basieren auf theoretischen Ansätzen
zur Internationalisierung des Bankwesens und der
geographischen Interpretation dieser Ansätze. Empirische Grundlage der Studie sind eigens für diese
Untersuchung aufgebaute Datenbanken sowie Ex-
pertengespräche mit führenden Bankmanagern. Die
Ergebnisse erlauben Schlußfolgerungen zur Position Osteuropas im weltwirtschaftlichen Gefüge
sowie zu aktuellen Trends der Internationalisierung
im Bankwesen.
Bd. 12, 1997, 352 S., 59,80 DM, br., ISBN 3-8258-3532-4

Christian Weikl
**Internationalisierung deutscher Klein- und
Mittelunternehmen**
Eine empirische Analyse unter besonderer
Berücksichtigung der Zielländer Großbritannien und Tschechische Republik
Während der letzten Jahrzehnte haben sich die
Standortbedingungen in Europa grundlegend
verändert. Dies gibt auch kleinen und mittleren
Unternehmen (KMU) neue Möglichkeiten zur Internationalisierung. In welcher Form KMU hieran
teilnehmen, welche regionalen Wirkungen hiervon
ausgehen und welche Rolle der grenzüberschrei-
tende Transfer von Know-how spielt, ist bislang
jedoch kaum untersucht worden.
Die vorliegende Untersuchung stellt diesen Fragen empirisch fundierte Antworten zur Seite und
überprüft zugleich die Erklärungsgüte ausgewählter
Internationalisierungstheorien.
Auf Grundlage dieser Analyse werden Überlegungen zur Tragfähigkeit einiger wirtschaftspolitischer
Strategien angestellt.
Bd. 13, 1998, 264 S., 48,80 DM, br., ISBN 3-8258-3856-0

Jürgen Specht
**Industrielle Forschung und
Entwicklung: Standortstrategien und
Standortvernetzungen**
Am Beispiel der Regionen Rhein-Main, Bo-
densee und Dresden
Die Rahmenbedingungen für industrielle For-

LIT Verlag Münster – Hamburg – London
Bestellungen über:
Grevener Str. 179 48159 Münster
Tel.: 0251 – 23 50 91 – Fax: 0251 – 23 19 72
e-Mail: lit@lit-verlag.de – http://www.lit-verlag.de
Preise: unverbindliche Preisempfehlung

schung und Entwicklung (F+E) haben sich in den letzten Jahren entscheidend geändert. Damit ist gleichzeitig eine grundlegende Neuausrichtung der F+E-Organisation im Industrieunternehmen verbunden. Welche internen und externen Strategien Unternehmen im Bereich von F+E verfolgen und wie Regionen in diese F+E-Strategien eingebunden sind, ist bisher weitgehend unbeantwortet geblieben.

Auf der Basis theoretischer Konzepte der Unternehmensorganisation und der Regionalökonomie gibt die vorliegende Untersuchung empirisch überprüfte Antworten auf diese Forschungsfragen und zeichnet somit ein umfassendes Bild über die Auswirkungen von Unternehmensstrategien auf die Wachstumsdynamik von F+E-Regionen.
Bd. 14, 1999, 264 S., 49,80 DM, br., ISBN 3-8258-3926-5

Cordula Neiberger
Standortvernetzung durch neue Logistiksysteme
Hersteller und Händler im Wettbewerb: Beispiele aus der deutschen Nahrungsmittelwirtschaft
Der verstärkte internationale Wettbewerb zwingt die Unternehmen zu einer neuen strategischen Ausrichtung und flexibler Marktanpassung. Die damit verbundenen Rationalisierungsbemühungen greifen über Unternehmensgrenzen hinweg, weshalb die Beziehungen zwischen Unternehmen neu überdacht und definiert werden müssen. Für die Beschreibung der Vorgänge wird das Schlagwort der "Kooperation" ebenso häufig verwendet wie "der Kampf um die Wertschöpfungskette".
Die vorliegende Studie untersucht die in den letzten Jahren erfolgten Umstrukturierungsprozesse im Logistikbereich zwischen Nahrungsmittelindustrie und Einzelhandel. Sie geht dabei von transaktionskostentheoretischen Überlegungen aus, analysiert deren Erklärungsgehalt für empirische Befunde und diskutiert weiterführende soziologische Erklärungsmuster. Ziel ist es darzulegen, inwieweit die zu beobachtenden organisatorischen Veränderungen zwischen Unternehmen räumliche Veränderungen im Sinne einer neuen standörtlichen Vernetzung hervorrufen.
Bd. 15, 1999, 208 S., 48,80 DM, br., ISBN 3-8258-4017-4

Stefanie Lowey
Organisation und regionale Wirkungen von Unternehmenskooperationen
Eine empirische Untersuchung im Maschinenbau Unter- und Mittelfrankens
Unternehmenskooperationen sind seit Anfang der 90er Jahre nicht nur ein vielerprobtes Mittel zur Entwicklung von Unternehmen, sondern auch von

Regionen. Doch müssen Kooperationen, die für Unternehmen positiv sind, nicht auch für die Regionalentwicklung förderlich sein. In dieser Studie wird ein theoretisches Konzept zur Evaluierung von Unternehmenskooperationen im Hinblick auf deren regionale Wirkung entwickelt. Vor diesem Hintergrund werden in einer empirischen Untersuchung Kooperationen im Maschinenbau in Unter- und Mittelfranken analysiert und aus den Ergebnissen ihre Wirkungen im Hinblick auf eine längerfristig erfolgreiche Regionalpolitik abgeleitet.
Bd. 16, 1999, 264 S., 49,80 DM, br., ISBN 3-8258-4104-9

Geographie der Kommunikation
herausgegeben von Peter Gräf (Geographisches Institut, Wirtschaftsgeographie der Dienstleistungen, Rheinisch-Westfälische Technische Hochschule –RWTH – Aachen)

Jürgen Rauh
Telekommunikation und Raum
Informationsströme im internationalen, regionalen und individuellen Beziehungsgefüge
Die Nutzung der Telekommunikation, die räumlichen Strukturen und Intensitäten telekommunikativer Interaktionen bilden wesentliche Bestandteile einer Geographie der Kommunikation. In Hinblick auf die Entwicklung raumwirksamer Investitionsplanungen im liberalisierten Telekommunikationsmarkt liegt hierin der inhaltliche Ansatzpunkt der vorliegenden Untersuchung. Sie bietet auf der Basis umfangreichen empirischen Datenmaterials einen Einblick in die räumlichen Muster telekommunikativer Beziehungsgefüge auf verschiedenen räumlichen Maßstabsebenen. Ziel ist dabei nicht nur die Suche nach modelltheoretischen Erklärungen und Telekommunikationsströmen im Raum, sondern auch eine praxisorientierte Netzplanung.
Bd. 1, 1999, 328 S., 79,90 DM, br., ISBN 3-8258-4379-3

Martin Grentzer
Räumlich-strukturelle Auswirkungen von IuK-Technologien in transnationalen Unternehmen
Information und Kommunikation gewinnen in einer globalisierten, wissensbasierten Gesellschaft auch für wirtschaftsgeographische Betrachtungen räumlicher Strukturen immer mehr an Bedeutung. Die vorliegende Untersuchung formuliert einen theoretischen Ansatz einer "Geographie der Kommunikation". Empirische Fallstudien belegen IuK-bedingte Implikationen für einen SIEMENS-Standort und damit zusammenhängende räumliche

LIT Verlag Münster – Hamburg – London
Bestellungen über:
Grevener Str. 179 48159 Münster
Tel.: 0251 – 23 50 91 – Fax: 0251 – 23 19 72
e-Mail: lit@lit-verlag.de – http://www.lit-verlag.de
Preise: unverbindliche Preisempfehlung

Auswirkungen. Neben geographischen, gesellschaftlichen und technologischen Grundlagen werden insbesondere neuere ökonomische Ansätze hinzugezogen, um das veränderte wirtschaftliche Handeln im Raum näher zu beleuchten. Das kritische Hinterfragen traditioneller (industrie-)geographischer Auffassungen eröffnet neue Perspektiven für ein junges und höchst komplexes Forschungsfeld.
Bd. 2, 1999, 248 S., 39,80 DM, br., ISBN 3-8258-4380-7

Hannoversche Geographische Arbeiten (HGA)
herausgegeben von der
Geographischen Gesellschaft
zu Hannover e. V. und dem Geographischen
Institut der Universität Hannover

Peter Könemann
Der Sand- und Kiesabbau im Wesertal an der Porta Westfalica
Bd. 50, 1995, 252 S., 38,80 DM, br., ISBN 3-8258-2394-6

Javier Revilla Diez
Systemtransformation in Vietnam
Industrieller Strukturwandel und
regionalwirtschaftliche Auswirkungen
Bd. 51, 1995, 240 S., 38,80 DM, br., ISBN 3-8258-2636-8

Tobias Behnen (Hrsg.)
Beiträge zur Geographie der Meere und Küsten
Vorträge der Jahrestagung des Arbeitskreises
"Geographie der Meere und Küsten"
Bd. 52, 1996, 192 S., 48,80 DM, br., ISBN 3-8258-3163-9

Heike Seeger
Ex-Post-Bewertung der Technologie- und Gründerzentren durch die erfolgreich ausgezogenen Unternehmen und Analyse der einzel- und regionalwirtschaftlichen Effekte
Bd. 53, 1997, 216 S., 34,80 DM, br., ISBN 3-8258-3193-0

Arbeitsberichte zur wirtschaftsgeographischen Regionalforschung
herausgegeben von Helmut Nuhn
(Philipps-Universität Marburg)

Helmut Nuhn (Hrsg.)
Entwicklungsprobleme und Perspektiven der Industrie in der Universitätsstadt Marburg
Eine Untersuchung in den Gewerbegebieten
Bd. 1, 1992, 140 S., 34,80 DM, br., ISBN 3-89473-485-x

Helmut Nuhn (Hrsg.)
Gewerbliche Wirtschaft in Stadtallendorf
Struktur, Entwicklung und Probleme
der Industrie eines ehemaligen
Rüstungsstandortes
Bd. 2, 1992, 140 S., 34,80 DM, br., ISBN 3-89473-509-0

Helmut Nuhn; Astrid Berthold;
Andreas Stamm
Auflösung regionaler Produktionsketten und Ansätze zu einer Neuorientierung
Fallstudien zur Nahrungsmittelindustrie in
Deutschland
Bd. 3, 1995, 150 S., 34,80 DM, br., ISBN 3-8258-2680-5

Martina Fromhold-Eisebith;
Helmuth Nuhn (Hrsg.)
Großforschung und Region
Der Beitrag von Forschungszentren des
Bundes zu einer innovationsorientierten
Regionalentwicklung
Bd. 4, 1995, 240 S., 34,80 DM, br., ISBN 3-8258-2681-3

Helmut Nuhn (Hrsg.) unter Mitarbeit von
Cordula Neiberger, Michael Plattner und
Hans-Peter Wildermuth
Thüringer Industriestandorte in der Systemtransformation: technologisches Wissen und Regionalentwicklung
Bd. 5, 1998, 254 S., 48,80 DM, br., ISBN 3-8258-3698-3

LIT Verlag Münster – Hamburg – London
Bestellungen über:
Grevener Str. 179 48159 Münster
Tel.: 0251 – 23 50 91 – Fax: 0251 – 23 19 72
e-Mail: lit@lit-verlag.de – http://www.lit-verlag.de
Preise: unverbindliche Preisempfehlung

Abhandlungen zur Geschichte der Geowissenschaften und Religion/Umwelt-Forschung Neue Folge

Herausgeber: Prof. Dr. Dr. Dr. Manfred Büttner
(Bochum)

Stefani Klos
Der Beitrag von Mission und Kirche zur ländlichen Entwicklung in Rwanda
Zur Problematik kirchlicher Entwicklungsarbeit mit einer Dokumentation ausgewählter landwirtschaftlicher Ausbildungszentren
Christliche Missionen zählen - neben Kolonialverwaltung und Wirtschaftsinteressen - zu den wichtigsten externen Faktoren, die die Entwicklung in weiten Teilen Schwarzafrikas bestimmt haben. Am Beispiel des ostafrikanischen Binnenlandes Rwanda werden die Auswirkungen der Missionstätigkeit auf die Organisation der Landwirtschaft, die Entwicklung des Bildungs- und Gesundheitswesens, die Siedlungsstruktur sowie auf Handel und Gewerbe detailliert und räumlich differenziert nachgezeichnet. Dabei werden die verschiedenen Formen und Folgen kirchlicher Entwicklungsarbeit von ihren Anfängen bis heute aufgezeigt sowie Handlungskonzepte und entwicklungspolitische Potentiale der in Rwanda aktiven Kirchen kritisch diskutiert. Die nahezu vollständige Zerstörung fast aller ökonomischen und gesellschaftlichen Strukturen im Jahr 1994 hat die Arbeit unversehens zu einer einmaligen Dokumentation zur Missions-, Wirtschafts- und Sozialgeschichte Rwandas werden lassen. Nicht zuletzt durch ihr umfangreiches Abbildungsmaterial (Karten, Diagramme, Photos) bietet die Arbeit zahlreiche Anregungen und Informationen für Kulturgeographen, Ethnologen, Agrar-, Sozial- und Religionswissenschaftler sowie für Praktiker der Entwicklungszusammenarbeit.
Bd. 1, 1997, 456 S., 38,80 DM, br., ISBN 3-89473-719-0

Andreas Schach
Carl Ritter (1779 – 1859): Naturphilosophie und Geographie
Erkenntnistheoretische Überlegungen, Reform der Geographie und mögliche heutige Implikationen
Bd. 2, 1996, 200 S., 58,80 DM, br., ISBN 3-89473-637-2

Jürgen Hamel
Die Vorstellung von der Kugelgestalt der Erde im europäischen Mittelalter bis zum Ende des 13. Jahrhunderts – dargestellt nach den Quellen
Scheibe oder Kugel? Welche Vorstellung von der Erdgestalt beherrschte das mittelalterliche intellektuelle Klima? Mußte die antike Erkenntnis der kugelförmigen Erde der rohen Anschauung einer Erdscheibe, als Ausdruck völligen Niedergangs des Naturwissens weichen? Auch wenn seit langem kritische Stimmen vor einer Überbewertung einzelner Beispiele warnen, stand doch die hierauf gerichtete Bearbeitung der mittelalterlichen Literatur in größerem Umfang bisher aus. Dieses Desideratum historischer Forschung sucht der Autor, Diplomphilosoph und promovierter Wissenschaftshistoriker, auszufüllen.
Die vorliegende Studie beruht nicht auf Vermutungen und Spekulationen sondern spürt den weit verstreuten Quellen nach. Als Ergebnis liegt eine knapp kommentierte Sammlung von Belegen für die Anerkennung der Kugelgestalt der Erde und der Existenz von Antipoden für das gesamte Mittelalter, seit dem 6. bis zur Mitte des 13. Jahrhunderts vor – geschöpft aus der "Artes"-Literatur, enzyklopädischen Schriften, Genesiskommentaren sowie kleinen theologischen und naturkundlichen Abhandlungen oder Gelegenheitsschriften. Die Liste von etwa 60 Autoren und anonymen Traktaten enthält gleichermaßen klangvolle Namen, wie auch in der Wissenschaftsgeschichte kaum bekannte Persönlichkeiten mittelalterlicher Gelehrsamkeit. So entsteht einerseits das Bild einer regen geistigen Auseinandersetzung sowie andererseits die Frage, inwieweit die Scheibengestalt der Erde, von einigen wenigen literarischen Belegen abgesehen, überhaupt eine größere Verbreitung im Kreis der Gebildeten erlangte.
Bd. 3, 1996, 112 S., 29,80 DM, br., ISBN 3-8258-2751-8

LIT Verlag Münster – Hamburg – London
Bestellungen über:
Grevener Str. 179 48159 Münster
Tel.: 0251 – 23 50 91 – Fax: 0251 – 23 19 72
e-Mail: lit@lit-verlag.de – http://www.lit-verlag.de

Preise: unverbindliche Preisempfehlung